The Hidden History of the Smock Frock

Fashion: Visual and Material Interconnections

Series editor: Rebecca Arnold, The Courtauld Institute of Art, London, UK

This interdisciplinary series explores the ways that the visual and material interact to create and sustain fashion cultures, both historically and today. Published in association with the world-renowned Courtauld Institute of Art, the series seeks to unpack the ways looking, seeing, wearing and being interconnect with wider visual, material and technological cultures of fashion. Through focused studies of specific themes and case studies in fashion and dress history, the series comprises exciting, new research that foregrounds fashion as a lived, emotional and sensory experience. Including both national and transnational examples, ranging from fashion film to periodicals to fashion photography, it fosters and facilitates new ways of thinking about dress as a local and global phenomenon. Titles in the series draw upon fashion studies and dress history, in addition to art, architecture, design history, philosophy, memory studies and the history of emotions.

Published

The Hidden History of the Smock Frock, Alison Toplis
Prêt-à-Porter, Paris and Women: A Cultural Study of French Readymade Fashion, 1945–68, Alexis Romano

Forthcoming

Fashion After Capital: Frock Coats and Philosophy from Marx to Duchamp, T'ai Smith
Danger in the Path of Chic: Violence in Fashion between the Wars, Lucy Moyse Ferreira

The Courtauld

The Hidden History of the Smock Frock

Alison Toplis

BLOOMSBURY VISUAL ARTS
LONDON · NEW YORK · OXFORD · NEW DELHI · SYDNEY

BLOOMSBURY VISUAL ARTS
Bloomsbury Publishing Plc
50 Bedford Square, London, WC1B 3DP, UK
1385 Broadway, New York, NY 10018, USA
29 Earlsfort Terrace, Dublin 2, Ireland

BLOOMSBURY, BLOOMSBURY VISUAL ARTS and the Diana logo are trademarks of
Bloomsbury Publishing Plc

First published in Great Britain 2021

Copyright © Alison Toplis, 2021

Alison Toplis has asserted her right under the Copyright, Designs and Patents Act, 1988, to be identified as Author of this work.

For legal purposes the Acknowledgements on p. viii constitute an extension of this copyright page.

Series design by Adriana Brioso
Cover image: Arthur Smith of Bledlow Ridge, 1872, Victorian Prisoner Photographs
© Centre for Buckinghamshire Studies, Buckinghamshire Council, reference:
Q/AG/23–26 Prisoner 4621

All rights reserved. No part of this publication may be reproduced or transmitted in any form or by any means, electronic or mechanical, including photocopying, recording, or any information storage or retrieval system, without prior permission in writing from the publishers.

Bloomsbury Publishing Plc does not have any control over, or responsibility for, any third-party websites referred to or in this book. All internet addresses given in this book were correct at the time of going to press. The author and publisher regret any inconvenience caused if addresses have changed or sites have ceased to exist, but can accept no responsibility for any such changes.

A catalogue record for this book is available from the British Library.

Library of Congress Cataloging-in-Publication Data
Names: Toplis, Alison (Writer on clothing and dress), author.
Title: The hidden history of the smock frock / Alison Toplis.
Description: London ; New York : Bloomsbury Visual Arts, 2021. |
Includes bibliographical references and index.
Identifiers: LCCN 2020036652 (print) | LCCN 2020036653 (ebook) |
ISBN 9781350212640 (paperback) | ISBN 9781350126114 (hardback) |
ISBN 9781350126121 (pdf) | ISBN 9781350126138 (epub)
Subjects: LCSH: Smocks–History. | Work clothes–History.
Classification: LCC GT1860 .T67 2021 (print) | LCC GT1860 (ebook) |
DDC 391.4/809–dc23
LC record available at https://lccn.loc.gov/2020036652
LC ebook record available at https://lccn.loc.gov/2020036653

ISBN: HB: 978-1-3501-2611-4
PB: 978-1-3502-1264-0
ePDF: 978-1-3501-2612-1
eBook: 978-1-3501-2613-8

Typeset by Newgen KnowledgeWorks Pvt. Ltd., Chennai, India
Printed and bound in India

To find out more about our authors and books visit www.bloomsbury.com and sign up for our newsletters.

Contents

List of Illustrations vi
Acknowledgements viii

Introduction: Form and definition 1

1 The smock and rural England 11

2 Histories of the smock frock 21

3 Making 37

4 Selling and buying 61

5 Appearances 79

6 Into the twentieth century 109

Conclusion 135

Notes 139
Bibliography 193
Index 205

Illustrations

1.1 British Pavilion, Paris Exposition 1937. © The British Library Board, LOU. LD83 16
2.1 Waggoner Playing Card, from a set satirizing the Rump Parliament, *circa* 1660–5, 1896,0501.917. © The Trustees of the British Museum 23
2.2 John Laguerre (1688–1746), *Hob Taken Out of Ye Well*, *circa* 1730, oil on canvas, B1981.25.392. Yale Center for British Art, Paul Mellon Collection 26
2.3 *A scene near Cox Heath, or the Enraged Farmer … May 1st 1779*, Acc. No. 1941-224. © The Colonial Williamsburg Foundation 27
2.4 Detail from *A Windy Day*, George Morland (British, 1763–1804), oil on canvas, 92.5 x 143.5 cm, 1790s, Acc No. PD.105–1992. © Fitzwilliam Museum, Cambridge 28
2.5 Feather stitch needlework, including spirals, on a nineteenth-century linen smock frock. © Author's collection 34
3.1 Arthur Smith of Bledlow Ridge, 1872. Victorian Prisoner Photographs. © Centre for Buckinghamshire Studies, Buckinghamshire Council, reference: Q/AG/23–26 Prisoner 4621 42
3.2 Bill from Thomas Hyde & Co., QS1854/4/F2/1b. © Oxfordshire County Council – Oxfordshire History Centre 46
3.3 *Hereford Journal*, 30 April 1828. ©Herefordshire Archive Service 50
3.4 *Evening Journal* (Adelaide), 21 August 1869, 4 51
4.1 Bill from Edward Meates, 8 December 1832, Ombersley Parish Accounts, 3572/13. © Worcestershire Archive and Archaeology Service, Ombersley Parish Church 64
5.1 Edward Varney of Westcott, 1872. Victorian Prisoner Photographs. © Centre for Buckinghamshire Studies, Buckinghamshire Council, reference: Q/AG/23–26 Prisoner 4984 82
5.2 Joseph Collier of Haddenham, 1872. Victorian Prisoner Photographs. © Centre for Buckinghamshire Studies, Buckinghamshire Council, reference: Q/AG/23–26 Prisoner 5059 83
5.3 A short linen smock, MERL, 52/151. © Museum of English Rural Life, University of Reading 84
5.4 A short smock. © Image used with kind permission of Oxfordshire County Museum Service, Slop; OXCMS: 1982.213.3 85

5.5 Joseph Hazell of Amersham, 1871. Victorian Prisoner Photographs. © Centre for Buckinghamshire Studies, Buckinghamshire Council, reference: Q/AG/23–26 Prisoner 4232 86

5.6 William Larner of Stokenchurch, 1872. Victorian Prisoner Photographs. © Centre for Buckinghamshire Studies, Buckinghamshire Council, reference: Q/AG/23–26 Prisoner 4702 90

5.7 John Smith of Newport Pagnell, 1871. Victorian Prisoner Photographs. © Centre for Buckinghamshire Studies, Buckinghamshire Council, reference: Q/AG/23–26 Prisoner 4328 93

5.8 William Quarterman, 'on the tramp', 1871. Victorian Prisoner Photographs. © Centre for Buckinghamshire Studies, Buckinghamshire Council, reference: Q/AG/23–26 Prisoner 4295 95

5.9 A short cotton smock, MERL 81/147. © Museum of English Rural Life, University of Reading 96

5.10 George Olney of Newport Pagnell, 1871. Victorian Prisoner Photographs. © Centre for Buckinghamshire Studies, Buckinghamshire Council, reference: Q/AG/23–26 Prisoner 4194 97

5.11 George Scharf, *between 6 & Seven O'Clock morning, Sumer*, watercolour, circa 1834. 1862,0614.1194. © The Trustees of the British Museum 98

5.12 S. T. Gill, *Prospecting*, plate 21 from *The Australian Sketchbook* 1864. Colour lithograph, 17.7 × 15.2 cm (image) 28.9 × 42.6 cm (sheet), purchased, 1953, 3049.22-4. © Courtesy of National Gallery of Victoria, Melbourne 106

6.1 *Carter's Illustrated Seed Catalogue of Tested Seeds for the Farm*, 1903. Special Collections, MERL, TR CAR P2/A14. © Museum of English Rural Life, University of Reading 116

6.2 Ellen Terry and her husband, James Carew. Postcard. © Author's collection 118

6.3 Detail from a postcard, 'Rural scenes, village gossip in a quiet corner', 'EAS', circa 1908–10. © Author's collection 120

6.4 Alfred Stieglitz. *Georgia O'Keeffe*, 1918–1919. Gelatin silver print, 8 11/16 × 7 7/16 inches. Museum Purchase [2014.3.56], Georgia O'Keeffe Museum 125

6.5 *The Landswoman: The Journal of Land Army* 1, no. 8 (1 August 1918): 160. © The British Library Board, Lou.Lon.596 127

6.6 John Galliano, knitted silk smock dress, 'Fallen Angels' collection, Spring/Summer 1986. Lot 155, Sale 18 June 2019. © Courtesy of Kerry Taylor Auctions 132

6.7 Molly Goddard, green smock, Autumn/Winter 2019. © Ben Broomfield (photograph), Molly Goddard 133

Acknowledgements

Looking back, from Kate Greenaway books to my mum's home dressmaking, as well as baby photographs of me wearing one, I now see that smocks have been a fairly continuous presence throughout my life. However, academically, this book has grown from ideas formulated during my PhD research into the provincial clothing trade, which turned up some interesting production and retailing methods for smocks that seemed to require much more investigation. As I have found, once you start looking for smocks, they turn up regularly and, sometimes, in unexpected places. Various people and institutions have helped me along the way, sparking new avenues of research and assisting me with the extant material evidence of this research. These include staff at the Berkshire, Oxfordshire, Herefordshire, Worcestershire, Bradford, Wiltshire and Buckinghamshire Record Offices, Archives, and History Centres; Somerset Museum, Valence House Museum, Hampshire Museums Service, Oxfordshire Museum Service, Abingdon Museum, Worcestershire Museums, the Ellen Terry Museum at Smallhythe Place, the National Army Museum, Bradford Museum and many of the staff at the Museum of English Rural Life in Reading, particularly Ollie Douglas.

I have had interesting discussions about various details with many people including Nancy Cox, Pat Hudson, Sam van de Geer and Sarah Thursfield, which have set me off on new paths. The Centre for the History of Retailing and Distribution workshops at the University of Wolverhampton have been essential for testing out my ideas. Janet Ivimey-Cook has proved an invaluable reader of my early drafts. Laura Ugolini has been a supreme mentor and an inspiration as always. The anonymous peer reviewers of this work along the way have also given me encouragement and challenged me to think in different ways.

Thank you to the staff at Bloomsbury Visual Arts for believing in this book, particularly Frances Arnold and Yvonne Thouroude. Thank you also to the Centre for Historical Research at the University of Wolverhampton for contributing to funding for the illustrations and for supporting me as an honorary research fellow. Vivienne Richmond, as editor of *Textile History*, added invaluably to an article which forms the basis of Chapter 6 and I would like to thank Taylor and Francis and the Pasold Research Fund for permission to re-use this in this publication.

The author and publisher gratefully acknowledge the permission granted to reproduce the copyright material in this book and thank the institutions and individuals listed on the previous pages and Rev. Stephen Winter of Ombersley

Parish, for permission to reproduce illustrations, particularly those who have done so gratis. Seeking final permissions to publish images during lockdown for the COVID-19 pandemic has not always been straightforward. My thanks to those around the world responsible for giving permissions for continuing to do their best for me and find ways around a difficult situation, often while working from home, allowing this book to proceed. Every effort has been made to trace copyright holders and to obtain their permission for the use of copyright material. The publisher apologizes for any errors or omissions in the list and would be grateful to be notified of any corrections that should be incorporated in future reprints or editions of this book.

This book would not have been possible without the faith of Rebecca Arnold, who has also become a great smock spotter for me throughout the annals of fashion.

And finally, thank you to my family, John, Isobel and Milly, who have put up with me and my 'slight' obsession for too long and, although I don't think that this is possible, now know more than they might want to about smocks.

Introduction: Form and definition

A common garment in the mid-nineteenth century, my own and many people's male ancestors wore the smock frock. This book will investigate this ordinary everyday mass-produced easy-care workwear that labouring men used day in, day out. By examining how smocks were produced, bought and sold, and how they were worn, including their wearers feelings about them, variations emerge which differ from traditional perceptions about the garment. As Bridget Yates, a costume curator, remarked in 1973, 'I have always approached … [smocks] with caution, as, believing it to be an emotive subject redolent of Old England, I have never been totally convinced of the reliability of my information'.[1] *The Hidden History of the Smock Frock* will also cautiously approach the subject, seeking to disentangle the multitude of garments which come under the simple heading of 'smock'. Though worn with and alongside trousers, jackets and waistcoats, which are still used today and indeed have not changed that much from their mid-Victorian equivalents, the male smock frock has disappeared. Generally associated with rural labourers, including the stock 'yokel', this book will examine how this connection has hidden the widespread use of the smock frock by many nineteenth-century working men. It will investigate why and how this happened, and the smock's resonances across time.

Although this book concentrates on the smock frock in a British context, its form of construction, the basic 'tunic', is common across many cultures. It is created from squares and rectangles of full widths of fabric gathered in for shaping, a method widely used from at least the Roman period onwards.[2] Men's shirts and smocks used this cut of 'the utmost simplicity' into the nineteenth century.[3] Constructing garments in this fashion was efficient, also meaning that no fabric was wasted, since cloth was more expensive than the labour needed to make it up.[4] It is a simple style that is found in variants of working dress across history and throughout Europe, including Germany, Austria, Sweden, Russia, Switzerland, Spain and Italy and, perhaps, most famously in the loose, often blue, shirts/smocks of France, during the nineteenth century.[5]

What makes the smock a smock and not a tunic, blouse or shirt, is the way that the fabric is manipulated and gathered into both the centre back and the front, and on the sleeves, decorative stitching worked to hold the gathers in place forming horizontal bands, the smocking, a later descriptive term for this needlework. This also gives the garment a certain elasticity and its fit. The application of smocking techniques to male working dress using self-coloured thread, at least in the first instance, made it unique to Britain and, from the scanty evidence available, seems to date from the eighteenth century. There are three main types of 'smock': the round smock, which is the same in the front and back, so technically reversible;[6] a shirt-like form, which has a partial opening at the front; and one that is completely open down the front, reaching its fullest development with caped collared smocks popular in the Welsh borders, resembling overcoats.[7]

The aim of this book is to examine the smock in its broadest form, the scope of the study extending beyond the 'typical' smock frock ossified in nostalgic images. It has become apparent that the terms 'smock frock' and 'smock' cover a wide range of garments, from highly decorated examples worn as Sunday best with a new one costing 6 shillings or more,[8] down to something utilitarian, functional, ready-made and sold new for a couple of shillings or a few pence as second-hand. Looking back in time, the identification of a 'smock' can also be slippery due to the use of words imbued with meanings which are no longer clear, as well as local complexities and regional variations.[9] As with all clothing, it is difficult to know what is being described without seeing a corresponding illustration. Although different types of smock, round and open, for example, survive in museum collections or are depicted visually, their form is not often distinguished in written texts. This lack of distinction has, to a degree, hidden how common the smock was, with various descriptive terms used in different areas, which were even confusing to contemporaries. In some parts of the country 'slop' was also an interchangeable term with smock. The term 'slop' is similarly problematic. Originally a loose outer gown in the fifteenth century, later meaning a sailor's loose ready-made trousers in the seventeenth and eighteenth centuries, slops were general ready-made clothing for sailors sold to them on board ships. Thus by the nineteenth century, a 'slop' was also an inferior, cheap ready-made garment.[10]

In 1875, a newspaper printed a list of 'Provincialisms Common to Leicestershire and Lincolnshire'. Their description doesn't really help us: a 'Slop, or Smock-frock – A loose outside garment, worn by a farm-servant or labourer', aside from confirming that they could be one and the same thing.[11] In a case of theft in Leicestershire, the thief concealed a stolen ham between his waistcoat and the 'outside shirt, called a smock-frock', supporting this definition.[12] Around this date, as dialects were being diluted and fast disappearing due to urban migration, provincial dictionaries were produced. In 1874, a Hallamshire (Sheffield) vocabulary was published. The smock entry was for 'a woman's dress, 'Cum lass, get thee smock on'… (formerly) for a woman's under garment … It is now used for the smock frock of the agricultural labourer',[13] not really narrowing down the nineteenth-century usage. Gillian Holman suggests 'smocks' were for rural areas, 'slops' for urban, with Flora Thompson in *Lark Rise to Candleford* calling an unbleached drill jacket a 'sloppy'.[14]

However, the terminology seems more complex than this as shown by a court case in Grantham in Lincolnshire. Thomas Goodson of Great Gonerby was charged with stealing a 'smock frock' from George Bilson in 1857. Having caught the train together at Corby, they both lodged the night at the Blue Sheep beer house in Grantham and spent the evening drinking. In the morning Goodson had gone and so had Bilson's 'slop' and some money. Goodson's wife eventually handed over the 'smock' to the police, providing the evidence for a trial.[15] The three terms are used interchangeably in this one report, in both rural and urban settings, the term 'slop' appearing in quotation marks, as if it was colloquial language.

In an advertisement for absconders in Lincolnshire in 1807, again both 'slop frock' and 'smock frock' are used, the smock being short and white.[16] Similarly in a court case at Taunton Guildhall, a garment taken off and put down in a turnip field is described as 'a slop, or smock frock', though it is subsequently called a 'slop'.[17] A man wanted in connection with a stabbing in Stokesay, Shropshire, is noted as being from south Wales and dressed in 'a slop smock frock with round collar, and open down the breast'.[18] In Cardiff, '"a slop" or short smock frock' was stolen from the shop of Messrs. Rogers and Davies, suggesting that a slop might be of a short length.[19] Certainly by the 1850s, the short smock was identified with the navvy.[20] Whether these 'slops' were similar garments in different parts of the country or just local slang is another question.

A case heard at the Hertfordshire Lent Assizes in 1840 sums up this difficulty, going into detail about what the terms meant. Emma Norris and Samuel Abrahams were caught up in a semantic case regarding the theft of 'a garment called a slop'. After working on the railway by day, George Dealey purchased 'a slop' which, after drinking in several pubs in Tring, he left on a pub table while tipsy. As he was a railway worker, this might suggest that it was a short smock. The case hinged on whether it had been stolen and then passed to Abrahams or given to Emma Norris to look after, or exchanged for money. However, it soon deteriorated into a battle of semantics between the terms of slop and smock, to match the charge on the indictment, the question asked in court, 'Is there any difference between a slop and a round smock?', the reply being, 'I don't know'. A few jurymen suggested that slops and smock frocks 'were differently made and could not be mistaken'. As 'slop' was on the indictment, the case was initially dismissed.[21] However, a few days later Norris and Abrahams were back, retried for stealing a round frock, confusingly for the court, also described as a 'smock frock, a round frock and a railway frock'. Robert Brice, a draper from Hemel Hempstead called the article 'a round slop' and said that if a man came and asked for a slop, this is what he would show him, as it was generally termed 'a slop'. He went on, in the cross-examination:

> Other things are called slops generally, but not literally; this is undoubtedly the only garment specifically called a slop; the general denomination is a round slop or slop; working on the London and Birmingham Railway, are men from all parts of England, and they have come into my shop and asked for a slop, meaning the very article now produced; I have heard in court that there is another article called a slop; these articles are called railway frocks in the invoices from Reading, where they are made: ... if a man came and asked for a round frock, I should give him one that comes down to the calf of the leg.[22]

Alfred Bisshenden, an apprentice to a tailor and originally from Yorkshire, confirmed the use of this terminology in that area too. However, a navigator (navvy), James Alison, was also questioned. He said that in Middlesex it would be called a slop, but here it was called a smock frock. The confusion continued with William Pollard, a draper of Hertford, stating:

> We sell slops generally; slops include all ready-made goods; if a man should come and ask for a slop, I should know what to give him; it would be an article very different to the one in question; I only know one garment called a slop; I have been asked for 'a slop' and have given a very different article; the manufacturers call these garments smockfrocks; I never heard the garment produced called a slop.[23]

The jury had to decide if a slop was the same as a smock frock, round frock and railway frock, and if it was a proper term and not just slang. They eventually found that it was not 'properly' called a slop but a smock frock, the judge retorting that this was not the question but whether it was a garment well-known as a 'slop'. They then found it was not, and the prisoners were retried for the theft of a smock frock using the evidence from the previous week. The trial then collapsed, the prosecutor, Dealey, 'falling in a fit' while giving evidence, Norris fainting as the two prisoners were acquitted. The contemporary confusion over terminology is evident, as well as the differences in usage within short geographical distances. Of course, we don't know what the original garment in this case was like, but there seems to have been no particular defining characteristics for either garment.[24] Across the country, smock frocks and slops were different articles in the same shop stock so there must have been some differences.[25] However, if contemporaries found it difficult to distinguish the terminology, tying themselves up in legal knots over it, it would seem nigh on impossible now.

Other terms used included 'jumper', found in a case involving the theft of a smock frock in Plymouth, the use of quotation marks in the report again suggesting colloquial language.[26] In Southampton, Charles Gifford, a labourer employed on the mud barges used in the dock entrance, was accused of being involved in a plot to assassinate Queen Victoria and Prince Albert with a pistol. Appearing in court, Gifford dressed in a smock frock, 'or surplice, as it is here called', suggesting a link to the white linen ecclesiastical garment.[27] Nineteenth-century rural protest often used religious imagery and biblical allusions, which the smock may also have been part of.[28] A 'kettle smock frock' or 'kittle' was a term used in Somerset.[29] A court case from 1846 reveals what this was. Charles Binning, a witness and a carrier working between Clewer and Bristol, saw two men; 'one had a short "kittle" and a high-crowned hat; the other a Jim Crow hat and kittle (this is a short smock frock)'.[30] This is backed up by a local newspaper report in 1908: 'A smock which reached only to the waist, and was gathered in with a tight band, was called, in Somerset, a kettle smock, or slop'.[31] Kittel is also German for smock. Defining what a smock frock was, away from the idealized nostalgic picture of one, is difficult, as it was for contemporaries as well.

By 1941, the smock frock was seen as 'a garment peculiar to Sussex in former days' and the terminology discussed in the fifteenth edition of the *Sussex County Magazine*. William Grantham favoured smock, while the editor favoured 'round smock', a former draper settling the matter by suggesting that if it had smocking it was a smock frock, if without this then a round frock.[32] Seemingly, historically, there was no consensus on what a smock frock was, despite our very fixed view of the garment today. The complexity of the nomenclature, to some extent, underlines the importance of the smock trade with expansion in the ready-made sector into the mid-nineteenth century, giving wide availability and subtle distinctions between types of the garment to reach different male consumers.[33] Some of these terms were descriptive, some colloquial, some just invented on the spot. Within the previously detailed three broad categories, there was both further definition and lack of agreement between contemporaries. When the garment is written about historically, without illustration or further description, it is thus impossible to know which type is being referred to. This book will therefore, for simplification purposes, use the generic term 'smock' to disrupt the received picture of the history of the 'smock frock' as we have come to understand it.

The Hidden History will take as its basis, the article published by Anne Buck in 1963, for which she surveyed 121 smocks.[34] Over twenty-five years ago, a friend of my father's knew Anne Buck well and, as I was undertaking my master's in the history of dress and she was one of the most respected figures in the discipline, arranged that we should meet for tea at her house. It was a beautiful summer's afternoon in Bedfordshire, my very own country idyll, and we sat outside on Miss Buck's terrace to take tea in her flower-filled garden. As a retired museum curator, working principally at Platt Hall in Manchester, she had built up an unrivalled knowledge of dress history over her long career. She had published seminal books on eighteenth-century dress and Victorian costume, helping to establish the subject as a core element of social and cultural history. I wish now that I had quizzed her more about her smock research, rather than just feeling a bit overawed in her presence as a mere novice student. Although she is no longer with us, her article has stood the test of time and has proved the foundation to many studies of the smock frock, including this one.

Building on and expanding this core material object research, this book includes evidence gathered from the relatively new resource for nineteenth-century historians, the online searchable archive of nineteenth-century newspapers held by the British Library. Although I collected over 3,500 references, this remains a sample, the online archive also being continually added to. I know from previous research, completed the old-fashioned way by manually winding through microfilm in a records office, that there are references that should have come up online but do not. It is therefore not a fail-safe way to extract every conceivable reference but, with these caveats, it certainly makes searching newspapers much easier and quicker than it was ten years ago. Newspaper research has shed light on areas not represented in other sources, particularly the manufacturing and retailing of smocks, but also, for example, important evidence about smock wearers from court reports. Of course, this reportage has limitations, filtered either through a journalist or by the person placing the advertisement, or indeed by the availability and survival of the newspaper itself, but it has revealed, if only partially, the complex social and economic networks that the smock trade was part of.

My newspaper sample has thus become the foundation for this 'microhistory' of the smock frock. The detailed observation and analysis about one particular community, family, individual, work of art, or in this case, garment, seeks to reveal unknown complexities and new meanings in structures, processes and human interactions. The concentration on one thing may deliberately be narrow, but the methodological range which encompasses that subject can be broad as it will be here, analysing a diverse range of sources including printed and archive material, literature, surviving garments and visual evidence.[35] One of the innovations that this book offers is the focus on the life cycle of the garment as well as on its production. It also looks at how men acquired smocks, what they felt about their garment choices, and how they used them. *The Hidden History* shows how this evidence can be interpreted to impact wider social and cultural developments. By focusing on the particular, surprising evidence can be found to change the whole debate about broader historiographical issues, in the case of smock frocks, for example, encompassing the clothing industry, English identity and Victorian working men.

Of course, in the field of dress history, many books have been written about one type of garment including smock frocks.[36] However, with its relatively short time span and direct correlation to its historical context, the smock frock makes an ideal candidate for a more in-depth study. The majority of the population of nineteenth-century England were labourers of some sort, or in a family with one, mine being shepherds and labourers in the villages around Avebury in Wiltshire, and likely to have worn such working clothing. Yet, even now, surprisingly little is known or written about working clothing. As John Styles notes in his groundbreaking survey of non-elite dress in the eighteenth century, occupational clothing has been seen as 'a utilitarian, vernacular counterpoint to fashionable clothing, rooted in the functional imperatives of particular forms of manual labour and resistant to change'.[37] While this is true to a degree due to the specific nature of their use, as Styles notes, such garments also often have a more complex development, their relationship to a particular occupation rarely fixed or exclusive.[38] Examining artefacts, especially utilitarian mundane ones, can help to probe unwritten history, a history which is otherwise ignored, and in the case of smock, obscured and hidden by perceptions of what it has come to represent.[39]

This is also a history of everyday sartorial practices and the resulting social behaviours of the male working classes, who left few traditional archival records.[40] As Peter Andersson notes in his study of street life in Victorian London, a broadening of scope is required, with a more imaginative use of sources to research ordinary practices, oral cultures and mundane behaviour, when this is not formally recorded. He suggests studying pictures, autobiographies and trial reports, where people mention or display such practices and have no reason to be untruthful.[41] I would add their clothing practices to this list: how clothing was used and affected behaviour, and perceptions of behaviour, particularly everyday clothing such as the smock frock. Pat Hudson urges, in her article on Welsh woollen clothing, for the necessity of looking beyond an object as a signifier of cultural convention and fashion, which often neglects the working-class population, to how objects were experienced and used, and how objects themselves influenced the person's life.[42] Barbara Burman and Ariane Fennetaux, in their history of the tie-on pocket, explore the capacity for both change and continuity within one object revealing what they see as a corrective to dominant fashion history narratives. The complex and fluid mundane sartorial practices that they uncover for women across all social classes are echoed in this research.[43] The clothing practices of working people in general need much further investigation, this research contributing to this field with an exploration of one male garment.

Historians have begun to acknowledge the complexity of the culture of appearances in the working population.[44] Clothing was vital and could be used to perform a role, whether to appear respectable or to dress in a particular way to fit in with a peer group.[45] The smock is unusual for working clothing in that large numbers of garments survive, whereas many common garments did not. Appearing to be a straightforward garment worn by a specific group, this research shows how an in-depth investigation instead reveals a very different picture, which myths and half-truths have hidden from view. By setting out to consider seemingly straightforward aims, reflected in the chapter headings, that is to investigate fully how smocks were made, bought and sold, and who wore them, complex findings are revealed. In order to be able to put this research about a predominantly nineteenth-century garment into context, it is also necessary to trace where the smock as an item of clothing came from and how we arrived at the view we have of it today.

Chapter 1 will therefore examine how the smock became associated with rural England, and particularly southern England, by considering the nostalgia for the countryside during the late Victorian/Edwardian period and interwar era, as the rural landscape appeared to alter dramatically. The male smock frock became ossified at this point, categorized as 'folk' dress, rural, unchanging and obsolete for modern life. By showing why smocks were collected for museums and the way that authors used them in their texts for a particular purpose, we can begin to understand where our misrepresentation about their history has come from.

Chapter 2 investigates the history of the smock from the medieval period to the nineteenth century. It will question why working men adopted smocks and why they remained a core part of their wardrobe for around a century. The idea of working-class male fashion is discussed with reference to the smock, as well as their decoration, including the embroidery worked by women makers. As a garment outside mainstream fashion, their increasing embellishment is contextualized as part of working-class clothing cultures.

By moving on to examine how the majority were actually made, in Chapter 3, the utilitarian purpose of the smock emerges, an item of workwear rather than a piece of folk art. The newspaper evidence shows widespread ready-made manufacturing of various types of smocks from different sized factories and workshops. It investigates in detail some of these manufacturers including Hyde of Abingdon and Bousfield of Reading, emphasizing the impact that manufacturing smocks had on the development of ready-made clothing production in general.

The counterpoint to making clothing is how consumers are sold, or acquire, garments, and this is investigated in Chapter 4. This highlights the widespread use of the smock by working men, across the country, and the importance of the smock trade for many clothing retailers, from a variety of outlets, large and small. For some, it became the mainstay of their business. The role of the working-class male consumer is explored as a purchaser of his own clothing and the homosocial environments which ran alongside this.

Linking to these male purchases of smock frocks, Chapter 5 considers how wearing a smock was related to various occupations, including those of navvies and dustmen. It examines the nineteenth-century culture of visualization and how smocks could be used to classify people by appearance and also to deceive others by using perceptions about this categorization. It moves on to investigate the broader global use of the English smock in the United States and particularly in Australia, where, overcoming its class connotations, it was taken up and adapted into a piece of egalitarian workwear suitable for all.

A different trajectory for the smock occurred in Britain, as it became seen as old-fashioned and then quaint, as Chapter 6 will show, linking back to Chapter 1. The decline of the male smock is thus explored, as well as why concurrently women and children began to wear the garment. The idea of smocking as a handicraft is also investigated, especially its promotion by organizations such as the Women's Institute. The smock is now seen as part of the vocabulary of fashion used when designers want to evoke a particular feeling, often relating to childhood or the freedom of a bohemian lifestyle. The book will conclude with a brief discussion about how the smock became part of mainstream fashion, via the United States, designers currently using the garment on catwalks in both women's and menswear shows.

What has emerged has been surprising and helps to shed light on the often hidden, vibrant clothing communities of working people. Questions are raised about clothing manufacture, retailing clothing to working people, as well as how masculinity and manliness was and is represented through clothing. First, in Chapter 1, let us turn to discuss what the smock has commonly come to represent and how it became linked to its now strong association with the rural.

1 The smock and rural England

Today 'smocks' are most commonly connected with children's wear, artists or perhaps coastal life, with the sailing and fisherman's smock. For artistic and marine wear, the smock is a plain 'non-fashion garment' that allows the adult wearer, male or female, to concentrate on higher purposes or physical activity, signifying a lack of interest in appearance.[1] However, if you talk about 'smock frocks', often the first thought is of a rural 'yokel' dressed in one, wearing a hat, chewing straw, often with unkempt facial hair, and drinking a flagon of cider. This image is usually located somewhere in the past, often combined with other rural clichés such as cottage doors, folk traditions and bucolic farmyards.[2] The smock and smock frock have been differentiated to evoke different feelings; one still a useful and practical garment, the other picturesque, unpractical, and so often comic, quaint and obsolete.

As discussed in the introduction, the nomenclature of the garment has historically been fluid, slippery and difficult to grasp. During much of the nineteenth century, at the peak of the smock trade, the smock and the smock frock were one and the same thing. However, during the late nineteenth century, the smock frock began to be associated with both a very specific type of garment and a particular wearer. While this iteration is as valid as any other, the aim of *The Hidden History* is to dispel the notion that this is the only version and, in doing so, to open up the complexities and multidisciplinary approach needed to fully analyse working dress across an extended period. This chapter will therefore first establish how this representation emerged so completely to subsume and hide how men used to wear the smock/smock frock earlier in the nineteenth century. There is a large body of research into the representations of rural England, including why the idea of Englishness and the countryside of southern England became so closely associated. *The Hidden History* will instead focus on how the smock became part of this symbolism, principally through its categorization as folk dress and the feelings that the garment induced. It will conclude by considering if surviving smocks in museum collections have also coloured our understanding of how they were used by the majority of men during the nineteenth century.

From the late 1870s, as crisis hit contemporary agriculture,[3] a version of a rural idyll deeply rooted in the past emerged centred on a southern vision of England, particularly the 'Home Counties', what has been called 'deformed nationalism'.[4] Parallels were drawn between the degeneration of urban life, particularly in London, and the fall of a debauched ancient Rome, country people uncontaminated by such vices and false values.[5] *Country Life* magazine (founded in 1897) illustrated the unattainable rural idyll that urban elites yearned for. With the 'back to the land' movement of the 1890s as rural depopulation became a problem, value was given to aspects of rural life such as folk songs, as collected by Cecil Sharpe,[6] and the vernacular architecture of the cottage. Popularizers, for instance, Helen Allingham, Edward Lutyens and Ralph Vaughan Williams, broadened this reach to a wider audience. With seemingly less physical countryside now in existence, writers such as George Sturt in the early twentieth century, eulogized about the passing of an old order, where self-sufficiency and industriousness were the virtues of an idealized peasant community.[7] The smock thus began to gain a symbolic significance, incorporated into the construction of a mythologized and sentimental rural existence, a 'simple' life, with a strong folk culture, particularly appealing to urban elites, offering consolation in a time of change, but which, in reality, perhaps never existed.[8]

This late Victorian and Edwardian idea of 'Englishness' – rural, anti-modern and traditional – however, remained very much a minority view of the artistic, articulate and literary elite, an attempt to recapture an apparently threatened way of life, and for both those on the left and right of the political spectrum, to find a better way to live.[9] For the mass of the population, who moved from the countryside to be urbanites, often within living memory, traditional rural society was class-ridden, hard, anachronistic and often feudalistic. By the late nineteenth century, rural working-class youths regarded 'the smock frock as an abomination, and farm work as a nuisance', with working on the land something to be 'despised'. There was a new aspiration for higher education which conservative factions saw as destroying 'Those idyllic days of which we get a glimpse in romance and ballad'.[10] Manners were changing in rural villages too, with youths no longer doffing their hats or bowing to parish priests as they had when wearing smock frocks.[11] A change in clothing, which certainly visually closed the status gap, at least at first glance, also equated with the disappearance of expected deference to the elite.

During the nineteenth century, there was a decline in the hegemony of the countryside as power shifted to the commercial and urban middle classes. With overspill house building and railways for example, the countryside itself was increasingly built on and accessible. What remained of the 'rural' began to be perceived as an exotic 'other' life, removed and isolated from the ordinary. Visiting this 'park' became a popular urban pastime, an escapist retreat from the stresses of modern town life.[12] The accessibility and comfort of rural images, from the mid-nineteenth century onwards, reinforced this visually, with landscape artists portraying views untouched by modern improvements, the emphasis being on the natural or the countryside as a site of recreation accessed via the railway.[13] A long tradition of writers, from the classical period onwards, also mythologized the idea of people in the countryside being happier and more virtuous, creating the notion of a lost paradise, or arcadia, verdant and blossoming.[14] Often this is the lost rural past of the writer's childhood or of tales passed down through the family.[15] Typically, the writer may have moved to a town to pursue a career and remembered their childhood as William Cobbett did in his *Rural Rides*. William Howitt is another example, the son of a yeoman farmer, he describes the farmer living 'like a rural king' and wistfully remembered the social harmony needed for events such as the harvest.[16]

Thomas Hardy too, although credited with realistic portrayals, was writing for a middle-class audience with a distinct whiff of nostalgia for the perceived rural idyll of his youth in the 1840s and early 1850s. He created an ideal of a timeless rural social order pitted against increasing changes derived from urban culture visually expressed through clothing, including the disappearance of the smock as working clothing for men.[17] For example, in *Far from the Madding Crowd*, Hardy compares fast-changing urban modernity with the timelessness of the countryside where 'Five decades hardly modified the cut of a gaiter, [or] the embroidery of a smock frock, by the breadth of a hair.'[18] Discussing the 'Dorsetshire Labourer' in his essay of 1883, Hardy ignores disagreeable conditions and seething discontent to romanticize elements, suggesting that rural labourers were not revolutionary or antagonistic about class differences, but content, unthinking and harmless, thus deliberately ignoring the political reality and pandering to the views of his urban middle-class readership.[19] Hardy used the smock frock as a construct to reflect contemporary ambivalence about urban values overtaking those of the idealized unchanging countryside.[20] Then, as now, scenes of traditional agriculture appeal to our nostalgia for the pre-industrial, supposedly unpolluted world, where life was thought to be simple and stable, with social harmony in accord with nature, albeit often in a man-made landscape. With a further connection to a remembered perfect rural childhood, and the emotional experience of recalling this lost time and place, that is nostalgia, the smock began to take on a different meaning.[21]

With urbanization, industrialization and mass consumerism enveloping British society at an increasing rate, there was a scramble to preserve cyphers of rural and popular, or folk, art.[22] The smock, then fast disappearing as everyday wear, became categorized as one of the only English examples of 'national peasant costume' or folk dress, ossified and preserved for special occasions, such as traditional rural events.[23] It became particularly associated with southern England and Sussex, obscuring its history elsewhere. Folk 'is a four-letter word', difficult to pin down and fluid in its meanings, including the vernacular, rural, naïve, self-taught and indifferent to change.[24] These seem, at first glance, appropriate descriptions for the smock. Often at times of collective crisis, in the 1880s, 1910s and 1930s–50s, the necessary reassertion of national identity used the smock frock as a concept, and, to a certain extent, reinvented it for that era.[25] It was 'quaint, primitive, picturesque, and serviceable garb',[26] and smocking 'one of the few peasant crafts which we have in England'.[27] A century earlier, in 1821, a report recorded that 'there is nothing very distinctive in the dress of any of the lower classes', and no British or English costume as such.[28] Although worn in the 1820s, in the intervening century the smock gradually filled this gap by becoming 'folk' dress, associated firmly with a particular place, the pre-industrial rural England of yesteryear, countering the modernity of contemporary fashions which supposedly alienated working people from their often recent rural origins. This perceived loss of rural identity through a change in dress formed part of the elite collective memory of England's golden past and led to the smock's preservation by them.[29]

During the interwar period, alarmed at the contemporary cultural poverty of rural life, artists and designers seized upon the spontaneous freshness of traditional primitive or 'peasant' work.[30] There was a nostalgia for such things, made slowly by hand to last a lifetime and, on these, rich narratives could be constructed beyond the object's humble usage. As Tanya Harrod points out, the recurring paradox of the period was that an important part of being modern was to be anti-modern. There was an anxiety about the quality of objects, the essence of things, threatened by synthetic materials and mass production. To counter this, the lost simplicity and plainness of crafted objects remembered from childhood were evoked.[31] The stories of smocks and their embroidered patterns, published in books such as one by Alice Armes in 1928, were part of this.[32] In search of the pre-industrial rural world, collectors and artists harked back to the eighteenth century, to an unenclosed English landscape, where workers may have been poor but were happy and deferential to the elite. This idealized portrait sought the authentic object, shaped by toil and by life, a timeless piece, requiring many hours in a domestic environment to make it. The smock was thought of as one of the only 'vernacular' pieces of dress to survive and was thus revered as a pre-industrial authentic object. It fed into the notion of the idealization of peasant life as being better than urban life, where hand-spun and handcrafted objects were signs of prosperity, commercially produced clothing a sign of poverty.

During the early twentieth century, the smock frock therefore seemed to fit with the ideas of folk art: the borrowing and reiteration of forms passed down from generation to generation manifested in smock embroidery patterns; a timeless and ahistorical feel; and the idea of the multiple – that there was less concern with uniqueness, one smock looking much like another. Makers were able to distinguish themselves by their own patterns within the conformity of producing a garment.[33] They were emblematic of the dress of old country 'folk' and photographs of smock frock wearers were points of curiosity for readers of *Country Life* magazine during the 1940s and 1950s, as the mythical 'good old days seem[ed] very far away'.[34] The smock was therefore imbued with sentiment about a lost childhood and nostalgia for the now changed landscape that this had been set in. The inter-materiality of text, image, surviving object and emotions about these representations conveyed and fixed upon smocks new meanings for different audiences. Moved to a new locus and used to demonstrate this lost intangible past, the reimagined smock has changed its meaning and also lost its original purpose.[35]

Thus a vision of Englishness, formed as the smock disappeared from normal male usage, and strongly re-evoked in the late twentieth century, still holds sway today as the ideal, the 'imagined community' of rural England.[36] In 1937, a photo mural designed by Oliver Hill was included in the modernist British Pavilion at the Exposition Internationale des Arts et Techniques dans la Vie Moderne in Paris. This reflected a pastoral vision of England, with quasi-feudal overtones, the focus on country sports and leisure in the countryside, such as hunting, shooting and fishing, marginalizing modernism. In the middle of photographs of cricket matches and scenic spots looms a man in a smock and gaiters (see Figure 1.1). The smock was now part of the pastoral, associated particularly with shepherds, not agricultural workers in general. Though located in the modernist British Pavilion, this man adds to the myth of 'Merrie England,' traditional and rural, the countryside available for pastimes and leisure, recreation for those who could afford it.[37]

The smock's authenticity as a working garment within living memory firmly connected it, in the minds of those who sought its preservation, to 'place', in this case rural southern England, its production supposedly being antithetical to commercial concerns and its immutability and handcrafted feel theoretically ensuring against its commodification in the past. Along with the sun bonnet for women, the smock therefore played a significant role in the cultural construction of this elite rural idyll rooted in undefined previous centuries. Today, this mythologizing has repressed the varied and culturally diverse history of the smock frock, and

FIGURE 1.1 *British Pavilion, Paris Exposition 1937, Frontispiece,* The Architect and Building News, *July 1937. © courtesy of The British Library Board, LOU.LD83.*

as one writer about them points out, 'The facts about them are fast eluding us.'[38] Unlike other clothing for manual labour which rarely survives or was collected, the smock was thus valued for its decoration and craft, and the feelings that it evoked for collectors, changing our perceptions of both what rural life was and about the garment itself.[39] The rural reality, then as now, was more usually poverty, distress, hard labour and class conflict.[40] However, this elite vision was and remains an active concept, seeping into 'middle England' to create mythical traditions, a cultural ideal, 'a modern superstition,'[41] where the perfect childhood is still seen as allowing offspring to roam the countryside and build dens.[42] The strength of this vision makes it undeniable, and in a sense tangible, existing as an idea now in many forms for different people, used to reassess our lives or to sell us new things from tourism to TV shows, and even music festivals in muddy farm fields.[43] John Lewis-Stempel wrote in *The Running Hare: The Secret Life of Farmland*, published in 2016, of 'how you think of England: rolling meadows, hangers of trees, meandering brooks, red telephone boxes, deep lanes, [and] thatched black-and-white cottages'.[44] This almost reactionary identity, 'a little Englander', rural and in opposition to 'urban' and 'Continental' excesses, is a common trope, as national identity, especially Englishness as opposed to Britishness, is increasingly polarized and contentious.

The survival of smocks in museum collections

Surviving smocks are therefore just as much representations as are the images of smocks in paintings and photographs or accounts in literature.[45] Certainly in the early twentieth century, the elite collected smocks to preserve them as an example of something which was disappearing or had disappeared, perhaps to capture their nostalgia for the past. They took on the projected values of their collectors, with the invention of a 'tradition', much like tartan or the Aran jumper.[46] Smocks are also donated to museums because they are an heirloom so they have been preserved intergenerationally for a particular reason. Rather than plain, workaday mundane smocks, elaborate handcrafted examples were more attractive to collectors and to curators for display, linking to the idea of 'peasant' craft. Having been filtered, their typicality and representativeness can perhaps therefore be questioned, their survival obscuring the standard garment.[47] As Rachel Worth has also noted, it is the embroidered smocks which survive rather than the 'despised' shoddy ready-made suits worn by those who cast aside their smocks in the name of fashion.[48] Museum curators did not seek out and preserve the clothing that replaced smocks, at least not until the end of the twentieth century.

In 1910, a surgeon made an early donation to the Buckinghamshire County Museum of a dark brown smock frock, with the name of its actual wearer noted.[49] As the *Bucks Herald* stated, collections were already seeking objects with 'distinct local interest', and should 'not confine … [themselves] to specimens of great intrinsic worth, but … rather strive to acquire a number of comparatively common objects, which when collected together, are undoubtedly of historical and educational worth'. This included everyday articles, tools 'and other objects used by our forefathers, such as the smock frock … would make a most interesting and instructive collection … Doubtless many such things get destroyed or lost when houses change hands, or an industrious housewife goes in for spring-cleaning'.[50] A perfect specimen of a smock was then said to be worth around 10 pounds, an imperfect one, about 3 pounds.[51]

However, the ambivalent attitude towards smocks by some early curators is summed up in 1923, when a correspondent from the *Western Times* visited Dorset, where his grandparents came from, to see if the life of the agricultural labourer was being preserved. Asking at the Dorchester County Museum, the attendant, busy with flints and potshards, matter-of-factly directed him to a draper if he wanted to see a smock frock. The article bemoaned the fact that while the everyday life of other civilizations was being preserved in the museum, that of the Dorset labourer was not.[52] By 1930, the *Western Gazette* reported that local museums now preserved once everyday items used in village life which were otherwise destroyed, such as agricultural tools and smock frocks, with the help of organizations such as the Women's Institute. According to the report, the most interesting local museum was the 'one that illustrates the history of the little town that owns it, and which contains nothing but [that which] has a connection with its home. And it is cherished by its owners'.[53] The positive feeling of connection to the past, whether through grandparents or place, and the value given to those emotions, is emphasized, the sought objects, including the smock, imbued with new meanings reflecting these sensibilities.

The survival of so many smock frocks in provincial museums, at first glance all very similar and many anonymized of their provenance, collected as representative of rural life and folk art, as well as perhaps for their exceptional needlework, has maybe led to a quandary as to what to do with them, not having the context of their social history.[54] The extant smock nonetheless has multiple histories encompassing practical, symbolic and aesthetic elements. We need to try and unpick its multifaceted narratives to gain a fuller understanding about the garment and its social context.[55] Clothing is a form of material memory, having an intimate relationship with the body which leaves an imprint. Signs of practical use and wear on surviving smock frocks make even mass-produced examples unique and relate them directly to their wearer's life.[56] Smocks were mended, patched, darned, washed and dyed, each creating a personal biography of its owner or owners.[57] By using diverse sources, including surviving garments, the following chapters will explore parts of some of these personal histories, including the value and emotions that a wearer attached to a smock. Considering how men used the smock and identified (expressed) themselves in wearing it and who the wearers were, as well as how the lived experience of a labourer using the garment changed its meaning and significance for them, offers an innovative approach to set within the context of research into working clothing.[58]

The dress of yokels

Over the last 150 years, life in the countryside has changed enormously. However, particularly in periods of crisis or national anxiety, a yearning for the rural or nature, or a desire for a simple living from the countryside, is often part of England's collective self-imagining. This usually recalls the countryside of an unspecified yesteryear, perhaps drawn from childhood memories or the influence of novels, television and film. Until the mid-twentieth century, nostalgia about, and preservation of, the smock was symptomatic of this, perhaps recalling Victorian and Edwardian childhoods. Smocks were emotional objects generating particular feelings. The cypher of a disappearing childhood, as well as a disappearing countryside, smock collections are thus partly an elite construct, a supposed reflection of this traditional pre-industrial rural life, folk objects, unique, and with almost a ritualistic use as part of countryside customs.

With much evidence about smock wearers collected around the turn of the twentieth century frequently relating to aged country 'folk', the mainstream view is that rural, usually elderly, labourers wore them. Perhaps this has also distilled into the character of the yokel as the primary smock wearer for more popular perceptions. As we will explore in Chapter 6, there were specific reasons why the smock was the dress of elderly rural men by the late nineteenth century, when collectors first began to acquire smocks for museums and photograph their wearers.[59] This representation hides the fact that while the smock was regarded as handmade and the dress of rural men, at the same time, it was also being mass-produced and worn by other working men such as navvies, across all geographical areas. Today, the smock still evokes the sentimentalism of childhood memories, and, in particular, the home-sewing of smocks for children, often by their mothers, their continuing use as children's wear reinforcing this.[60]

Thus, the following chapters of *The Hidden History* rescue the smock from the realms of the picturesque, nostalgia and folk dress, redressing the balance between perceptions of smocks being unfamiliar and extraordinary to that of their mundanity, seeking, in the process, to uncover more about our 'minimal knowledge of the unknown majority'.[61] They seemingly had very little to do with 'Englishness', 'craft' or 'folk' dress, at least until the turn of the twentieth century when commentators ascribed these qualities to the garment for posterity. Having examined both the constructs of the idealized rural past and of the common elderly smock-wearing rural labourer here, the next chapter turns to look at the history of the smock and how and why it fitted into the working-man's clothing needs.

2 Histories of the smock frock

As I have indicated, unpicking the history of the smock frock is problematic and, as Anne Buck noted, well-documented examples are rare.[1] As with most clothing, there are different qualities and costs associated with garments bearing the same descriptive name, although as we have seen, the name was also open to interpretation in the case of the 'smock frock'. This chapter will discuss the history of the smock frock, stories about the smock's origins having obscured and hidden the development of the garment. These narratives will be traced, before examining the smock and its relationship to male working clothing and the female makers of this clothing, particularly during the nineteenth century.

The medieval and Tudor period

The origin and antiquity of the smock was periodically debated in the press from the mid-nineteenth century onwards. A piece in the architectural journal, *The Builder*, in 1857, notes that fashions for 'male agriculturalists' had not changed for '2,000 years ... in a remote part of Suffolk ... the shepherds ... dress in close-fitting leggings, smock-frock and wide-brimmed felt hat ... looking ... as if they had only recently given a sitting to one of our old Saxon illuminators'. The article observes the adherence to this 'old costume' in the country, particularly in the south, and states how the wheel of fashion had stood still for 'the peasant class'.[2] During the 1890s, the smock frock's supposed origin from ecclesiastical garments was also discussed. This suggested that ornate Catholic vestments given away or sold to labourers and the poor during the Reformation were then copied, giving rise to the contemporary garment.[3] However, ecclesiastical garments themselves derived from secular late Roman dress, although it was suggested that the slits at the side of the smock were an echo of the Saxon tunic of a bondsman.[4] As the country moved politically towards enfranchisement for all men, including labourers, the smock frock was increasingly linked to the 'Anglo-Saxon peasantry', the true 'English', who held the land before the Norman Conquest, a symbol of a rural, ordered, if not feudal, arcadia, now fast disappearing.[5]

However, the Saxon word 'smoc', translating as 'a garment to creep into' and similar to the Norse word, 'Smjuga' with a related meaning,[6] had originally meant a female undergarment, with fine sixteenth- and seventeenth-century examples elaborately embellished with embroidery around the neckline and hem, as well as on the long sleeves.[7] The mundane variety of the female linen smock was sold ready-made during the sixteenth century, essential for wearing next to the skin, for withstanding frequent washing and keeping more expensive woollen clothing in a better condition for longer.[8] The medieval female smock transmogrified into the shift between 1650 and 1750 and then, later, the chemise, as successive names for essentially the same undergarment became imbued with too much innuendo for respectable society.[9] In 1843, this change in the use of language was acknowledged, with the description of a smock as an inner garment for a lady in the time of Shakespeare, before the shift took its place, 'A shift? A change in linen!' as the report wittily put it, 'to shift' originally being the verb for changing into clean linen/underwear. However, as this too became suggestive, the chemise took its place, the article speculating about 'she-mises' and 'hemises'.[10]

Seventeenth century

During the seventeenth century, a 'smock' thus generally refers to female garments while a 'frock' was male clothing.[11] In a collection of inventories of chapmen and salesmen transcribed by Margaret Spufford dating from the late seventeenth century, the male 'frock' as a protective garment seems well-established and the source of the eighteenth-century smock frock.[12] Diana de Marly suggests that plain 'smocks' without smocking spread from the Netherlands during the seventeenth century, Jayne Shrimpton proposing that they derived from farm carters' loose linen or canvas coats worn during the same period[13] (see Figure 2.1, for an example). Danae Tankard, researching clothing in seventeenth-century Sussex, has found references to ready-made frocks being sold in the second half of the century. For example, Samuel Jeake, a merchant from Rye, bought a linen 'frock' for 5 shillings in 1676, which Tankard suggests was a practical garment, perhaps for use as an overall when moving stock around his warehouse.[14] When James Farndon disappeared in the mid-seventeenth century, he had 'a canvas

FIGURE 2.1 *Waggoner Playing Card, from a set satirizing the Rump Parliament, circa 1660–5. 1896,0501.917. © The Trustees of the British Museum.*

coat called a frock' with him.[15] Randle Holme helpfully states in his description of a carter in 1688, that he was a 'Man in a Frock (or Linnen or Canvas Coat)', with an illustration of a plain coat very similar to Figure 2.1.[16]

In John Dryden's translation of *Amaryllis, or the Third Idyllium of Theocritus* in 1684, the garment in line 55 is translated as a 'Shepherd's Frock'.[17] As a translation of a Greek bucolic poet writing pastoral poetry, this seems to be the first association of frocks with shepherds and therefore as a specifically rural garment.

Ready-made fustian frocks, worn as a protective overgarment, were also a feature of men's working dress since the late seventeenth century. Runaways in 1675 and 1685 carried fustian frocks with them.[18] In Gregory King's 'Annual Consumption of Apparell', a table formulated in 1688, 200,000 frocks were sold for 4 shillings each alongside other garments.[19] Chapmen travelled around the countryside, going out from drapers' shops, to sell clothing accessories and textiles from which larger garments could be made up. *The Plain Dealing Linnen Draper*, published in 1696 as an aid for linen drapers and seamstresses, sold for a few pence and suggested that customers buy a double-woven fustian 'dyed sad colour', for 'Men's Frocks'.[20]

Around the same time, during the 1670s and 1680s, the East India Company began to sell ready-made male shirts and shifts for women, contemporarily also called a smock as a female undergarment. Made out of cotton calico rather than linen, the peak of this trade was in the 1680s when the company auctioned off 200,000 ready-made cotton shirts and shifts in England.[21] As the East India Company was good at doing from the start, they differentiated their various products for different social categories with precise instructions for their Indian manufacturers.[22] Although probably referring to female garments, some clothing was to be embroidered on the breast, sleeves and collar. These sound like embryonic smock frocks. With a glut of Indian textiles in the market, this venture initially failed with a surplus stock of over 100,000 shirts and shifts left in the company warehouse in 1685. A stuttering market continued into the 1690s, but after 1699 no more requests for ready-made Indian cotton shirts or shifts are noted, although fabrics specified for use in making shirts were imported by the company into the eighteenth century.[23] Army contracts during the English Civil War and garments required for overseas markets, both for sailors and colonial settlers, along with the surplus East India Company stock, may have helped stimulate ready-made markets well into the eighteenth century and the subsequent development of the ready-made smock frock.[24]

Eighteenth century

Ready-made frocks continue to appear in shop inventories in the early eighteenth century. For example, in 1703, Robert Amsden, a salesman of Canterbury, listed '12 Men and boys frocks at 3s 6d apeice [sic]'; Thomas Webb, a salesman of Tonbridge, similarly stocked '2 Mens unlined frocks' for 15 shillings and '3 Lads frocks at 4s 6d' as well as '½ a Dozen of Round frocks' for 15 shillings in 1721, signifying some variety in style and size by this date.[25] The price differences suggest that perhaps the round frock was more utilitarian and maybe not made from fustian. From the early eighteenth century, in dictionaries of common words, such as Nathan Bailey's *Dictionarium Britannicum* of 1726, the smock was still a female undergarment, the frock 'a Garment to wear over the Apparel to keep it clean' as an overall.[26]

However, young men from a higher strata of society adopted fustian frocks as outer garments from the 1710s onwards, perhaps, as Philip Sykas proposes, aping coachmen's dress which they perceived as being sporty.[27] Many such 'fustian frocks' seem to be like loose, unfitted coats with turned down collars and buttons down the front, as with a butcher's frock in 1742, with '12 Plate Buttons'.[28] By the mid-eighteenth century, many elite men wore the 'frock', now a full-skirted plain coat, not necessarily fustian, for informal occasions such as for riding, sports or to wear in the country. Alongside this, working men continued to wear the fustian frock as an overall, unshaped and purely protective in function.[29]

Fustian ranged in colour from white to buff and yellow, and so had a similar palette to the later male smock frock.[30] White fustian frocks became a common article during the first half of the eighteenth century, often cited in descriptions of the appearance of criminal suspects. Their use as a disguise by the criminal fraternity, much like the smock frock a hundred years later, suggests that they were a popular article of dress for working men. Fustian frocks were also stolen, incidences peaking in the mid-eighteenth century, falling off sharply after 1770. Sykas suggests that this decline was due to competition from other fabrics, for example 'canvas drilling', a coarse linen also used for frocks, on which new duties were suggested to protect fustian manufacturers.[31] Thomas Ives, of Spalding in Lincolnshire, erected a 'factory' in 1746 for hemp and flax manufacture to make 'drill' suitable for 'Men's Frocks'.[32] Similar industries were undertaken in other towns such as Abingdon, later a centre of smock frock production.[33] By the second half of the eighteenth century, large quantities of ready-made 'frocks' were routinely included in slop orders for the navy, often in canvas or duck.[34] The *Purefoy Letters*, dating from the 1740s, note Edward and Francis Fell of Chipping Norton making working frocks,[35] and Henry Purefoy describes a 'strange' man from Lincolnshire wearing a 'white ffrock [sic] over, buttoned at his hands like a shirt,' so this was unlikely to have been made from fustian.[36] By the 1790s, fustian had become associated with country wear for farmers and gentlemen, used for breeches and jackets, its pile shedding light rain and drying out quickly, so giving it practical advantages. Hardwearing and useful, but unable to be shaped or tailored, fustian was subsequently relegated to the working-man's wardrobe during the nineteenth century and, ultimately, alongside the smock, became a symbol of the labourer.[37]

During the 1730s and 1740s the long frock was also used on the London stage to dress country bumpkins in comedy roles. The character of 'Hob' appeared in various productions including *The Country Wake* (1696 and 1711–29) and *Flora*, a ballad opera of 1729, for which engravings of scenes were produced, initially to illustrate a songbook.[38] As seen in these contemporary depictions (see Figure 2.2), the frock in linen, duck or canvas, with its loose cut and long length was antithetical to the fashionable urban male. Thus with comedic and rural associations, the garment may have also been termed a 'smock' pejoratively at

FIGURE 2.2 *John Laguerre (1688–1746)*, Hob Taken Out of Ye Well, circa *1730, oil on canvas, B1981.25.392. © Yale Center for British Art, Paul Mellon Collection.*

first, with the word's recent link to female underwear, the term perhaps advanced for comic effect on stage. However, by the 1750s, newspaper descriptions of the appearance of runaways begin to use the term 'smock frock', although as this is parallel to the successful development of provincial newspapers, it is difficult to judge if the lack of mention before this date is therefore particularly significant. In 1752, at Upton Lovell in Wiltshire, two men were trying to sell a suspected stolen horse to a blacksmith, one wearing 'a white Canvas Frock', the other a 'Carter's Smock Frock', which they left behind.[39] Alabe Angles, from Tadley, Hampshire, with 'some Pimples in the Face' and a carpenter by trade, from the 11th Regiment of Foot and Captain Scott's Company, absconded in Portsmouth in 1756 wearing a linen 'smock frock' with a green waistcoat and black breeches. Another deserter, from Captain Robinson's Company, John Combs, a labourer from Wiltshire, also wore a linen 'smock frock', old brown waistcoat and dirty leather breeches.[40] In the poor law records of Hagworthingham in Lincolnshire in 1752, women spun hemp and men wove cloth to make up articles including 'smock frocks for men'.[41] Thomas Smith, a husbandman, was described as 'generally wears a

FIGURE 2.3 A Scene near Cox Heath, or the Enraged Farmer... May 1st 1779. Acc. No. 1941-224. © The Colonial Williamsburg Foundation.

Smock-Frock for his upper Garment', when he left his wife to be taken care of by an Ipswich parish in 1769.[42] The Old Bailey records show that the term 'smock frock' appeared during the 1770s, first in 1774, with a more common usage in the 1780s and thereafter, as the trade in fustian frocks fell off.[43] Therefore by the late eighteenth century, the male labourer's linen smock frock was everyday wear.

This development is backed up by the earliest known surviving smock from Mayfield in East Sussex, said to date from 1779 and held in the Victoria and Albert Museum. This is smocked, but is not embroidered further.[44] Unlike fustian, linen, in particular, can be manipulated and, to a degree, shaped by pleating. Holding pleats down with bands of stitching was decorative and practical and, due to the work needed to accomplish this, resulted in a more expensive garment than a plain one.[45] 'Smocking' seems to take its name from the smock frock, later becoming a specific type of needlework, with similar pleating techniques and 'honeycomb' effects also used on female dress during the 1770s.[46] Susan North suggests that the practice of finely pleating the sleeves of shirts and shifts began during the 1770s, so they could more easily fit under increasingly tighter coat and gown sleeves.[47]

These were not permanent, unlike smocking, the pleats disappearing after washing and needing to be reset. However, this practice may be linked to the increasing amount of smocking seen at this time. During the 1790s, as styles for ladies' dresses became looser, 'waggoners frocks' were depicted in satirical fashion plates.[48] *La Belle Assemblée* fashion magazine in June 1809 featured a 'gaged waggoner's sleeve and collar' for morning dress. Mrs Gill of Cork Street also 'invented' a morning dress of white muslin, illustrated in *Ackerman's Repository of the Arts* in May 1812, with 'waggoner's cuffs' and a panel of rolled muslin, imitating smocking, embellished in the same areas as a smock. By using the 'picturesque' and unique elements of the garment, the smock frock shape and detailing entered the fashionable discourse.[49]

Prints by artists such as James Gillray, Thomas Rowlandson and George Cruikshank from the 1780s and 1790s still depict the smock frock with no embroidery and often minimal smocking[50] (see, e.g., Figure 2.3). As cheap workwear for labouring, not everyone needed, nor could afford, a decorated one. During the French Wars of 1792–1815, rural genre paintings by artists such as George Morland were popular, portraying honest and hard-working rural people in a nationalistic light, toiling for the good of the country. Although Morland's paintings have often been seen as sentimentalizing rural life, he also depicted a divided discontented society, the, often scornful, poor usually clad in cheap smock frocks.[51] While small panels of honeycomb smocking, particularly around the neck opening were evident in many of these representations, and practical to contain surplus fabric as in the Mayfield smock, there is little decorative embroidery.[52] The ornamental embroidery on the shoulders in Figure 2.4 is a rare depiction.

FIGURE 2.4 *Detail from* A Windy Day, *George Morland, (British, 1763–1804), oil on canvas, 92.5 x 143.5 cm, 1790s, Acc No. PD.105–1992. © Fitzwilliam Museum, Cambridge.*

In William Alexander's *Picturesque Representations of the Dress and Manners of the English* from 1814, a smock on a farmer's boy, worn like a shirt, is described as 'stitched or plaited in a fanciful manner' on the front, shoulders and back of the neck, although decorative embroidery as such is not mentioned.[53] The middle classes could use such books to distinguish and categorize working people, a guidebook to various occupations with generic attributes and cyphers to identify them, which started to include the smock as rural dress.[54]

Working-men's fashions during the nineteenth century

Plainness was regarded as a distinctive characteristic of normal English dress, ostentation and decoration eyed with suspicion. Especially in the last quarter of the eighteenth century, the fashionable man dressed down, incorporating plebeian rural and sporting influences, including the frock coat, for a pared back, muted look which eventually dominated first, elite male fashions and then, menswear more generally. Plain dark clothes came to be seen as representing male modernity by the nineteenth century.[55] Appearance was moderate, restrained, an idealization of Arcadian simplicity which embodied England and civil liberties during a time of revolution.[56] Of course, with Beau Brummell, who came to epitomize the early nineteenth-century version of this look, less was more, using unforgiving plainness and sophisticated tailoring.[57] This ideal of manly virtue stood in opposition to luxury and effeminacy, epitomizing sobriety and integrity and contrasting with feminine style in particular, but also extravagant displays by the aristocracy and workers.[58] As David Kuchta has argued, this inconspicuous consumption was adopted by both the middle class and the elite during the nineteenth century, and although still differentiated within this cohort, it excluded working-class men both from being able to dress in this way and the power that this implied.[59]

Elite dressing absorbed items of plain plebeian clothing, including garments such as the frock, jacket and trousers.[60] Nonetheless, showy 'flashy' clothing remained part of working-class culture in both rural and urban settings, differentiating between their clothing and that of the elite, and elite and mass taste. Young men of poorer classes in both rural and urban areas enjoyed a certain amount of dandyism, from colourful neckerchiefs and buttons to, perhaps, ornamental smock frocks. The 'dandy' in this context is not associated with a historically specific Brummell-like figure but generalized to encompass usually young men who were preoccupied with their dress and appearance, showing off with some kind of overt display or parade with the aim of attracting partners. Although their blatant ostentation may have set them apart from the majority of men, many men went through this phase, when they were young or bachelors, before their income was diverted for other resources.[61] William Howitt noted in 1848, for holiday or Sunday wear, if not wearing a smock that had 'never yet been defiled by touch of labour', rural labourers wore a coat over a waistcoat that 'must be showy' and in a 'glaring' colour, with wide trousers, often turned up to reveal a white lining, a 'flaming' handkerchief with ends like streamers and walking with their hands in their pockets, posture an important part of self-presentation.[62]

Self-fashioned leisure clothing resisted easy identification by outside observers, being separate from the sphere of directed labour and beyond middle-class control. Dressing up for the statute day fair, on 1 May 1848, in Lincolnshire, the ploughmen wore 'a coloured shirt with a gay handkerchief tied loosely round the throat, a ruby or violet-coloured velveteen shooting jacket, a double breasted party-coloured waistcoat with glass buttons', along with fustian trousers.[63] No longer defined by occupation, men might wear flashy, fashionable and ornate clothes, including the smock, such display and experimentation accepted at particular times in certain localities without too much ridicule.[64] How clothing was worn and slight changes in appearance, for example, hairstyles and cleanliness, could signal closer affiliation to peers, or deviation from a group, the meanings of which are now indecipherable.[65] Contemporaries knew that it was possible to manipulate the reaction to their appearance and social position by using these minute changes.[66]

For working men to dress in an ostentatious way, whether choosing colour and/or decoration, was aspirational, the outward sign of prosperity visible to all, a far more public symbol than a well-furnished home, for example. It made economic sense to display prestigious dress in this way as a type of security, for everyone to see. The goodwill this engendered might be called upon in a crisis, although only if being perceived as respectable within that community's mores.[67] Here the smock had an advantage over flashy waistcoats, for instance, which might be perceived as too outré and pushing the boundaries of what was locally acceptable. Ostentation was also personally pleasurable and contrary to elite masculine ideals where concern about appearance or dressing uniquely was seen as unmasculine, showiness the antithesis to the industrious and respectable country gentry and merchants, for example.[68]

Young working-class men seemingly developed a separate flamboyant fashion system, involving items such as neckties, waistcoats and fancy shirts.[69] The urban, 'dandy cockney' was a familiar figure from the 1830s to the 1880s, personifying proletarian flashiness and sartorial confidence, embodying a pervasive vulgarity which was unsettling to middle-class contemporaries.[70] As Chris Breward notes, about the London-based dandy style of dressing in the late nineteenth century, part of it was the joy of wearing something brighter than working clothes and the parade of those clothes was a source of pleasure, allowing for the performance of a range of fashionable identities.[71] However, those living in rural areas, or coming into provincial towns for work or leisure, also participated.[72] For example, Ben Powell deserted his family at Ullingswick, Herefordshire, in 1812, wearing a smock frock, light-coloured breeches, fustian jacket, yellow striped waistcoat and red silk handkerchief, a template for similar descriptions of absconders in Herefordshire and Worcestershire from 1800 to 1820.[73] In 1805, when the apprentice William Barker ran away from his master in Loxley near Uttoxeter, he was wearing a blue coat, red waistcoat with black spots, a red and yellow handkerchief and a smock frock.[74] Joseph Woolley regularly bought new neckerchiefs in early-nineteenth-century Nottinghamshire, commenting about the right way to tie them.[75] To assert their particular masculinity, working-class men appropriated a variety of fashions, including those from within peer groups or localities, or even those of the elite.[76] The collective impulse towards personal display, whether in smocks or other garments, created a complex aesthetic which defied traditional social hierarchies.[77]

Some smock frocks were embellished in the late eighteenth century, although self-coloured embroidered examples were perhaps also more difficult to paint and so do not show up often in the visual evidence. In 1795, James White of Westgate Street, Gloucester, advertised ready-made clothes for town and country, including carters' smock frocks, 'plain or worked'.[78] In his Cheap Ready Made Clothes Warehouse in Derby in 1819, Henry Mackenzie offered a variety of blue and white 'Russia Duck' smock frocks for sale. Ranging in price from 4 shillings to 10 shillings and 6 pence, some were 'neatly flourished'.[79] It is not clear whether this is additional embroidery or just a reference to 'honeycomb' smocking. Such ornamentation can be seen as part of the counter reaction to pared down elite fashions, friendly competition within peer groups perhaps resulting in increasing elaboration.[80] The smock frock represented a way of dressing that was antithetical to fashionable male dress, 'an island of identity' which suggested some other world that the elite were not party to, beyond their control and grounded in community pride and the practical realities of this environment.[81]

Smock frock embroidery

Working-class clothing was therefore fluid and changing,[82] the development of the ornate embroidered smock frock suggesting that within communities there were differences in smocks, the most elevated being the embellished ones. What started out as a modest utilitarian garment gradually became showier. Anne Buck suggests dating this development to around 1830–70, in parallel with more embellishment in fashionable dress. As smocking became a popular needlework technique for middle-class women by the 1880s, the use of working smocks had declined, the availability of other cheap ready-made clothing being one reason for this.[83] However, as Buck remarks, the development of stitching of varied patterns in deepening bands onto panels of increasing size on the smock owed nothing to fashionable dressmaking or embroidery of the time. As one book of 1847 notes, for respectable women embroidery was 'nearly out of fashion' and a 'sad waste of time'.[84] Buck also suggests that there was a dilution in the differences between working and Sunday dress, the relatively cheap smock used for both, signifying a fall in the living standards for labourers at this time. This dating also parallels the now evident rise of large-scale ready-made smock manufacturing. Ornamental embroidery was one way to differentiate and personalize a basically functional everyday garment for Sunday and more regular wear.[85]

The notion of respectability is elusive and varies between communities, but to appear respectable within a particular locality required sartorial display to signal that position and an adherence to a behaviour that was deemed appropriate for that group.[86] Embroidering clothing, even if 'unfashionable' for the mainstream, perhaps offered social kudos within working communities. An embroidered smock made it less of a marker of poverty and added distinction to it, above the uniformity of the garment and of men's clothes generally. It may even have been a type of one-upmanship either economically, in being able to afford a finely worked one, or socially, in having access to a needlewoman with the skills and time to complete a personalized smock, particularly for special occasions such as weddings. A shepherd in Hertfordshire recalled that his smocks were bought plain, presumably ready-made, and then embroidered and personalized, his with shepherd's crooks, by the women in his family.[87]

Since Buck's article was published, it is increasingly apparent that there is no linear development in the smock during the nineteenth century and different styles and patterns can be found in the same place and at the same time. Perhaps this suggests that both practicality and personal preference played a large part in selecting a smock and also that there were many types to choose from. From the late eighteenth century through until the twentieth century, an unembroidered smock closely related to the eighteenth-century shirt remained prevalent in the Surrey, Sussex and Hampshire area. Men in these counties continued to favour this type of smock, often with very fine smocking, despite the development of more ornate smock embroidery during the nineteenth century.[88]

A distinctive smock could distinguish a man from the masses and possibly promote him and his trade, as suggested by one with very large shoulder coverings worn by a market gardener from Llanbister, Radnorshire.[89] As Vivienne Richmond notes, sewing and femininity were so intertwined that a woman was still likely to assert her ability to sew even as cheap ready-made clothing became available and a time-saving alternative for many.[90] A way to still show off skills was by embellishing these ready-made smocks with embroidery. This type of work was also outside the sphere of elite influence, having little to do with markers of mainstream social status, and indeed, was thus ridiculed.[91] Although, by the Victorian period, there was general disquiet and suspicion over the character of the 'male peacock' for middle-class commentators, decoration per se was not considered unmanly by working men, as was also the case in non-European cultures.[92] The evidence is so scarce for how working men, prior to the late nineteenth century, felt about and regarded their clothing that such decorative impulses should also be given consideration as part of their identity formation.

Working-class embroidery

Whether the desire to embroider a smock therefore came from an individual man asserting their preference or a female maker affirming their skills is impossible to know. A tradition of plain sewing dated back to the eighteenth century and, certainly, teachers trained in the previous century might instruct women working in the 1820s.[93] From the 1840s into the twentieth century, needlework dominated school life for girls, taking up half the day.[94] It formed a central part of the elementary school curriculum from 1862, minutely detailed in a code of regulations but embroidery was vetoed: 'darning, mending … and knitting … but no fancy work of any kind may be done in school hours'. Girls were to be taught how to make clothing suitable for themselves, particularly underwear, along with basic stitches and mending. Embroidery served no practical purpose being suggestive of social aspiration for working-class girls and women, although, as a middle-class feminine attribute, it was associated with goodness, meekness and obedience.[95] Under elite control, such school needlework was therefore limited to functional stitching in minimal colours, for example, darning samplers or professional whitework stitching for the lace or Ayrshire work industries.[96] Thus 'finery' was prohibited, with only plain sewing and the construction of basic useful garments taught, skills needed for servants in middle-class households, with similar attire distributed through clothing clubs and charities.[97] However, smock embroidery could be seen as a development from functional stitching worked on linen, carried out usually in just one colour and generally using no more than three stitches, including feather and chain, in a regimented manner[98] (see Figure 2.5).

Embroidery on smocks also served a practical purpose acting as reinforcement and padding over areas which might wear, the shoulders and chest, adding durability and texture to the garment and keeping it together for longer.[99] As Cally Blackman points out with regard to working dress in the west of Ireland, clothing was valuable and prolonging its life with patching or reinforcing,

FIGURE 2.5 *Feather stitch needlework, including spirals, on a nineteenth-century linen smock frock. © Author's collection.*

protecting the investment, was part of the innate frugality of working people.[100] Women educated in sewing at school could make and embroider smocks, either as an outworker or privately for a family member. However, in contrast to Ayrshire work, for example used for fashionable and expensive female accessories such as collars and cuffs as well as baby clothes, the smock maker's male social peers often chose and bought smocks for themselves, perhaps appreciating their workmanship within the community.

Aside from the practical and respectable aspects of the smock, the care and embellishment lavished on them, as Rachel Worth says, 'are testimony to the value given by the poor to their clothing', and, perhaps, also a source of self-regarding pleasure especially when completed outside of elite surveillance.[101] According to oral testimony from Lincolnshire, only the head shepherd wore a decorated smock, others just wearing a plain smock to cover working clothes, even on a Sunday.[102] Plain and decorated coexisted at the same time, serving different purposes and engendering various responses from the local community, which may not be obvious now. This also suggests that there was a ready market of working men, discerning consumers, who wanted to buy ornate and more expensive clothing, creating an area that ready-made manufacturers quickly moved into.[103] Beyond the workplace, individual men defined themselves by the way that they spent money, the buying of goods and services, whether smocks or beer, being an important part of the social dynamic in confirming community position and reputation.[104] Although middle-class observers might think of showy clothing for working-class men and women as morally suspect, this censure did not seem to extend to the smock at its most ostentatious, beyond disapproval for the ignorant rustic labourer wearing a ridiculous and cumbersome garment unsuitable for work. The smock and its wearer were two different entities. So while criticism focused on girls' and women's dress in particular, modest dress reflecting inner purity, at least for the elite, and the perceived idea of female morality which went with this, the smock and its decoration seems to have fallen outside this condemnation.[105] The individuality of hand embroidery, whether the pattern was the same as another or not, gave them charm for the artistic elite from the mid-nineteenth century onwards. Smock embroidery was increasingly linked to the English historic love of surface patterning.[106] From the 1820s, alongside pleating, ruching and gathering, 'honeycombing', the basic smocking stitch, was also used in fashionable female dress as a way to manipulate fabric, to shape the increasing size of female sleeves and contour form-fitting bodices.[107] This may have helped to mitigate any criticism of these needlework techniques.

Hidden history

Surviving smocks without provenance are therefore problematic to contextualize, their original location and time period often uncertain, with the complicated, and un-linear, history of the smock.[108] Developing from the linen frock used as a utilitarian overall in the seventeenth century, the 'smock frock' is first noted by the mid-eighteenth century. Already associated with the rural and used for comedic effect on the London stage, the smock frock was low status, cheap, ridiculed and anti-fashion. However, as an inexpensive, often ready-made, overall, it was also an extremely useful garment for working men. Especially during the first half of the nineteenth century, the smock became part of the way that working men could differentiate their appearance from mainstream menswear. Increasingly embellished, both with smocking and embroidery, the garment could change in status within some working-class communities from a dress purely for manual labour to a usage for rituals such as Sunday wear and other similar occasions requiring 'respectable' dress. This needlework could be completed by local women to reflect increased status as well as individualizing them, particularly those which were bought ready-made. The impetus for such embroidery and embellishment seems to have come from within working-class communities, partly as an affirmation of a needlewoman's skills and partly from the love of showing off and ostentation in working-class fashions. Working men were not excluded from flamboyant sartorial display and they played an active role in developing their self-presentation, as will be explored in Chapters 4 and 5.

The smock, as a garment in its many forms, played a large part in male working-class identity formation through clothing, its appearance actively changing and adapting to suit local mores and an individual man's sense of visual self-presentation and perception of status. From the late nineteenth century, as will be investigated in detail in Chapter 6, the garment assumed a passive role, undergoing a process of traditionalization, associated with the rural and seen as unchanging for hundreds of years, echoing nostalgia about the countryside then itself in flux. As this chapter has shown, this story, which has continued to cling to the garment, has hidden the dynamic development of the smock during the first part of the nineteenth century within working-class communities. However, the use of the cheap smock by such communities was also a reflection of the parlous economic state that they found themselves in. The next chapter will turn to examine where smocks were manufactured, and how they came to be so cheap for men to buy and modify.

3 Making

The smock frock has come to epitomize the home-made garment crafted by skilled, yet amateur makers.[1] In actual fact, many women had little time or means to undertake such unpaid needlework.[2] Looking back at parish records for outdoor poor relief in Ampthill, Bedfordshire, around 1816, that is assistance which could be applied for outside the workhouse, the writer in 1932 is surprised to find dozens of applications for smocks for boys and shirts for men, commenting, 'Can it be that Ampthill women had already at that period lost the art of shirt-making and smocking!'[3] Smocks were more usually produced by skilled paid outworkers for retailers or manufacturers, or by a local professional needleworker. Now often categorized as 'shepherd's smock' or something similar, emphasizing their supposed rural origins, this has obscured the fact that the majority were bought ready-made.

Manual labourers, then as now, require an overall of some kind to offer protection and warmth when needed, providing manufacturers with large markets to sell to.[4] John Styles suggests that smocks became general wear in southern England and the Midlands in the late eighteenth century, at a time when wages came under pressure, unemployment was rising and living standards declining. Adopted because they were cheap ready-mades, they were also practical in being durable and washable. They could protect good clothing or conceal poor garments, so presenting a suitable appearance to enable agricultural and other employment. Overseers for Theydon Garnon in Essex recognized their value for clothing the poor, including smock frocks on a list of garments procured from one supplier in the 1790s.[5] By the early nineteenth century, the trade was well-established with ready-made clothes sellers across the country listing them as part of their stock and often making them as well.[6]

Tracing the specific firms of Hyde and Bousfield, before surveying manufacturers across the country, this chapter will investigate how widespread the smock trade was and its importance as part of the ready-made clothes manufacturing business. It will explore how this trade developed and was exploited by entrepreneurs to become part of the foundation of clothing manufacture in England by the mid-nineteenth century, providing cheap but decorative garments for many working men. As Madeleine Ginsberg states: 'The commonly held notion is that clothes were always home-made and hardly an article of commerce, an idea untrue of any historical period and of any place in the mainstream of economic development'.[7] This viewpoint is particularly applicable to the history of the smock frock.

The ready-made clothing trade and smocks

From at least the sixteenth century onwards, simple pieces of clothing, such as aprons, caps and shirts, were manufactured in quantity to sell ready-made to the large sizeable market of the 'middling sort' and below.[8] Large government contracts for ready-made clothing for organizations such as the army and the navy accelerated this process, with the 'slop' trade developing from the late seventeenth century to fulfil these demands.[9] Since at least the eighteenth century, outworking in the industry with specialization in particular products or processes was common practice.[10] The industry boomed in the second quarter of the nineteenth century, possibly with stimulation from numerous government contracts during the Napoleonic Wars and the subsequent sale of surplus clothing after the end of the conflict. Although this may have led to some lowering of prices, for the male consumer cheap ready-made clothing became more readily available and this included smocks.[11]

As the smock was an unfitted garment, it did not have the sizing and fitting problems of other male clothing. Badly fitting or loose clothes were synonymous with poverty and marginality, suggesting initially second-hand origin and, later, ready-made manufacture.[12] Ultimately, the looseness of the smock contributed to its decline, but for the nascent ready-made clothes industry this, along with its simple construction, was an advantage. Aside from well-known centres in Newark-on-Trent, Nottinghamshire, and Haverhill in Suffolk, there has been little exploration of this branch of the ready-made industry despite the huge potential market.[13] Male agricultural labourers were the predominant workforce in the first half of the nineteenth century, the 1851 census recording over 1.4 million men working as agricultural labourers, farm servants or shepherds. More than in any other type of employment, this situation continued until the 1901 census with the majority of the population still physically living in the countryside.[14] To provide cheap working garments for this population, the ready-made industry expanded.

The trade was particularly prevalent in towns which had a textile tradition but were struggling, by the early nineteenth century, to compete with the northern textile industries. Ready-made manufacturers took advantage of this existing skilled labour before the mechanization of the industry.[15]

An examination of nineteenth-century trade directories reveals how widespread the smock trade was. Manufacturers are found in Liverpool, Stone (Staffordshire), Sheffield, Leeds, Chesterfield and Nottingham, as well as in Oxford, Reading, Bristol and Syleham, Suffolk, in the south. In Bristol, part of the export market for the slave trade was the manufacture of cheap slops, which included 'frocks'. In the mid-1770s, three dozen canvas frocks were supplied to a ship bound for West Africa to buy slaves and the city became known for manufacturing shirts, particularly for export, during the nineteenth century.[16] To be listed in a directory as a smock maker implied that this was a substantial part of a business. However, there were smock makers on a smaller scale, usually drapers, who employed local women to make smocks for retail. For example, in 1842, sixteen to eighteen new smock frocks were stolen from George Dexter, a draper in Tuxford, Nottinghamshire. It is likely that he had these manufactured for sale in his shop, as one of the women who made them came with him to court to identify the smocks.[17] Charles Gresham was a tailor, draper and hatter, running a Cloathing [sic] Establishment in the High Street of Grantham. His ready-made clothes and smock frocks for men 'have been made up under his own inspection, and can … be recommended for workmanship and quality'.[18] Likewise workmen for W. Chaloner, tailor, draper and hatter of Lincoln, made 'Blue, Drab, and White Smock Frocks in various patterns and all sizes'.[19] For these retailers, an initial capital outlay was needed to make stock for their own shops, but they retained control over the manufacturing process. James Rooke's 'Home-made Clothes Warehouse', in Salisbury, in 1835, advertised his 'strongly made"shepherds' and carters' clothing' and 'Russia' smock frocks.[20] This suggests that some of these retailers also had a centralized workshop, enabling scrutiny of the design process and quality control, the quality being particularly emphasized in advertisements, and a necessity to withstand physical labour, along with the availability of a variety of patterns.[21]

Smock frocks were thus a common stock item for many clothing sellers from country shopkeepers to city dealers, with retailers often in charge of commissioning their manufacture. Russell and Dorrell, drapers of Worcester (whose business existed until 2011) gave material to Hannah Wainwright in 1858 to make up six smock frocks, of which she illegally pawned two to raise money.[22] In 1851, George Russell also advertised smock frocks 'of all shapes and sizes' for sale in a separate department within his shop.[23] Certainly in villages around Worcester, making up smock frocks along with making up gloves, or gloving, was a common female occupation. John Salt, a farm labourer from Bransford, told the Parliamentary Commission that his wife made smock frocks, but, by 1867, that the 'work is going out', women then not being able to earn 3 shillings a week for it.[24] Thus, wherever smocks were sold across the country, local women made them up for drapers to sell ready-made.[25]

Of course, during the same period, female family members still made smocks for male relations, perhaps if they were also making them commercially and particularly those for special occasions such as a wedding. In Withington, Herefordshire, a fellow agricultural labourer stole the smock of Elisha Powell. The accused was found wearing it, Powell's two sisters, who made and repaired it, identifying the smock in court.[26] Anecdotal evidence from Worcestershire suggests that some women might travel around to make up several smocks at the same time for one farm. A smock with no embroidery, made by 'the woman who came and stayed in the house and made all the smocks' at Willersey Farm near Broadway, is now deposited in the collection at the Museum of English Rural Life (MERL).[27] Where one woman made up smocks for a village or small local area, these were likely to have a similar construction, design and patterns, although complexity would depend on an individual's ingenuity and skill.[28] Working for a large manufacturer, a local retailer or for a specific private order, this female work was seen as a low-status occupation and as an offshoot of plain sewing linen to make inner-garments such as shirts and underwear. It was often undertaken to help make ends meet, even if earning only a few pence each day.[29] The Old Poor Law regularly created such female labour as a method of offering support, with women employed in various care and provisioning jobs, including making up shirts and smocks. Elizabeth Beale performed this task in Castlemorton, Worcestershire, providing a cheap service for the parish and a small wage for herself.[30] However, it is the large-scale professional manufacturing of the garment that has so far been left out of clothing histories.

The cost of fabric decreased continuously during the eighteenth and nineteenth centuries, reflecting global trading and the development of factory systems for weaving textiles. The price fell by 75 per cent in the first half of the nineteenth century, with a sharp fall in the cost of cotton fabrics in the 1830s and 1840s. This aided the rapid development of ready-made clothing produced by hand, helped by a reduction in sweated labour rates, which left little incentive to mechanize at first.[31] The purchasing power of sections of the working classes thus increased, with the routine buying of new ready-made clothing rather than relying on second-hand garments.[32] The increasing specialization and economies of scale therefore came before mechanization, the first half of the nineteenth century offering unprecedented opportunities for innovative tailors, drapers and clothing dealers, who would substitute ready-made clothing for bespoke or second-hand items further stimulating consumer demand.[33]

There was a need for a firm to focus on a particular specialized area to be able to grow in size beyond the general ready-made clothing wants of the local population. This included uniforms for prisons, charities, asylums, the military, workhouses and railway employees, the latter forming a speciality for the ready-made manufactory of Hyam in Colchester.[34] As they were also often used in workhouses, smocks were another potential area for ambitious entrepreneurs to focus on.[35] Such businesses followed a typical pattern for slop clothing, employing cheap female outworkers in making garments which did not directly compete with male artisan tailors who worked under guild control until the 1830s (see Figure 3.1).[36] The integration of manufacturing, wholesaling and retailing, plus effective advertising, within one business were features of this market.[37] Drapers initially had more capital than ready-made clothing sellers but by the mid-nineteenth century, after the boom during the 1840s and the scaling up of their businesses, London slop dealers also began to move into the lucrative smock trade.[38] Although frequently missed in the existing literature about ready-made entrepreneurs and rural clothing industries, the smock trade was critical for the prosperity of particular towns and villages, one example being Abingdon, Oxfordshire.[39]

Hyde's of Abingdon

Abingdon has been associated with clothing and textile production from the medieval period onwards, its position on the banks of the River Thames probably helping with access to distribution networks.[40] As also happened in East Anglia, the decline in weaving industries left a ready pool of labour used to working with textiles and with skills that could be adapted to manufacturing clothing.[41] However, what emerged in the mid-nineteenth century was on an unprecedented scale. Now largely forgotten, by 1850 the town was home to one of the leading clothing factories in the country. Providing local employment for many with both indoor and outdoor work, smock making, at least initially, was the company's main business.

There was already a tradition of producing ready-made smocks in the area. William Petty and Son, tailor and salesman, Market Place, Abingdon, included smock frocks 'of their own make' in their wholesale and retail stock in 1788.[42] Fisk's Clothing Warehouse in the Corn Market in nearby Oxford was also an early advertiser of smock frocks, promoting them in 1816 as 'cheaper than most houses in the trade … [and] made under his own inspection', by his workmen.[43]

FIGURE 3.1 *Arthur Smith of Bledlow Ridge, 1872. An agricultural labourer, aged fifteen, convicted of stealing a rabbit, wearing what would seem to be a cheap ready-made smock, crudely smocked, with wide spacing of the 'tubes' and little ornamental embroidery. Victorian Prisoner Photographs © Centre for Buckinghamshire Studies, Buckinghamshire Council, reference: Q/AG/23–26 Prisoner 4621.*

From around 1817, John Hyde ran a draper's shop in Abingdon High Street.[44] His move into manufacturing smock frocks apparently began when a debt was repaid with bale of linen. A speculative smock was made from this, which was easily sold to a labourer. More were then made to supply this demand, or so the legend went.[45]

The Hydes were an old Abingdon family, John Hyde junior succeeding his father in the business in 1833 at the age of 35. He began to focus on the wholesale market rather than just retailing, in 1840, being listed as a wholesale clothes manufacturer, along with Harris and Tomkins, the earliest directory reference to his manufactory. Both firms were specifically wholesale 'Slop and Frock Makers' by 1844, when Hyde bought a former hemp manufacturing factory on the same street as his house.[46] In 1847, the Hyde family's shop in Reading advertised: 'One of the most important articles of domestic economy … is DRESS … [at] J. Hyde's Round Frock, Ready-Made Clothes … Warehouse, 22, King Street'.[47] Leeds manufacturers of clothing for men from the 1880s, such a Hepworth's, also used this system, selling their own products alongside other goods in their family retail outlets.[48]

From 1852, the building known as the Clothing Factory was constructed in East St Helen Street, Abingdon, and enlarged with the purchase of adjacent properties in 1862, 1866 and 1869.[49] Hyde maintained the retail side until 1857, when he sold out to his partner to concentrate on the wholesale business and, in particular, manufacturing.[50] John Creemer Clarke from Devon became a partner in the factory in 1863.[51] Although the capital outlay was small in comparison to industries such as the railways or steel, it was still substantial and increased as more sophisticated equipment was required. As the company expanded into general clothing and gradually became mechanized, Clarke's involvement and his capital was perhaps needed, enabling the factory to continue to thrive into the late nineteenth century.[52] What may have started as a speculative move to use up an unwanted linen bale, within forty years had developed into a fully fitted-out clothing factory.[53]

The focus of the firm from the start was on manufacturing ready-made clothing, particularly smock frocks, rather than weaving. Through occupations listed in the census, the impact of the firm on the town is apparent. Before the factory was established, in the 1841 census there is little evidence of the ready-made trade in the local area. John Hyde himself was listed as a draper. However, in the 1851 census, John Hyde senior, aged 72, is described as a 'cloth manufacturer employing fourteen hundred person[s] making garments', presumably mainly as outworkers.[54] On West St Helen Street, outside the factory, fifty female 'slop tailoress[es]', women and their elder daughters, are listed as working from home.[55] Also noted in the census were two male slop cutters who would work in Hyde's receiving room, where material was cut up into garment pieces and given out to women make up into clothing.[56] A cutter was always male and at the top of the factory workers' hierarchy, often trained through one of the only apprenticeships in the factory system. They were responsible for ensuring that there was as little wastage as possible when pieces were cut out from material to assemble into 'bundles' for completion.[57] This gender division of labour continued in clothing factories, with women doing 'unskilled' work and men the skilled cutting out.[58] By 1861, mechanization was underway, James Althrope and George Abbott, brothers-in-law, coming to Abingdon from Kettering, Northamptonshire, to work as machinists. Cutting machines were used along with sewing machines made by Grover and Baker, although at first, mechanization caused 'consternation' among the women and 'a small riot'.[59]

Hyde's bought material in Manchester and made up garments also including waistcoats, trousers and coats. The gradual move into a factory during the 1850s and 1860s enabled more regulation of their production as well as facilitating some sort of quality control particularly in standard sizing, especially as this was before the full mechanization with sewing machines.[60] Smocks were already made in several sizes including boys, youths and adult, a policeman describing a smock in 1846 as a 'Full man's size'.[61] Smocks were measured in nails (two and a quarter inches), the various lengths being noted on labels.[62] Despite the projected image of the firm to the press as making clothing 'for the middling class of people', the smock frock remained a major part of their business into the 1860s.[63]

At the beginning of the American Civil War period (1861–5), Clarke initiated the buying of quantities of cotton fabric before the so-called cotton famine, which lead to a dearth of raw cotton imports for northern cotton weavers.[64] Manufacturers, like Hyde, who had stored finished cotton fabrics were able to continue to develop and mechanize their ready-made clothing operation, aware of the potential growth in the sector to fulfil the need for cheap ready-mades.[65] Periods of war, such as the Crimean War or the American Civil War during the 1850s and 1860s, were also an opportunity for clothing manufacturers with the necessary infrastructure to mass manufacture uniforms as well as civilian clothing.[66] A clothing entrepreneur was a capitalist, financier, works manager, merchant, salesman and, in some cases, a community builder.[67]

When John Hyde senior died in 1864, the firm was reported as 'one of the most extensive of the few modern model factories and wholesale houses in the kingdom for the manufacture and supply of machine made clothing for the home trade', with employee numbers increased to 1,500 outworkers and 350 '*employès*' in the factory.[68] These numbers were not unusual for towns involved in clothing manufacture. Colchester too, had similar employment figures by the late nineteenth century, mainly women and girls being employed as outworkers, as did Haverhill.[69] Commentary in the local press usually regarded the factory and the Hyde family favourably for bringing prosperity to the town and building the community. The owners were seen as paternalistic, for example, taking 500 employees by train to the Crystal Palace in London in 1867, and similarly 2,000 employees in 1871 to visit the International Exhibition in London.[70] It is possible that they were exhibiting goods and so could show their employees the kind of company that they worked for, boosting staff morale and work identity to compensate for this expense.[71] A newspaper report commented that there was a 'good understanding between master and servant in that extensive factory', and other factory owners in small towns used similar benevolent but despotic models, viewing their companies as a familial extension, hierarchical and strictly structured but with secure employment and occasional treats for workers.[72]

Outside the town, Hyde's outworkers were scattered in villages in a radius of about 7 or 8 miles around Abingdon and were usually young married women who combined their slop work with domestic and family duties. As Keith Snell suggests, rural women were less frequently employed in agricultural work during this period so needed to make up family incomes in other ways.[73] 'Slopping' could add 2 to 3 shillings to their weekly income, a shilling more without distractions. A local surgeon, William Lightfoot, described the working conditions to Parliamentary Commissioners noting that women preferred fieldwork to needlework, 'plenty of which they can get from a tailor's establishment at Abingdon', although the same was not true of girls.[74] Older women spudding thistles questioned at Culham, very close to Abingdon, suggested that they earned more at 8 pence per day for eight hours work than a woman doing slopping would, although the wear on their clothing, and particularly their shoes, was more. However, overall, field work was seen as healthier than 'slopping' and popular for women aged 30 to 40.[75] By the 1860s, the work was described as making clothing for the Oxford and Abingdon ready-made clothes shops, trousers, waistcoats and smocks for railway labourers or navvies rather than for agricultural labourers.[76] Employment in the surrounding hinterland was bound up with firms such as Hyde's.

After John Hyde junior's death in 1872, with employees of the firm then numbering around 2,000, 'which is considered one of the largest, if not the largest, in the kingdom', the factory continued as 'Clarke's' into the twentieth century and was known for its production of corduroy trousers.[77] Certainly, looking back from the early twentieth century, Hyde's importance was recognized: 'This, then, is the birthplace, cradle, and nursery of the provincial clothing trade. The purchase of a piece of duck, and the cutting it up into smock frocks – Mr. John Hyde's first textile enterprise – was the origin of an industry which has now spread all over the country and become one of Britain's most important trades.' The subsequent factory was seen as a benefit to Abingdon, allowing families to find work in the area.[78]

Parallel to the Abingdon business, Thomas Hyde (John Hyde junior's younger brother) ran a similar manufactory in Oxford from 1839, with various partners.[79] Sometime during the 1840s, he took over another premises giving him more retail space in Queen Street at Carfax, along the road from his manufactory, which may well have been an outlet for the Abingdon factory too. Named The Oxford Clothing Establishment, located at the city's central crossroads, a photograph of the shop from around 1900 under a different ownership is still in existence.[80] In the 1851 census, as a frock and clothes manufacturer (see Figure 3.2), he is described as employing 604 men and women, and 28 children.[81] By the mid-1850s, their promotional image was that of superior ready-made clothing, their long experience as manufacturers guaranteeing the quality of their garments. The factory was mechanized by 1867, Thomas Hyde advertising his 'steam power' manufacture as well as being an agent for 'Grover and Baker' and Wanzer Family sewing machines. However, in Headington Quarry outside Oxford, women still made smocks for a local factory, possibly Hyde's, one account suggesting that they earned 9 pence per smock.[82] In 1869, Hyde sold out to his manager, who built

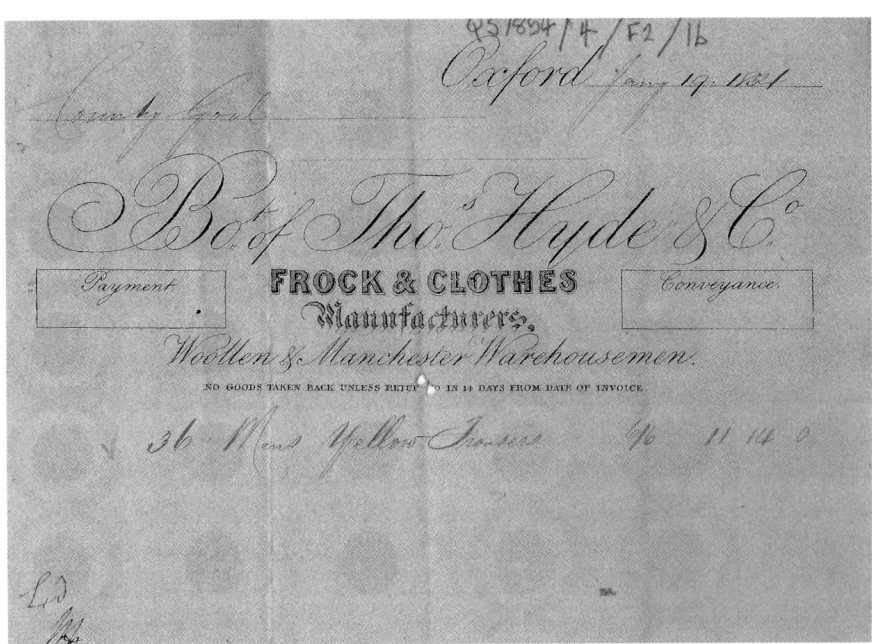

FIGURE 3.2 *Bill from Thomas Hyde & Co., QS1854/4/F2/1b. © Oxfordshire County Council – Oxfordshire History Centre.*

a new factory backing onto Shoe Lane, at the rear of the original warehouse.[83] Like their other family business, this had grown from originally manufacturing smock frocks.

Bousfield's of Houndsditch and Reading

As clothing production expanded, with types of garments categorized, at least superficially, by occupation, this gave both retailers and manufacturers an opportunity to make very similar items but sell them to different markets. T. Palmer in Crewkerne offered ready-made clothes for sale in 1868 including brown and white slops, 'Engineers, Railway and Smock Frocks', all seemingly similar items but differentiated for their particular markets.[84] 'Railway frocks' for navvies were sent from Reading and sold in Hertfordshire in 1840 alongside other types of smocks.[85] One of the businesses involved in the smock frock trade in Reading, Berkshire, also on the banks of River Thames, were the Bousfield family. They were well-known London slop wholesalers, working out of Houndsditch and St Mary Axe, the traditional heart of the slop and second-hand trade in London.[86]

After arriving in London from Cumbria in the late eighteenth century, William Bousfield was in partnership with Samuel Favell as slop sellers in Tooley Street. In a complicated mesh of familial and business links, the firm gradually developed. Samuel's father, John Favell, had initially run the business, listed as a slop seller in 1765. Favell was involved with another company too so, by the 1790s, William's eldest son, also named William, joined the Favell and Bousfield partnership.[87] William the elder died in 1804, his younger son, John Richardby, coming into the business by 1810, when they also moved to 12 St Mary Axe. Over the next forty years, the firm expanded to 126/7 Houndsditch, under the title John R. Bousfield and Company, Favell and Bousfield remaining at St Mary Axe.[88] From around 1830, they built their business by exporting clothing to the colonies, in particular to Australia, and importing wool into London in return, advertising widely in the Australian press for consignments.[89] John Muston, a draper from Hobart, Tasmania, approached Favell and Bousfield to supply slops on the same terms to him as they supplied others in 'Van Diemen's Land' in 1835.[90] T. Towle, who ran Cheapside House in Geelong, advertised in 1851 that his ready-made clothing suitable for the town or 'bush' was manufactured by Favell and Bousfield to his orders.[91] This business with expatriate communities was a major factor in the expansion of the ready-made clothing industry, a report from 1875 noting the 'global' trade.[92] William's children, William, Thomas and Samuel, also worked for the firm along with John Richardby's sons John and Robert, who ran a different branch of firm as J. R. Bousfield & Co., from 1851 to 1863, with Favell and Bousfield continuing to operate alongside.[93]

In 1843, *Lloyd's Weekly Newspaper* carried an article 'Grinding the Poor', highlighting the unfairness of the London 'slop' trade in using the cheap labour of workhouse inmates as well as convicts in Brixton and Millbank prisons. Independent seamstresses and outworkers could not compete with the so-called protected poor in workhouses. Bousfield came under direct criticism, replying that they paid the same wages to those inside and outside the workhouse, which failed to silence their critics.[94] This was not just a metropolitan practice though. Inmates of Worcester County Prison manufactured a whole range of shoes and clothing, for example, men's smock frocks listed for sale at 8 and 9 shillings each, undercutting local businesses.[95] Despite their reliance on outworkers, Bousfield also had a sizable factory at their Houndsditch address, a model similar to Hyde's. This is evident from newspaper reports in 1851, when a fire destroyed the new four-storey building. The business was described as 'one of the largest at the east end of London', with losses variously set at between thirty and fifty thousand pounds and 'upwards of 2000' workers who were now unemployed.[96] They were major players in the slop business, particularly the export trade. Their 'stout Halifax frocks' sold at auction in Hobart in 1842, around the same time that they began to expand further into the smock trade, setting up a new hub in Reading.[97]

Kelly's *Directory* of 1847 lists Bousfield and Co. as 'Outfitters', at 57 King's Road South, Reading, implying the sale of ready-made clothing. An advertisement in the *Reading Mercury* from 1848 sought an assistant in the 'round frock trade', already a recognized business in the town.[98] By 1852, John Robert Bousfield & Co., were listed as 'round frock manufacturers' at the same address, with Robert Poulton as agent/manager for the firm.[99] This specific listing continued into the 1860s.[100] Presumably Poulton, using his experience of the smock trade, was in charge of the day-to-day running and female outworkers, while the Bousfield family provided the manufacturing set-up and capital. They placed advertisements in the local press for workers, for example, in 1856 for a warehouseman with experience in the 'smock frock trade'.[101] The business operated very much under the Bousfield name, smock frocks being described in 1865 as the 'property of Mr. Bousfield, wholesale clothier, London'.[102] J. & R. Bousfield also exported to Tasmania and Melbourne in 1855, and this large export market may have been the primary function of the Reading business.[103] It is unclear where the textiles used to manufacture Bousfield's smocks came from, but there were several regional centres which specialized in producing such fabrics.[104]

Unlike Hyde's, where there seems to have been a certain amount of respect for the paternalistic attitude of a locally born proprietor employing a resident workforce, Bousfield's were often criticized, as we have seen, particularly about their wage rates in London but also, indirectly, in Reading. In 1862, Caroline Child was charged with assaulting Emma Emmett and ordered to pay a 10 shilling fine. She was questioned about her ability to pay the fine – Child said that she worked at smock making, was paid 2½ pence per smock and could 'make three in a day'. The newspaper noted comments about whether 'the profits of smock making, less the expenses of living, will yield the amount in question by the day named, as being doubtful', the magistrates remarking that 'she evidently cannot afford the luxury of assaulting her neighbours'.[105] This also suggests that the smocks she made were not elaborate and were put together very quickly. Bousfield's may have come to Reading with the expectation that wage rates would be lower than in the capital, with less work for women available locally.[106] Pamela Sharpe notes, in relation to Hyam, that by the 1840s the complexities of subcontracting on this scale, through various middle men, hid the fact that masters such as Hyam, Bousfield and Moses were highly capitalized and engaged in the large-scale production of garments. By seeking country labour, they could perhaps avoid, although not altogether successfully in Bousfield's case, being tarred with the brush of cheap manufacture which sullied their garments made in London.[107]

Despite the reservations of commentators, the cachet of London was felt to be important for clothing and was a feature of promoting ready-made garments across the country. The fact that clothing was London made and so of London 'fashion', was highlighted in the promotional literature.[108] However, the 'home made' and locally manufactured smock frock could compete alongside those of the larger manufacturers, as shown by advertisements in the Hereford press in the early 1840s (see Figure 3.3 for Turner's Hereford Manufactory with 1,000 'frocks').[109] This also seems to be the case in Lincolnshire, suggesting, perhaps, that in some areas, the locality of manufacture was important, perhaps with its links to local employment, whether these claims were actually true or not. Along with wage rates and a ready trained labour pool, a provincial manufacturing hub in Reading or Colchester might provide some authenticity for certain garments made for clothiers otherwise based in the City.

By 1861, Bousfield's in London were advertising for 'Thomas's Machine Hands', workers to operate the new Thomas sewing machines.[110] The Bousfield's manufactories were relatively early adopters in mechanizing the production of ready-made garments, which may have included smocks. Some later smocks have machine-stitched seams, but these generally still required hand smocking and embroidery.[111] In Chatham, in 1861, Catherine Hopper was charged with

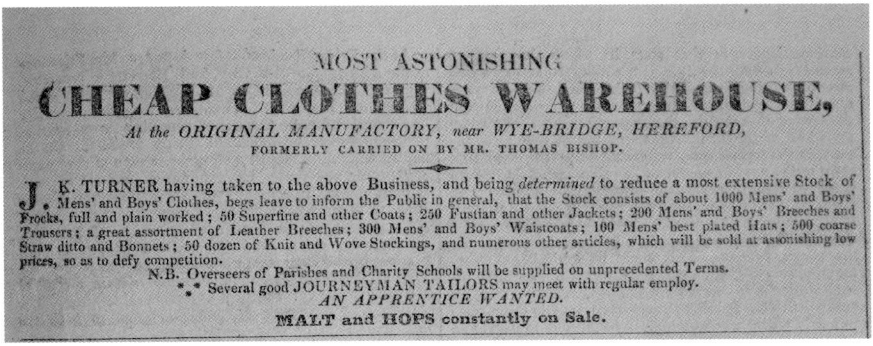

> **MOST ASTONISHING**
> # CHEAP CLOTHES WAREHOUSE,
> *At the* ORIGINAL MANUFACTORY, *near* WYE-BRIDGE, HEREFORD,
> FORMERLY CARRIED ON BY MR. THOMAS BISHOP.
>
> J. K. TURNER having taken to the above Business, and being *determined* to reduce a most extensive Stock of Mens' and Boys' Clothes, begs leave to inform the Public in general, that the Stock consists of about 1000 Mens' and Boys' Frocks, full and plain worked; 50 Superfine and other Coats; 250 Fustian and other Jackets; 290 Mens' and Boys' Breeches and Trousers; a great assortment of Leather Breeches; 300 Mens' and Boys' Waistcoats; 100 Mens' best plated Hats; 500 coarse Straw ditto and Bonnets; 50 dozen of Knit and Wove Stockings, and numerous other articles, which will be sold at astonishingly low prices, so as to defy competition.
> N.B. Overseers of Parishes and Charity Schools will be supplied on unprecedented Terms.
> *** Several good JOURNEYMAN TAILORS may meet with regular employ.
> *AN APPRENTICE WANTED.*
> **MALT** and **HOPS** constantly on Sale.

FIGURE 3.3 Hereford Journal, *30 April 1828.* ©*Herefordshire Archive Service.*

stealing a jacket from the Axe Brand Sewing Machine Warehouse, owned by the Bousfield family.[112] However, the same year Mr Griffith's, who ran a ready-made clothing establishment in St George's, now part of Telford, Shropshire, and whose stock included smock frocks, advertised that his ready-made clothing was 'not made by machinery'.[113] While the sewing machine was transforming the business of large slop wholesalers, and to some extent side-lining smock production for them as a hybrid and therefore complex manufacturing process, the traditional method was still seen as worthy of promotion to local consumers, maybe as an assurance of value and durability.

Perhaps to counter press criticism, Bousfield developed tag-lines recommending the quality of their ready-made clothing. In an 1851 advertisement for a Leeds shop, with 'cheapness and excellence displayed in their goods', their overcoats were in direct competition with Nicoll's, also a well-known London ready-made manufacturer.[114] Continual reassurances that guaranteed quality and a certain standard helped to overcome any doubt about the ready-made manufacturing process, both for the retailer and the consumer. This advertising appropriated values associated with made-to-measure clothing, for example, tradition and fashion, alongside the innovation and modernity of the process.[115] Bousfield developed the Axe Brand, based on their address at 12 St Mary's Axe. By 1861, the Axe Brand appears to have become their trade name, part of a general movement from the 1860s as brands become more important than the specific reputation of individual merchants or retail outlets.[116] The protection of branded products was more viable from 1862 with the Merchandise Marks Act.[117] Advertisements began to promote brand awareness, and with the brand becoming the name, specific products were not described in any detail. Favell and Bousfield followed this method: 'The Axe in a Circle, surrounded by the Motto "Axe Brand best value for Money", is Favell and Bousfield's Registered Trade-Mark. Clothing without this ticket is not of their

FIGURE 3.4 Evening Journal *(Adelaide)*, 21 August 1869, 4. http://nla.gov.au/nla.news-page22383608.

manufacture'[118] (see Figure 3.4). With their clothing exports to Australia and New Zealand established for over thirty years, this branding was widely publicized in the Antipodean press. Such pictorial labelling was a way to make their products visually distinctive for consumers in a market full of clothing which looked very similar. The advertisement printed the genuine label to assure consumers of the authenticity of their choice, a strategy to guard against piracy, but also linking together the product, the brand name, the labelling and its promotion.[119]

By 1867, Bousfield used this advertisement in British newspapers, the 'Registered Trade Mark, Axe Brand', appealing to wholesale buyers of shirts and clothing for 'orders and contracts of every description'.[120] As manufacturers and wholesalers they may have sold through companies such as Atkinson & Co. who advertised themselves as 'Government Contractors' operating out of 198–212 Westminster Bridge Road, the other side of the river to the Houses of Parliament, where they had a large shop with numerous departments.[121] They specialized in furniture and furnishings, but also undertook to supply ready-made clothing 'in all Sizes, and for both sexes' for contracts for asylums, workhouses and hospitals. They employed manufacturers like Bousfield to fulfil specific contracts, for instance, one order in March 1866 for clothing for the Ross Union, Herefordshire, including men and boy's moleskin coats, waistcoats, jackets, shirts, as well as duck smock frocks for boys.[122] During the 1870s, the Bousfield firm was in decline for a variety of reasons, involving changes in business and family members.[123]

The innovative 'Axe Brand' reflected the complexity of consumer attitudes towards ready-made and mass-produced goods. If a manufacturer overtly advertised with, for example, labels and tickets on garments, this could signal its ready-made status and the implied cheapness and thus poor quality of the clothing.[124] However, frequent advertising was also a way to build up a relationship with customers so that they began to feel that they knew the 'brand', even an impersonal mass manufacturer. It gave people a means of relating to each other across vast national, and international, markets.[125] Although some retailers trumpeted their cheap ready-made clothing, others did not want to be seen selling it, even if they were, as this might have had a detrimental effect on their own reputation and individual brand. Their name remained their premier promotional tool, so they instead stressed the 'traditional' or 'home-made' qualities of their personally chosen stock.[126] This attitude perhaps also disguised the origin of many mass-produced smocks.

Gurteen's of Haverhill

Like the Hyde family in Abingdon, the Gurteen family were said to have transformed Haverhill 'from a small decaying place to a thriving little town' without the advantages of a canal or port, with Daniel Gurteen called, somewhat pejoratively, 'the "little king" of Haverhill'.[127] Haverhill is a town on the Essex/Suffolk border noted for its textile manufacturers, particularly of fustian, from the seventeenth century onwards, with many of the local population employed in these industries. The Gurteen family started making smocks in the 1800s, as seen by the sale of a ready-made smock in 1807.[128] However, Pigot's 1830 *Directory* only lists one smock maker, not Gurteen, although they were already making such garments.[129] A handbill from H. Hyam, clothier of Colchester, dated 1828, advertised 'Men's real Haverhill open slops' for 6 shillings 6 pence. These were likely to have been smocks, open at the front, which Gurteen and other firms in Haverhill made, along with the waggoner's 'slops' also listed.[130] Moving from fustian to drabbet production, diversifying and expanding their product range to make ready-made smocks, helped the Gurteen family form the basis of a successful company by the 1840s, although like Hyde and Bousfield, as manufacturers, they rarely advertised their product.[131]

Drabbet was a heavy cotton canvas (warp hemp or later linen, weft cotton – termed 'drabbet' from its colour, also dyed olive and slate)[132] which smocks were often made up from. However, as drabbet is relatively thick, it was difficult to embroider and so is associated with later, less decorated, smocks.[133] White's

1844 *Directory* notes Gurteen's as drabbet and smock frock manufacturers and that many women made up drabbet into smock frocks for various businesses in the town.[134] By 1856, Gurteen's threatened 'with the competition from other parts of England of large steam looms', put their capital into a steam plant and full mechanization and expansion followed.[135] This development differentiated them from other firms in the area and pulled them out of a recession that they had suffered in the 1840s and 1850s.[136] By the 1861 census, Daniel Gurteen employed 130 hands in his manufactory.

Gurteen's also relied on outworkers, a precarious existence for women undertaking this. A report in 1850 noted that although older daughters of cottagers of Castle Camps, close to Haverhill, earned 1 shilling 6 pence a week by 'smocking', there was currently no trade and so no work.[137] Skilled needlewomen earned wages making garments, but these wages were unlikely to be high enough to enable them to buy new clothing for themselves.[138] Anne Buck obtained oral histories from families which noted that a carrier brought out the material to local villages on Monday morning, one woman pencilled out designs and then handed out the pieces to other women in the neighbourhood for working. These were later collected and sent back to the factory on Friday for making up.[139] Patterns were also inked on from stencils or from blocks for the women to follow.[140] As the business picked up in the 1860s, outwork remained a feature of local female employment. In 1867, Rebecca Andrews of Helions Bumpstead, a small village near Haverhill, was given ten drabbet 'slops' belonging to Gurteen to work on and was then prosecuted for their theft.[141] *The Royal Commission on Employment of Children, Young Persons and Women in Agriculture* the same year noted weekly wages of around 2 shillings 6 pence to 3 shillings for outwork for women and girls in the town and surrounding villages, about the same as that paid by fieldwork. Although wage rates were similar, girls and young women tended to do 'slop-work' in their own homes rather than fieldwork. However, Rev. W. John, vicar of Shudy Camps complained: 'Slop-work (sewing) for the ready-made clothes dealers seems to me to be worse than field work for the girls, taking them earlier from school, keeping them from service, and exposing them to temptations.' Even though fieldwork was increasingly being seen as unsuitable for women, the clergy around Haverhill also saw slop work as a problem, a letter from Castle Camps Rectory noting that: 'I do not think this has any favourable result on their morals, or fitness for domestic duties.'[142]

Gurteen's increased smock frock production from 1863 with the installation of hand-powered sewing machines set up in a factory in the garden of the family home in the High Street, although the smocks still required hand finishing.[143] By 1871, the trade had changed entirely, with further mechanization and the setting up of a Clothing Factory described as 'gigantic' in the local press.[144] There is no specific mention of frock or smock makers in the 1871 census. Daniel Gurteen still described himself as a Drabbet Manufacturer employing 150 workers, but also a 'wholesale Clothier' employing 2,000 hands, so on par with Hyde's factory in Abingdon. In 1888, looking back at how the company had expanded in the 1860s and 1870s, Gurteen's had gradually moved into ready-made clothes 'in a small way' as smocks 'went out of fashion', young female workers now sewing machinists with around sixty listed at the time.[145] By 1881, Gurteen was the only textile producer in Haverhill.[146]

A reporter was shown around the factory in 1888, who noted that they made no women's clothing, Mr Gurteen apologetically saying: 'We can't do everything you know.' With a rapid expansion in mechanization, there were now 400 steam-powered sewing machines and the band knife was used for cutting out sixty pieces at once. While the reporter characterized ready-made clothing as something the poorest would buy, Gurteen stated that they made clothing for all classes. Despite the lack of mention in other sources, they were still making smock frocks according to the reporter, 'brilliant green' ones for the Essex market and 'dull drab or nothing' for Lincolnshire. They also made other occupational clothing such as drabbet smocks for Yarmouth and Lowestoft fishermen and butchers' blue drabbet overalls, both being varieties of smocks.[147] Daniel Gurteen had not foreseen the decline in demand for the smock, but was able to refocus his drabbet manufactory into other areas such as military uniforms and the descendent of the smock, the working overall.[148] The growth in his business was said to have occasioned the prosperity and development of the town, the family contributing to projects such as a school for girls, an independent church, building the town hall in 1883 at a cost of £5,000 including a library and reading rooms, and thus making 'a community as respectable and moral a set of people as could be wished'.[149]

A report shortly before his death paraphrased Gurteen's views when he is said to have believed that 'vote by ballot and universal suffrage are of little benefit unless they are worked by a sober and educated people'.[150] His aim was to create a hardworking, dutiful and educated workforce. 'Christopher Crayon', the pseudonym of the journalist James Ewing Ritchie, visited Haverhill in 1885, portraying it as a kind of rural idyll compared to urban manufacturing areas, with everyone 'well dressed, healthy and well fed'. In a ventilated room in the factory, women were making up trousers, smock frocks and waistcoats, 'which the buyers might put on with impunity, not fearing that their garments were tainted with infectious disease or had been wrought up by some poor seamstress in her London cellar almost at the peril of her life'.[151] Here was ready-made clothing with no squalid undertones, the young women working in the factory, the married ones at home, a family earning a 100 to 150 pounds a year between them, as well as living in good housing provided by the firm at fair rents. When work was done, 'pleasant rambles' in the country could be undertaken, contrasting with factory work in the East End.[152] As at Hyde's, railway trips to Alexandra Palace were also organized for workers, 1,000 treated to dinner there at noon on one such trip in 1880.[153] Despite the misgivings of the local clergy about slop work for women, Gurteen was seen as having brought the area prosperity. Daniel died in 1893 and when his will was proved the following year, his personal estate was worth over £28,000.[154]

As businesses such as Hyde, Gurteen and Bousfield successfully expanded and diversified in the third quarter of the nineteenth century, becoming the primary focus of particularly female employment in the towns in which they were based, their very visible success lay them open to criticism about the treatment and payment of their workers, something which they tried to mitigate through paternal acts. The smock itself became part of this positive publicity as a handcrafted garment made by skilled and valued workers, Gurteen's continuing to include smocks in their product range shown at the Turin International Exhibition in 1911.[155] In a catalogue from the late 1930s, they were still offering 'long worked smock frocks to order in olive and drab drabbetts, olive linens and white duck', as well as short slops in white duck, as engineers' overalls.[156] Even today, as one of the oldest clothing companies in the country still under family ownership and in the same town, they continue to pay homage to their smock frock heritage in their publicity.[157]

Newark-on-Trent

Long thought of as a centre for smock manufacture, Newark-on-Trent in Nottinghamshire was famed for its blue smocks from at least the 1820s, using indigo dye from Coventry.[158] William Howitt, in 1848, was able to identify a 'Newark frock' worn in the Midlands area. Blue and smocked on the back and breast in a square, and on the shoulders and wrists, it was also embroidered in white thread with a little white heart at the bottom of the neck slit.[159] However, evidence for the involvement of the general population as outworkers is harder to find here than in Abingdon or Haverhill.[160] After 1841, the trade seems to have consolidated into the hands of a few manufacturers. For example, William, Thomas and Stephen Noddall of Middle Gate, were listed as smock frock manufacturers in an 1841 *Directory*, although the census entry from the same year classifies them as tailors and drapers.[161] Continuing in the smock trade into the 1860s, as with Hyde and Gurteen, by the 1870s they had refocused on making other ready-made garments, the firm of W. T. & S. Noddall, a well-known clothing company in Newark surviving into the twentieth century.[162] John Henry Morley at Barnby Gate was another manufacturer of smock frocks in the town. During the 1830s and 1840s he was in partnership with Reuben Moore.[163] He continued in the trade by himself, in 1851 described as a 'Smock Frock Manufacturer, Master' employing thirty women, and by 1861, was a 'Frock and Slop merchant', suggesting that he had a wholesaling role too.[164]

There was thus a specific colour and type of smock associated with the town, its own 'proto' brand, promoted by local retailers and gradually sold across the country. Resident tradesmen used this as a marketing tool, the advertisement of J. Jackson of Bargate, Newark, 'a dyer of ducks, linens and calicoes', appealing in 1843 to smock frock dealers to use his services to achieve a fast blue, 'the celebrated Newark-dyed Blues', for their white or grey garments.[165] Once dyed, other manufacturers outside the town also made up smocks in the seemingly popular Newark style. W. Angliss of Walker-gate, Grantham, advertised his new Emporium of Fashion in 1852 alongside his wholesale smock frock manufactory, 'the demand for his particular make of Smock Frocks being so great, [so as to] manufacture … them on a very extensive scale … N.B. W. A's Frocks are of the Newark dye and make'.[166] Metal blocks which were used for marking out embroidery patterns survive, with extant smocks in Nottingham and Lincolnshire Museums likely to have been embroidered from them. The patterns are simplistic, Anne Buck associating them with the later years of the industry and finding them 'much debased' in comparison to other more elaborate embroidery.[167] However, as part of the ready-made industry, their use to get a consistent pattern and style makes sense. The Newark smocks may have been simply decorated but they were colourful, helping to create the Newark 'brand' advertised by retailers and reinforcing the idea of the town as a centre of smock frock manufacturing, which endured into the twentieth century.[168]

Chesterfield and the north

Although now largely forgotten, from the early nineteenth century Chesterfield in Derbyshire was also a significant town for the smock trade.[169] The smock manufactory of Riggott and Wright in Burlington Street was noted in 1862 as a 'place … well known in the Smock Frock Trade, that Business having been carried on there for about Half a Century'.[170] An obituary of Henry Clarke, listed in the trade directories as a smock frock manufacturer from the 1830s to the 1850s, also noted that 'he pushed the business beyond local limits and ultimately made a large fortune out of it'.[171] However, the grandly named Midland Frock Manufactory – run by Charles Smith from 1849 and employing around three hundred people – garnered the most attention.[172] Charles Smith liked to be known as 'the Governor of the Midland manufactory' and attracted a lot of commentary in the local press as an 'eccentric' individual.[173] The son of a farmer, he trained at a drapers in Bakewell. He set up his smock business in Chesterfield and was seen to give himself airs above his station, leaving him open to ridicule. For example, he drove to church in an open carriage, the postilion with an 'erratic' coat of arms on his jacket, and Smith pretended to have a cellar of rare wines.[174] *The Derbyshire Times and Chesterfield Herald* published a mocking article in 1859 describing the 'Lord Mayor's Day', also called 'Natal Day of Charles Britain Smith', in some detail. Nicknamed 'Cloaky Pecksniff' in the article, so apparently affecting benevolence or high moral principles after the character in Charles Dickens's *Martin Chuzzlewit*, Smith 'resolved to honour the occasion', 'the front of the smock-frock, *alias* 'cow-gown' shop in Burlington Street, under[going] … a renovation quite wonderful to behold', decorated in red, white and blue with commemorative lettering.[175] The name of his business was locally recognizable, the winner of the ploughing match at the Heath Farmers' Club receiving a 'new frock' from the Midland Manufactory.[176] With his eccentric character openly ridiculed in the town, his personal reputation perhaps impacting on his business, Smith moved to York and his shop, manufactory and warehouse were put up to let and auction by 1862.[177]

Manufacturers have also been traced in Sheffield, Barnsley and Leeds.[178] Barnsley was described as having 500 looms in the town in 1789, weaving material for 'countryman's smock frocks' from the early nineteenth century, presumably as trade in the garment increased.[179] An accident reported in the press reveals the smock manufactory of Mr Morley, Barnsley, where, in a fit of passion, a male worker nearly killed a female worker.[180] By 1858, an article described how the trade had fallen off in the town, the Barnsley ducks used for making smocks now superseded by drabbet, which was cheaper and woven by power loom rather than by hand, as at Gurteen's.[181] However, in 1860, a draper from Winston in the Derbyshire Dales, requested blue smocks of a particular pattern from Barnsley merchants Hardaker & Co., 'as no other were saleable in the neighbourhood'.[182] Although primarily a weaving town, enterprising manufacturers also made up smocks to sell wholesale, a similar pattern emerging in the linen industry in eastern Scotland.[183] Keating & Co., 'Home and Foreign Outfitters' of Aberdeen and Dundee, supplied ready-made clothing for men including tweed trousers, 'stout wearing' suits, waterproof overalls and smock frocks, with their advertisements and directory entries dating from the late 1850s into the early 1870s.[184] Smock frocks were sold from 4 shillings 6 pence to 6 shillings 6 pence. From 1862 they were listed as merchant tailors and clothiers, operating from 4 High Street, Dundee, and 26 Union Street in Aberdeen.[185] Mrs John Calder's Clothing Establishment in Carmelite Street, Aberdeen, was still selling smock frocks as part of her stock of working clothing in 1882.[186]

Foundation of the clothing industry

The smock frock is therefore a good example of a garment which survives in quantity in museum collections, some of which were produced ready-made. Like ready-made quilted petticoats studied by Beverly Lemire and which similarly survive due to their decorative nature, there are standardized elements, a simple construction and adjustable sizing, with a lack of seasonal variation. The characteristic irregularity of petticoats in Lemire's study suggests that they were not quilted from templates but that individual needlewomen adapted and modified a design much as smock patterns were too.[187] Both smocks and petticoats were still made in the large part by hand, even after 1860, which as Tanya Harrod remarks, 'was no fun at all' in comparison to handicrafts for leisure.[188] This hand-work naturally gave customers distinction, the antithesis of typical ready-made uniformity and mass production. However, with standardization and regularity in their production, using straightforward needlework techniques and simple stiches, they were mass-manufactured for shop stock in an assortment of fabrics with variety in quality of workmanship and embellishments, attracting different prices and a range of male consumers.

Ambitious drapers developed this large-scale ready-made smock frock trade from the early nineteenth century by employing female outworkers in their own locality. Those successful in this specialization might expand production into 'factories' and produce more varieties of smocks in quantity. Their local economic influence also increased the social status of such entrepreneurs, many becoming part of their community's elite, for instance mayors, benefactors, Justices of the Peace and trustees of building societies, despite commentators' increasing misgivings about their production methods.[189] The 1860s has been seen as the nascent years for the wholesale clothing industry, coming to fruition in the 1870s with the construction of new factories and familiar names being established, such as Hepworth in Leeds.[190] Such growth appears to have been built on the development of ready-made clothes manufacturing in the second quarter of the nineteenth century, of which smock production was a major part. As the smock went out of use in the 1870s, those who were successful diversified into more complex garments such as trousers and increasingly men's and boys' suits, with menswear dominating garment mass-manufacturing by the late nineteenth century.[191] The substantial growth of the ready-made industry in the second quarter of the nineteenth century was paralleled in the United States, again with 'downscale' markets: rural consumers, slaves, gold rush miners, frontiersmen, railroad workers and soldiers.[192] By around 1880, emporiums in American port cities were selling thousands of ready-made garments to men across most strata of society.[193] Likewise in France, manufacturers such as Pierre Parissot produced work outfits from 1824 including 'blouses' and work shirts which required no fitting. His company, La Belle Jardinière, swiftly moved onto manufacturing cheap suits, the 'blouse' seemingly a catalyst in the development of the French ready-made menswear market.[194]

With continuing falls in clothing prices from the 1870s onwards, the quality and quantity of garment purchases increased, standard styles cheaply available and targeted at working men. Essentially the same styles were sold in multiple versions with fine price gradations to suit every pocket, purchased men's clothing being the norm. It was now as easy and as cheap to dress in what everybody else was wearing, the suit. Home-made clothing became a marker of relative poverty.[195] Manuel Charpy argues that using ready-made uniforms and loose unfitted blouses and smocks in three sizes as workwear familiarized men with standardized sizing so that their own personally chosen clothing was more likely to be ready-made.[196] Special 'working-class' clothing, such as the smock, was no longer required, overalls and occupational workwear becoming a small subsection of the industry.

The manufacture of smock frocks is a trade that reflects what historians have increasingly seen as the intersection between urban and rural spheres, fusing 'urban' and 'rural' occupations into hybrid communities. For example, in villages around Abingdon men might work as agricultural labourers and women as outworkers making smock frocks. Outwork depended on the cheap labour of women who worked within their own homes, whether rural or urban.[197] The ready-made clothes industry was thus partly a rural industry. Until the end of the nineteenth century, there was a massive growth in the numbers of women employed as rural outworkers, reflecting the importance of an industry initially sparked by manufacture of smocks.[198]

In this sector of the trade, as we have seen, manufacturing, wholesaling, retailing and exporting were commonly carried out within one extended family business for mutual familial advantage.[199] As Stanley Chapman notes, the ability to mass market clothing to large portions of the population seems more significant to the expansion of the industry than mechanization, especially when labour was so cheap.[200] Manufacturers who focused on utilitarian workwear, of which the smock was part, did not have the glitzy retail outlets of Moses for example, or the type of advertising that went with this.[201] However, the common or garden ready-made smock infiltrated many retailers' stocks both nationally and internationally, almost without fanfare, which will be further explored in the next two chapters. Introducing innovation without invention and new scales of production without new production methods, the smock trade was an enormously successful industry, its influence felt into the twentieth century by those firms who built generalized clothing businesses from this initial specialization.

4 Selling and buying

Investigating how and where men bought smocks from highlights both their widespread usage and the importance of their purchase. Some of the first references to smocks come from eighteenth-century shop advertisements. The earliest identified is from 1765 when George Boggis, a tailor, salesman and haberdasher of hats in St Clement's Fore Street, Ipswich, 'near the sign of Noah's Ark', advertised his new and second-hand stock, including twill frocks and duck smocks.[1] Peter Crickett, a tailor and draper in the High Street of Colchester, also sold 'Men's Smocks or Slops', and 'Thickset Frocks' by the early 1770s.[2] By the 1790s, many areas of England including Gloucester, Abingdon, Market Harborough and Newport Pagnell had shop advertisements which listed ready-made smocks for sale.[3] This chapter will investigate how these smocks were sold, by examining the rural and urban retailing of the garment as well as their more informal sale through markets and fairs. It will then turn to consider the male consumer and what attracted him to particular shops, emphasizing the importance of working men shopping for their own clothes, before concluding with a discussion about the second-hand market.

Newspaper references to smock frocks being advertised by, or stolen from, shops, across all areas of the country gives us an indication of how widespread the smock trade was from the late eighteenth century onwards. Of course, this is not exhaustive, with references depending on, for example, the type of local newspaper and whether a retailer could bear the expense of advertising, but does signal that the trade was more extensive and prolonged than previously thought. As might be expected, most references were found for the period of 1830–60, across all counties of England except for Northumberland, Durham and, surprisingly, Kent, Norfolk and Surrey, which were all known smock wearing areas. Retailers who advertised in the earlier period were located in Berkshire, Buckinghamshire, Oxfordshire, Warwickshire, Northamptonshire and Worcestershire, indicating a focus for the trade on a central area of rural southern England, although there are examples in surrounding counties, including Yorkshire by the 1800s and Lancashire by the 1820s. In the 1860s, there are strong clusters in Bristol, Birmingham and, particularly, Chesterfield, with examples still scattered throughout England, Wales and eastern Scotland. However, after 1870, there are only a further twenty-three references until the end of the century.[4] For retailers, the trade took off in the 1810s and flourished for around fifty years, aided by the development of the ready-made sector.

As cheap utilitarian clothing, sold without fuss, many retailers held a stock of smocks including market traders, village shops, drapers, ready-made clothing sellers such as clothiers and outfitters in towns and cities, as well as those in the second-hand trade. In Worcester in 1815, the stock of William Savage, described as a glover and draper, included, 'upwards of two hundred men and boy's hats, shirts and smock frocks'.[5] In Chaddesley Corbett, a small town in the north of Worcestershire, John Tetstell, tailor, draper and grocer, went bankrupt in 1810. His stock at the time included 'some ready made clothes, smock frocks … hats … stockings', as well as grocery items.[6] Likewise accounts from a grocer and draper's shop in rural Westoning in Bedfordshire from 1785–1800, show that a variety of smock frocks retailed there from around 4 shillings to 8 shillings 6 pence, whereas coats and waistcoats cost more.[7] The numerous outlets reflected the large consumer market for the garment by the beginning of the nineteenth century, with various opportunities for men to purchase one. Indeed, descriptions of men wearing smock frocks in the press were often preceded with adjective 'common'[8] or 'invariable',[9] suggesting their widespread usage.

From the late eighteenth century, there was thus already a variety in quality and how 'worked' a smock was, reflecting the differences in garments for various occasions, whether for work or for Sunday best, for example, and probably other small subtleties which reflected social gradations between individuals, including cost, no longer obvious to us.[10] The peak of the ready-made smock industry from the 1830s to the 1860s saw a further reduction in the price of the garment. Although cheap in comparison to other clothing, smocks still remained relatively expensive, costing around a week's wages for a labourer and so even 'factory' made ones would have been looked after with care.[11]

Rural retailers

In smaller shops and rural settlements clothing was often part of a mixed stock.[12] Customers might buy a ready-made garment when they came in for hardware or groceries. John Saunders was a grocer, linen draper and slop seller in Cradley, Herefordshire, on the main turnpike road, halfway between Hereford and Worcester. When his business went bankrupt in 1816, he had an extensive clothing stock including 105 flannel jackets, 152 waistcoats and 40 smock frocks.[13] The stock of a village shop in Wingrave, Buckinghamshire, was sold when its owner, Mr Grace, died in 1844. Alongside groceries, ironmongery, medicine and drapery, including fabrics suitable for making up working clothing such as fustian and jean, smock frocks were the only ready-made clothing that he stocked.[14] The elaborate billhead of William Corbett, a linen and woollen draper, grocer, tea dealer and tobacconist, drew on classical and exotic images appealing to local respectable society in Ombersley, Worcestershire. He, however, supplied the local parish overseers with smock frocks for 4 shillings each as well as other textiles, unadvertised stock which is otherwise invisible to us now.[15]

These types of shops also acted as wholesalers to smaller isolated shops and itinerant sellers. For example, Richard Andrews, a pedlar from Aldbourne, near Lambourn in Berkshire, was noted with a smock frock and gaiters in his pack in 1843, which he could have purchased from a town or country shop to sell on.[16] James Smith, 'late of the Bell, Lawrence Waltham, Berks, Draper and Victualler', whose stock included shawls, handkerchiefs, hose, smock frocks, ready-made clothes and hats also owned 'a useful hawker's cart on springs', suggesting that he possibly did rural rounds to cater to all consumers, wherever they lived.[17] A description of a village 'general warehouse' in 1857, notes matches, butter, candles, mousetraps, broadcloth, treacle, lace, black puddings and smock frocks for sale, all exhibited in one window and sold over one counter, in fact, not that different from a description of a mercer in Charlbury in the 1620s.[18] So although some rural retailers were enterprising in seeking out customers, many just eked out a living serving the specific wants of their locality as best they could. Rural consumers saved both time and money buying locally, rather than having to travel to town and, although there was probably less choice, even rural shops usually offered some variety in garments.[19]

Market towns and provincial cities

Retailers in provincial market towns and cities transformed the selling of smocks and men's workwear.[20] A rising demand for these garments stimulated local trade, with manufacturers and retailers in urban areas also acting as middlemen to sell to shopkeepers in the rural hinterland. The connection between production and distribution was very close, often in the hands of one business focused on localized supply networks. John Turner took over a cheap clothing warehouse and the 'Original Manufactory' in Hereford in 1828, thus suggesting that they

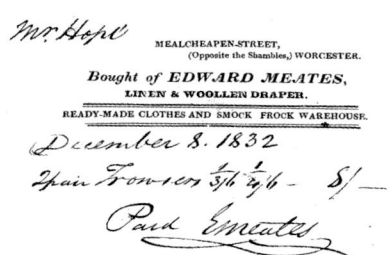

FIGURE 4.1 *Bill from Edward Meates, 8 December 1832, Ombersley Parish Accounts, 3572/13. © Worcestershire Archive and Archaeology Service, Ombersley Parish Church.*

also made the '1000 Mens' and Boys' Frocks, full and plain worked', advertised for sale alongside other male ready-made clothing[21] (see Figure 3.3). Reflecting the success of the wider market for working-class clothing, businesses in provincial towns and cities moved from general drapery to focus on lower status clothing. By 1832, Edward Meates, a Worcester draper, called his business a 'Ready-Made Clothes and Smock Frock Warehouse' (see Figure 4.1).[22]

This type of shop could offer a variety of smock frocks, in different colours and sizes, with various types of embellishments and embroidery. J. and W. M'Alpin of Gallowtree Gate, Leicester, tailors, clothiers and woollen drapers, offered 'an extensive variety of Drabbett and Blue and White Smock Frocks', allowing their customers some choice.[23] Likewise, in 1839, included in an auction of the stock-in-trade of Mr T. Miller, a hatter of Leighton Buzzard, were white, grey, olive and blue duck frocks.[24] The dressed masculine body was the primary public symbol of men's work skills, also reflecting small gradations in social and economic status, so it was important for a shopkeeper to have a selection of various types of the same garment for customers to choose from.

A progressive specialization by shopkeepers thus occurred as the market for ready-made clothing for men, including smock frocks, was realized. The author of *The Reminiscences of the Old Draper* noted that drapers in provincial towns all had their own specialities, one catering for sailors, another for the country trade.[25] In Banbury, Oxfordshire, William Baker's account books between 1814 and 1822 show that the focus of his business was on smocks and leggings (gaiters), that is in selling practical workwear to local men. His stock included smock frocks, loose frocks and slops, in three different sizes, and from 'best', 'full worked', and 'double worked', the most expensive, through to 'stout' and 'comon [sic]'. He apparently sold nine different patterns alongside each other, identified in his accounts by a numbering system of N1-N9, with N9 the last to be introduced, his customers including overseers.²⁶ J. White in Stamford, Lincolnshire, advertised his ready-made clothes in 1828 as 'consist[ing] of several thousands of garments, suitable for farm servants ... [with] a large stock of Farmers' Servants' Smock Frocks'.²⁷ The quantity and therefore choice available in his stock was emphasized as well as his direct appeal to rural workers, his largest market in the surrounding area. Prices were marked in ink on the inside of the garment or on a ticket.²⁸ So, by the 1820s, the consumer could choose a size and the decoration required on their smock in an already specialized marketplace. The burgeoning mass-manufactured ready-made trade of firms such as Hyde and Bousfield expanded this further in the second quarter of the nineteenth century.²⁹

Shop advertisements thus highlighted availability and choice and, as 'factory' made smocks came onto the market during the 1840s, also underlined their cheapness. F. Elmes in Aylesbury promoted his shop with a large red signboard over his door for easy identification. He sold a variety of cheap ready-made clothing, including white and coloured smock frocks in two sizes from 2 shillings, 'some extra worked', for male buyers coming into the market town.³⁰ In Hereford, from the late 1830s, Dan Evans sold items such as smock frocks claiming that he had 'the largest stock of Readymade Clothes and Frocks in the County'.³¹ In 1843, there was keen competition between ready-made clothing sellers in Hereford, including the smock trade, played out in the pages of the local press. Dan Evans's 'Cheap Mart' advertised boys' stout 'Russia duck' smock frocks from 1 shilling to 3 shillings 6 pence, men's the same, from 2 shillings to 4 shillings 6 pence, 'extra prime worked' smock frocks, presumably with embroidery, from 5 shillings 6 pence, and boys' and men's drabbet smock frocks from 2 shillings 6 pence to 5 shillings 6 pence.³² One of Evans's main Hereford rivals, Watson, advertised their 'well-sewed' and 'home-made' garments at the same time, also appealing for 'several good frock makers'.³³ The implication was that their ready-made clothing came from within Hereford, whereas Evan's bought his from outside manufacturers. Watson continued their campaign against very cheap prices, appealing to the common sense of their customers: 'The public must clearly perceive that if Prints be advertised at a farthing or 1d per yard ... or waistcoats at 9d each and Frocks 1s, they can be of no possible use to the purchaser'.³⁴ These prices were a direct reference to Evans's advertisement the previous April and were part of a campaign to appeal to male consumers to buy smocks of a particular manufacturing origin from a specific shop where their quality could be guaranteed. It was an early 'Buy Local' scheme although, then as now, the lure of cheap prices may have been too much for consumers to ignore.³⁵

Enterprising shopkeepers also sent out smocks on trial to male consumers in surrounding country areas, who otherwise could not get into town. In 1870, one Saturday evening, Hannah Lingwood went into the draper's shop of John Henderson in Ware, Hertfordshire. She asked for smocks that she could take home for her husband to try on and was given three with a total value of 8 shillings. She had also done this the previous week, returning two on Monday and paying for the third, so presumably there seemed to be a low risk of theft for the draper. However, she almost immediately pawned these smocks in Hertford, where she was detained. Lingwood had seemingly worked out a specific strategy to obtain cash, using the custom of shopkeepers sending out smocks for working men to try on at home, on approval. It being an offence to pawn other people's property, Lingwood admitted what she had done and, showing a valid reason for her actions, was found not guilty.[36] A case in 1877 showed a similar practice going on in Aylesbury, where 'it was the custom amongst Aylesbury tradespeople to send out goods on approval'. Here F. Elmes in Aylesbury gave an errand boy two smock frocks from his shop to pass onto a youth living in the village of Oving on a trial basis for three days.[37]

Smocks were hung at doorways and outside shops to catch the passing eye and entice customers, but this also made them vulnerable to the opportunistic thief.[38] This type of display was associated with downmarket shops, stock being informally placed outside, on window ledges, hung at doors or from fascia boards, and often led to conflict with those who wanted order in their streets.[39] A shop keeper in Halifax, Mr Spencer of Woolshops, was fined 2 shillings 6 pence for having smock frocks hanging from his doorway and projecting over the causeway.[40] In Devizes, Wiltshire, there was also controversy, in 1839, about goods being displayed in this way, when an inspector invoked the Devizes Improvement Act bringing several shopkeepers to court, including Mr Jones for displaying a smock frock over the edge of his property which flapped about projecting over the footpath.[41] The attempt to clean up the appearance of towns and remove unsightly articles, including flapping smock frocks, brought local elites into conflict with retailers and the majority of shoppers.

The wider trade

While it might be expected to find smocks for sale in market towns or cities with large rural hinterlands in southern and central England, there is evidence for more widespread retailing of smocks. Elizabeth Brown, a widow, originally set up the Brown Muff Department store in Bradford in 1817 as a 'clothes brokers'. By the 1820s it was a linen drapery selling stock for cash only.[42] The store continuously sold men's ready-made clothing throughout the 1820s and 1830s, including smock frocks, seemingly thriving on its specialization in male working garments. There were different types of smocks for sale, such as long and short ones, those made from various materials including 'Russia duck' and dowlas, as well as 'slops'.[43] This suggests a steady demand for a practical and useful garment, the quantity in stock in 1836 at one point being twenty-two short and forty-four long smocks, showing their popularity. Different prices in the account books probably indicated various sizes of garment and how well-worked, or embroidered, they were.[44] Likewise, B. Leach, a tailor, draper and ready-made clothes seller in Wakefield advertised his stock of 500 smock frocks and slops for sale in 1841. The reach of the smock frock seemed to spread across the north of England, although seemingly most popular in Yorkshire.[45] John Barran was a tailor and clothes dealer at 1 Briggate, Leeds, during the 1840s, his stock book of 1845 including 'smocks'.[46] From this shop, in the early 1850s, he developed his ready-to-wear factory, focusing on boys' and menswear and was an early adopter of the sewing machine.[47] By 1872, he employed some three to four thousand workers using 2,000 sewing machines and is seen as the founder of the industry manufacturing ready-made clothes for men in Leeds, the city later famed for firms such as Burton and Hepworth's.[48]

Clothing retailers in large cities therefore stocked smocks as they were worn by many working men across England. Edwin Butler was a clothier and outfitter in Birmingham High Street from around 1818 until his death in 1869. From the 1820s, his stock included 'Waggoners Smock Frocks', and by the mid-nineteenth century, he sold 'Railway and other slops … butchers blue Worcester frocks' as well. Like other similar urban retailers, his advertisements emphasized the vast quantity of stock that he held, 'Ten Thousand Blouses', and the cheapness of his prices.[49] Such stores in urban settings grew throughout the century selling all types of clothing for working men, reaching an apogee by the 1880s, with huge shops such as The Manufacturers Alliance at 249–53 Edgware Road, London. This establishment sold duck jackets, a replacement for the smock, at, what it claimed, were wholesale prices.[50] Within the smock trade there were different markets appealing to a variety of economic strata and the diverse occupations of the working-class male consumer who wore the garment, perhaps a trade more nuanced than might be expected.

Markets and fairs

Alongside shops, some retailers and manufacturers took a stall in a market or fair to connect more directly with their customers, who might be there on other business. A row erupted during York Thursday Market between two smock frock manufacturers running stalls on opposite sides of the road. John Tuke shouted out 'John Tuke's smock manufactory – no rubbish', implying that his competitor's smocks were inferior. An altercation arose leading to an assault for which a fine was issued.[51] Without this fight, the existence of these 'manufactories' would be unrecorded. Michael Charlton, also of the Thursday Market, brought a case at York Guildhall for the embezzlement of two of his smocks which were given out to Ellen Brearey to make up, but which she subsequently illegally pawned, one unfinished.[52] In 1859, Mr Williams in Tavistock sold smocks from a market stall for two days each week,[53] and Mr Gabbitas, a tailor from Newark, had two smock frocks stolen from his market stall.[54] Markets thus remained an important way to sell working clothing into the mid-nineteenth century, particularly, though not exclusively, in the north of England.[55]

Alongside the daily or weekly market, it was also common for shopkeepers to sell smocks at periodic fairs. In 1787, at the famous Weyhill Fair, three linen smock frocks were stolen with other fabric from the stall of Brice Graham, a draper from Lower Wallop.[56] William Sergeant, a slop seller from Bedford, was selling clothes at Ampthill Fair in 1821, when a smock was stolen from his stall. As a ready-made garment, he identified it from the ticket he had fastened onto it.[57] A fair in Edmonton in 1823 had sixty or so stands selling shoes, stockings, razors, pen knives, pottery and smock frocks.[58] In the mid-nineteenth century, William Howitt noted smocks being 'hung aloft at the end of the slop-vendor's stall, on a crossed pole, and waving about like scarecrows in the wind' and therefore catching the eye.[59] A report on the annual rag fair held at Whitchurch in Shropshire in 1869, noted the decline of the country fair, with people preferring instead to go by rail into town to visit larger clothing retailers, with little left of the usual trade in smock frocks and haberdashery.[60] Barclay Wills interviewed old shepherds in the 1920s, who went into Lewes for the fair every 21 September and bought their smocks from Browne and Crosskeys, a draper in the town. Packing cases were placed outside as seats for those waiting to buy, turning the event into a social occasion, with dogs to be left at the foot of the stairs![61]

A mixture of commerce and pleasure, statute or mop fairs also functioned as a labour exchange. Fitting in with the working calendar, they were furthermore a social occasion and an opportunity to spend wages and show off, sartorially or financially or both. An account of Barton Fair in Gloucester notes that people came into the city dressed in their best clothes, blue coats or 'snowy white smock frocks', with hats, 'for a country-man always wears a good hat on gala days', browsing shop windows which were specially 'arrayed' by shopkeepers for the occasion, accompanied by their female companions.[62] William Freshwater advertised his business in the centre of Coventry around the time of the city's fair with an appeal to 'Yearly [farm] servants' working within a radius of 10 to 12 miles of the city, who would likely seek new employment at the hiring fair, to come to his ready-made clothes shop. To identify his shop, 'giant's trousers and smock frock hang outside', both eye-catching and an indication of his stock.[63] Workers with their harvest-boosted cash might provide an annual bonus for shopkeepers, if they could promote their business in the right way. Men wore new smock frocks, 'fiery neck-ties, or waistcoats of terrific tint and pattern', for the Gloucester Mop Fair in 1853, where stalls sold Banbury cakes and the most popular dance was 'Pop Goes the Weasel'.[64] These fairs were an opportunity for both retailers and consumers. Canny shopkeepers traded on the idea of men having the right clothing both to find work and to fit in with peers for the sociability of the fair. There seems to have been a later romantic notion that the embroidery on a smock could identify the trade of the wearer and make such hiring easier. The act of putting on a smock would identify the wearer as a manual labourer, but closer specification was, it seems, in general kept for smocks worn on special occasions, perhaps as a celebration of that person's life, as at a wedding.[65]

Male shoppers

We tend not to think of nineteenth-century men engaging in any 'shopping' and, certainly for the middle classes, shopping was seen as an increasingly feminine preoccupation, the department store, for example, a safe environment for respectable women. However, as overseers, poor law guardians or charity trustees, local elite men enabled the purchase of working clothing such as smock frocks. Joseph Arch remembered his smock as a visible marker of poverty in his childhood, growing up in Warwickshire in the 1830s. He went to school and work, aged 9, in the same smock frock, clothing of the 'coarsest' type, as the family struggled to buy both clothing and food.[66] For families that could not afford to buy clothing, poor relief or charity was another way to obtain it and the local elite, who ran these organizations, often ended up as one of the largest purchasers of smocks frocks and other similar garments. Linen for round frocks was included in workhouse tenders by 1790, so Poor Law authorities had already recognized the smock's value for money and it's usefulness.[67] The overseers of Hindlip in Worcestershire bought a smock frock for 7 shillings 6 pence from a salesman in Worcester in 1812, whereas a coat from the same shop cost 18 shillings.[68] Another Worcester salesman, Stephen Burden, supplied the overseers of Powick with 170 items of clothing in 1818, a third of which were smock frocks or jackets.[69] Their cheapness was consolidated by the developing ready-made sector, as seen in the previous chapter. While they bought economically, overseers' purchases were not always the cheapest, account books showing other people buying cheaper versions of the garments that they chose.[70] In 1828, the overseers of Ombersley, Worcestershire, bought a 'best frock' for 11 shillings from William Corbett, the local draper, as part of their order for their workhouse.[71] However, James Horsley was able to supply the overseers of St Andrew's Parish in nearby Droitwich, with smock frocks costing only 3 shillings 4 pence in 1823, so the differences in price could vary greatly.[72] If overseers could afford and justify obtaining good quality clothing, then this reflected well on the parish.

In Abbey Dore, in rural Herefordshire, the overseers made frequent payments for male clothing, presumably to maintain men in work and allay the threat of higher relief costs being needed in the future. John Brace, an agricultural labourer, claimed smock frocks from the parish in 1816, 1822, 1824, 1827 and 1831, while James Pritchard was allowed 7 shillings to buy his son a shirt and smock from the Hereford clothing sellers to enable him to start work as a farm servant in 1807.[73] Overseers allowed different amounts for what appears to have been similar clothing at around the same time. In Abbey Dore in December 1814, John Williams's boy was given 6 shillings 6 pence for a 'frock', William Lewis's boy was given 4 shillings 6 pence for a 'smock frock', and three months later, in March 1815, William Lewis the father was given 10 shillings 6 pence for a frock. These varying costs probably reflect different sizing and smock types, as well as the decoration. Smocks were a respectable garment that people thought might be granted by the overseers and attire that they were willing to give out, fulfilling various purposes including maintaining appearances and allowing a man to work.[74] The preference of overseers for generally plain and decent garments could be seen as a guide to what they thought was a necessity and conversely, a luxury.[75] For retailers of working clothing, local elite men were therefore major customers, facilitating its purchase, although they may not have bought it in person.

Particularly during the eighteenth century, it is apparent through advertising that tradesmen viewed male consumers as a prime sector of the purchasing market for all types of goods, household included, although the focus of research has so far been on the middle classes and local elites.[76] Historians have posited that as male waged work outside the home became the norm, particularly into the nineteenth century, women took over the role of domestic consumer activity.[77] By the Victorian period, new codes of modern masculinity represented by sober plain dressing, separated respectable men from the day-to-day management of their home and reduced their interest in petty consumer activities.[78] However, many working men seemed to have maintained both the opportunity and the desire to fulfil their own consumer needs in terms of clothing and thus self-fashioning their identities. As Laura Ugolini has shown, with her investigation into the shopping habits of ordinary men in the late nineteenth and early twentieth centuries, shopping was not perceived as 'unmanly'. Men routinely bought certain, particularly masculine, items, for example, tobacco, hair oil and razors, with women not necessarily being trusted to do this. Clothes shopping was also routine, although as Ugolini notes, autobiographical material of the period tends to record only memorable clothes shopping trips.[79]

The ability to purchase new or better clothes was perceived as a mark of a successful and desirable manhood.[80] Rural workers were highly mobile, not static and isolated in one place, and there was a significant amount of migration and movement in localized areas, within a walking distance, which included moving between town and village.[81] Opportunities to engage in consumerism, in whatever context, were therefore never far away. Traditionally, new clothes were bought for the Whitsun holiday in May and again after the harvest wages had been paid.[82] Jesse Grant worked as a carter and agricultural labourer on Grants Farm in Bratton, Wiltshire. His employers, the Whitaker family, allowed him a generous 10 shillings 6 pence every summer, July and August, during the 1830s, to buy a smock frock. Described as having seven children by 1841, this perquisite was probably very welcome and would have allowed him a trip into town to make the purchase.[83]

As the primary breadwinner in a family, it was common for men to retain a portion of their wages to spend on alcohol, tobacco and their own clothing.[84] These three things were quite often combined. Men would go into a market town or city to purchase smock frocks, along with a visit to a public house, frequently in pairs or groups.[85] The son of a tailor described the operations of his family's shop in Stowmarket, Suffolk, at the end of the nineteenth century in an oral testimony. The 'old country bo's' would come and buy their clothing ready-made from them, his father keeping 4½ gallons of beer under the counter. Before buying an item, such customers were given a glass of beer: 'time was not a factor; they were in town for a bit of a spree as far as their money allowed them'. His father also took clothing out to the countryside for those who could not make it into town, setting up in a room in a public house.[86] The 'pub' was the most important site of plebeian leisure and culture throughout the nineteenth century and an ad hoc site for retailing, outside the gaze of 'respectable' society.[87]

The combination of enjoying alcohol and purchasing a smock frock during a visit to a local town was thus a regular occurrence, although it became almost a morality tale in the Victorian press. Men set off with good intentions to go and buy a smock frock, enabling them to work effectively and achieve a level of respectability, but succumbed to the lure of alcohol instead. Richard Moore went to Wantage to buy a smock frock and hat, with two other male friends.

After spending the night drinking in the White Hart and then the White Horse with new acquaintances, Moore was separated from his friends and violently robbed of his money and watch, his smock frock purchase never being carried out.[88] In Fordingbridge, Hampshire, William Roberts bought a smock frock before spending the night at the George where he was 'tipsy'. Here he lost his new smock, or it was stolen, depending on the version of events.[89] William Higgins left service and collected his wages on 1 May 1848 from Mr Mutlow, in Holme Lacey, a village outside Hereford. He then headed into the city and bought a smock frock for 6 shillings 6 pence before visiting the White Swan for a beer, where he was apparently robbed.[90] It seems to have been expected behaviour for men to congregate in a public house outside the vicinity of their home or neighbourhood, to fraternize and share drinks with strangers in similar social situations, contrasting with the kinship or friendship bonds of a 'local' pub.[91]

Some shops catered for late night shopping after a visit to the pub, when male consumers were perhaps most vulnerable. Charles Homsby spent Saturday evening in the Crown pub, Great Waltham, before going to Mr Brewer's shop between 11 and 12, where he was 'tipsy' and swore at the owner's wife. He managed to buy some goods including a smock frock, before walking home when he alleged he was assaulted.[92] Shops might also open on Sundays, Thomas Eagles, a shopkeeper and clothier of Springfield Hill near Chelmsford, caught open on a Sunday, three labouring men in the shop, one holding up a smock frock, 'as if to buy it'.[93]

Shops which sold smocks offered a comfortable arena where men, individually or in a group, could try them on as an outer garment to find the one that they liked best under the guidance of generally a male shopkeeper. In Wirksworth, Derbyshire, William Botham went into Mr Fryer's shop and asked to look at smock frocks. He tried on several and chose one which fitted him.[94] Sometimes supplemented by the imbibing of beer, such shops were usually a convivial, male homosocial environment. In Chelmsford, a 9-year-old servant boy was caught up in an attempted arsenic poisoning case, as when going to fetch castor oil as an antidote, he instead was found 'fitting on' a smock frock in the same shop.[95] Shops would sell to all consumers including young ones.[96] In a case which did not garner much sympathy in court, a youth, described as 'a stupid looking lout', had saved 9 shillings to buy a smock frock. He went with two other boys to Wellington, Shropshire, first to the Three Crowns for ale, then to a house where he requested a 'wench' and the other boys stole his money.[97] With his 'sociability', Yeomans had lost his savings and the chance to buy a smock frock. To counter such episodes, the Lincolnshire village of Sturton established a penny bank to encourage saving rather than the squandering of money on things such as alcohol. Youths who used the scheme continued to buy articles such as a pair of boots, smock frocks and gloves.[98]

The smock connoisseur

The purchase of a smock seemingly led to a certain amount of pride, with an awareness of the role that clothing played both in masculine identity formation and as a reflection of their economic circumstances. In 1853, John Colton, a servant to a publican in Moira, Leicestershire, bought a new smock which he hung on a screen in the kitchen, from where it was stolen.[99] Perhaps he was revelling in his new purchase, giving it pride of place, before he needed to wear it. When James Freeman stole money from William Sedgewick, who he apparently knew, after lodging at his house in Pelsall he then went straight to nearby Lichfield. Having bought 'a very good smock frock', a policeman found him in the Anchor pub and he admitted the crime.[100] He bought a better smock than perhaps he actually needed, possibly because he could afford it at that point. Thomas Weller lived in Whitchurch and crossed the River Thames to Pangbourne, Berkshire, where he bought a smock frock and three handkerchiefs. On his way back he stopped at a beerhouse in Whitchurch and also the Lawrence public house. Witnesses stated that he appeared 'quite drunk' and was showing off his bundle of new clothing to a man who was later accused of stealing and pawning it.[101]

In 1831, John Bishop of Bethnal Green, London, a carter, wore a smock when he met his accomplices in the Fortune of War public house opposite St Bartholomew's Hospital to drink rum and eat lunch.[102] James May admired his smock frock and asked him where he could buy one. Bishop took May to a Jewish clothes dealer and salesman, Davis, in Field Lane, Holborn, who sold them a smock frock 'worked in front'.[103] They also bought another with unusual stitching from a Jewish clothes dealer of Saffron Hill, to add to their smock purchases, the dealer later identifying them in prison when they were subsequently accused of the infamous Italian Boy murder.[104] Depicted in various court sketches wearing smocks, reportage about the case portrayed the accused dressing in this way as a disguise. However, John Bishop was a carter, so would have ordinarily worn a smock.[105] Therefore the desire to own a smock, and a good quality one too, was perhaps more of a motive for the purchases, giving an individual distinction within peer group conformity. Functional utility was not always the highest priority, decoration and ornament also important to men, along with displaying new clothing to peers to reveal their current financial status which did not always last very long.[106]

Men thus generally bought smocks. In a witness statement during a murder trial in Gloucestershire, an overheard argument between the accused husband and his wife was reported. The wife berated the husband: 'Why can't you behave yourself as well as other men, and breed up your children as tidy as other men do – buy a smock and take them to church – how much better that would be?' The husband then threatened her with violence.[107] The implication was that the smock ensured some propriety and signalled appropriate masculinity, enabling activities such as going to church to be undertaken so also garnering community respect. Although women made smocks, either as outworkers or for a particular individual, it was usually a masculine decision to choose a particular smock. Male shopping practices implied that men acquired a body of consumer knowledge about what they wanted and where they could buy items before they went shopping, derived from a variety of networks including relatives, friends and acquaintances.[108] This influenced which shops were patronized, with recommendations of quality, for example, as well as which garments were eventually bought.

As Ugolini suggests for the late nineteenth century, the clothes consumption of men was a social activity, the common occurrence of the pub in recorded shopping trips reflecting this. Sartorial decisions were influenced by fellow men around them, with a general awareness of how they would appear to others and fit into their community peer group as well as the various social environments negotiated in daily life. Where there was a transgression, the wearer laid themselves open to ridicule. Clothing associated with a particular group, for example labourers, was fluid but with conventions and unwritten rules about what was appropriate and acceptable within local boundaries to form a collective sartorial identity. An urban rural divide is perhaps spurious in terms of clothing choices, rural 'society' adaptive and accommodating to the 'urban world' from using trains to going 'shopping'. Most men also belonged to a variety of groups which might have different sartorial models, from work, to pub, to home, to church, as well as including broader issues such as age and location.

The most important group to signal membership of was that of being a man and wearing items associated with femininity could lead to accusations of effeminacy or unmanliness.[109] The men who bought smock frocks could have purchased other increasingly cheap ready-made clothing also available in the same shops, jackets for example, but they chose to buy smocks. Perhaps this was necessary for work and because they were expected to look a certain way. However, smocks were also seen as comfortable, practical, decorative and economically prudent, so their purchase may have been a personal choice. Maintaining the gender boundary was a primary function of clothing during the nineteenth century and, to modern eyes, one that the smock may have transgressed, as indeed it gradually became seen as doing and thus was ridiculed by the late nineteenth century.[110] However, in the earlier period, it was very much a masculine garment associated with those who laboured hard. Anticipation, browsing, socializing and the spending of money on both leisure pursuits and useful purchases such as smocks, were all bound together closely in the shopping experiences of the working man, both young and old.

The second-hand trade

The smock frock was so ubiquitous that labourers freely exchanged, lent or even stole the garment into the 1870s.[111] Smocks were overalls, so not intimately connected with the body and were taken off frequently to actually do physical work, so they were left lying around. John Smith, of Charlton, Oxfordshire, left his smock on a heap of stones while he worked on the nearby road, from where a tramp stole it.[112] As a capacious, generally ready-made garment with no fitting required, their ease of wear must have made smocks attractive to just pick up where they were found and illegally reuse. Although they were relatively cheap to buy in contrast to other garments, they remained expensive in comparison to wages. With seemingly an insufficient quantity to meet demand at the right price, hence their routine theft, such practices highlight gaps in the market which large-scale clothing manufacturers eventually filled.

The second-hand garment market was thus rife and saying that you had just bought it from a traveller on the road was a relatively common defence for those accused of stealing a smock, sometimes provable, sometimes not.[113] When John Thomas stole a smock frock from a wagon in Hereford city centre in 1837, he took it to an outlying village and tried to sell it, saying that he had just purchased it and it was too small for him.[114] Presumably he hoped to avoid detection this way, although he failed in this case. In 1839, in Basford, Nottinghamshire, John Matthews was working on the Mansfield road and put his smock by the roadside. Another man picked it up and quickly sold it on for 3 pence.[115] In another case, a smock frock was stolen from a stable where it was left overnight. It was quickly passed on at the local blacksmith's shop, 'a public gossiping place' and 'the usual place for assembling together' in country places, where it was sold for a few pence to the rag-and-bone man.[116] The speed of passing smocks on seems to have been key to avoiding detection, often sold randomly to a stranger who happened to be passing or at a gathering spot for people, whether an ale house or street corner.[117]

The swiftness with which stolen smocks changed hands would necessitate them being sold for only a few pence – whatever cash the buyer had on them.

However, in one case, a smock frock stolen from a barn, where it was left with 'a basket containing eatables', was taken into the nearest town, Newark, to be sold on the street for 3 shillings 6 pence, with the story that it was bought in Lincoln and needed to be sold to raise money to buy food. It was then resold for 5 shillings 6 pence, unfortunately to a man who worked with its original owner.[118] Obviously a good smock sold to the right buyer, or in this case, the wrong one, could raise a decent profit. There was apparently a ready market of male smock buyers happy to deal on the street or in a 'back room'. In the courts there was also some incredulity at where and when such deals might be done. Two labourers from Godshill were drinking together one Sunday evening in the White Hart Inn. Williams decided to sell his smock frock to raise more money to buy beer and so his companion lent him a waistcoat. The mayor adjudicating in court in the county petty sessions asked if it was likely that he could get money on his smock frock on a Sunday evening. 'Yes, sir, I have frequently seen it done' was the reply.[119] It is not clear whether a formal or backstreet pawnbroker was used here or if it was another deal on the street, but it was evidently not uncommon.

In 1857, James Evans, a labourer, came to Hereford for the second day of the May Fair. That evening he bought a smock frock and pair of braces from Mr Francis's stall in the marketplace. He then visited the Crown and Sceptre pub to meet his cousin, where his parcel of new clothes was stolen. The smock was quickly sold onto another man in a nearby pub a couple of streets away, although through a description of the thief, John Shepherd was identified as the man who took the package. As a seller of rings, cutlery and other small wares, and calling himself an optician, his defence was that he took the smock in exchange for two razors and a pair of spectacles, not knowing that it was stolen.[120] The smock frock had an associated second-hand value, which appeared to be widely known and used to formulate deals such as this, Shepherd selling it for 3 shillings 6 pence and a quart of ale. At a backstreet hucksters shop in Dolday, Worcester, a smock frock was left as security for payment to enable the purchase of other articles, presumably as its value would be widely understood.[121]

The context of the site for the sale of second-hand or stolen garments was seemingly as important as the actual garment itself. Everyday situations were used to exchange everyday garments – the middle of a field, the roadside, the pub – the seller presenting the opportunity as the one chance to get a bargain or to gain a smock that might be useful in the future. It was an on-the-spot purchase, with bartering, and a sale that may not have been considered if it necessitated a journey to a shop for a similar garment, even if at a comparable price. The convenience, the sense of getting a bargain, the consent and trust needed between buyer and seller, the value ascertained on accumulated knowledge of previous transactions, was perhaps more important than the garment itself which may have been only briefly glanced at. Purportedly buying directly from the garment's wearer, although many were stolen, could give assurances about quality and condition. As outerwear, the problematic nature of second-hand clothing's close association with their previous owner's body was also more easily overcome. With a recognized monetary value to sell as second-hand or to pawn, the buyer had knowledge that a garment's value could be unlocked at a later date, perhaps as a defence against penury, even if not immediately useful to wear.[122] A blue smock, 'nearly a new one', taken from a mashing tub where had been left in order to assist the ostler at the Fish Pub in Worcester, was pledged for 2 shillings, stolen specifically to raise this money.[123] They acted almost like an alternative currency, although if the need arose to get rid of a smock quickly, it might be passed on for just a few pence.[124] There may have been other types of value too for second-hand exchange, for example, indirect charity for someone fallen on hard times, which is now extremely hard to quantify.[125] There also remained a second-hand retail market in smock frocks, some ending up for sale, for example, in the stock of old clothes sellers in Houndsditch, London, the traditional centre of the second-hand trade.[126]

Purchasing smock frocks

Most men devoted some attention to appearance and many enjoyed the process of self-fashioning that image through the acquisition of clothing.[127] The working man's clothed and decorated body was the public site for the display of his status, both within peer groups and wider social spheres, reflecting his economic standing and occupation. Thus successful shopping could enhance manliness and self-worth, include other leisure activities and demonstrate social success to peers on a number of levels.[128] This routine shopping by men was not regarded as effete or feminine but as an essential part of life. Owners recognized their smocks, for example in court, through wear marks, patches, repairs and also the needlework on them. They were reminders of hard-won leisure time in the town where they were first bought, as well as being essential to maintain a respectable working appearance and a repository of monetary value when required. Thus the emotional response to losing a smock, reflected in the intimate knowledge that men retained about the quirks of their garment, meant that, for many, the effort needed to regain it was usually seen as worthwhile. Such apparel was an integral part of their life in many ways.

The smock frock trade was likewise an essential part of business for many retailers and so profitable for some that it became their only business. This chapter has traced the multiplicity of outlets and opportunities that there were to buy smocks across all areas of the country, highlighting their importance for retailers. For many nineteenth-century clothes retailers, selling ready-made clothing for men, including smocks, was the backbone of their business. As so few account books survive for such shops, examining court reports and overseers' accounts gives access to records of this stock, otherwise not recorded in advertisements and so often missed in historical accounts. The large markets for such clothing included elite men buying for groups such as the parish poor, including workhouse uniform. Some of this clothing was involuntarily given to male recipients, with no choice, but within some parish provision, there was also scope for sartorial differentiation. As discussed, sellers sold a variety of smock types, colours and embellishments from one site, whether a shop or market stall, reflecting the popularity of the garment for working men and catering for the many purposes that it fulfilled for different individuals. Indeed, by using the example of men wanting to buy a better smock, or a more unusual version, when economic circumstances allowed, whether through legal gains or not, the diversity of the market is shown. There was an expectation by male smock shoppers that retailers would provide a variety of smocks, at different price levels, which would allow them choice in their purchases. The next chapter will move on to investigate the range of smocks used by various working men.

5 Appearances

Categorizing people and their role in society, before we know who they are, by judging their clothing is nothing new.[1] As John Styles points out, for the eighteenth century, 'ordinary people reveal an acute sensitivity to sartorial distinctions', assessing others by their clothes, and a person could construct a visual identity through the use of particular types of clothing.[2] This culture of 'visualisation' continued during the nineteenth century, where display and observation were intrinsic to 'cultural processes and values'.[3] Working people were very much aware of the social and economic coding of dress and the need for particular garments to imply specific occupations or status. Appearance and associated perceived personal qualities were important for doing business, getting work and gaining credit in shops.[4] However, this was a system of classification and not identification; a way of saying that somebody looked like a waggoner, not that they actually were a waggoner, and so it was open to subversion. The description of a body of a stranger pulled from the river at Wilton in 1849, having 'the appearance of a drover', was due to his dress; a long smock frock, blue neckerchief, fustian trousers and two waistcoats, one worn over his smock frock.[5] In 1821, near Leicester, a man wearing a smock frock took and drove some sheep from Birtall to Leicester market where he sold them, his dress suggesting that he was either a shepherd or a drover. He 'undisguised' himself by taking off his smock frock in a local pub and then disappeared.[6] The sheer ubiquity and uniform appearance of smocks helped men wearing one to blend into the crowd. They anonymized appearance making the identification of one difficult from the many, like denim jeans or 'hi-vis' jackets today.

Appearance could thus easily be superficial, created for gain, and there was an acceptance that this 'identity' was easy to falsify and to use for deception.[7] An article from 1861, discussing the pros and cons of hiring fairs, notes that it was difficult to judge a man by his dress, especially if worn to deceive: 'The clean smock-frock may cover only inward uncleanness and villainy'. Many who came to hiring fairs to look for work were likely to be of bad character, the article observes, 'men of a roving, dissatisfied turn of mind, not fond of regular employment or steady labour', whereas good servants usually remained employed in the same place.[8] The subversive way that swindlers and criminals used the smock frock emphasizes this complex categorization by appearance. The minutiae of differences and signifiers in dress, including smocks, and what this meant to individuals, is quickly rendered invisible to those looking at it from a different time or place. Even contemporaries, such as William Tayler, a footman, could misunderstand the sartorial perception that he was creating. On his visits to the country he was various mistaken for a land surveyor, a school master, a beggar, a thief, a tailor, a grocer, an army captain and perhaps unsurprisingly, a swindler.[9] Knowing what occupation you were trying to portray and how to do this was an art and difficult to interpret correctly for those outside the locale, including us. Observers readily interpreted a person's identity, visualized through their dress, whether self-fashioned, for show, or imposed. This chapter will investigate the widespread use of the smock to create some of these many male working-class appearances.

When Anne Buck examined fifty-four surviving smocks in museum collections for her article in 1963, she concluded that it was not possible to connect the details or shaping of a smock to a particular occupation and, likewise, the embroidery designs were not usually linked to the wearer's employment, especially if ready-made.[10] Thus Gabriel Oak obtained 'a shepherd's regulation smock frock' in Thomas Hardy's *Far from the Madding Crowd*, but this was a ready-made item and not necessarily worn just by shepherds.[11] While these occupations and colloquial names, for example 'cow gown',[12] suggests a rural bias, working-class men in general used the smock widely in its many varieties.[13] William Howitt underlines this in 1848, suggesting that the metropolitan caricature of the 'English peasant' as a clown, 'silly-looking' in a white 'slop' was too simplistic. Protean and multifarious, Howitt lists some of the many occupations of the English 'peasant': day labourer, woodman, ploughman, wagoner, collier, worker in railroad and canal making, gamekeeper, poacher, an incendiary, charcoal burner, keeper of village alehouses and Tom-and-Jerrys [small beer houses], tramp, pauper, boatman, roadside stone-breaker, quarryman, journeyman bricklayer or his clerk, shepherd, drover, rat-catcher, mole catcher 'and half a hundred other things'.[14] Men working in many of these and other occupations wore a version of the smock. As discussed in the introduction, the nomenclature around the terms 'smock' or 'smock frock' was complex, even for contemporaries to follow. This chapter will discuss how this confusion over terminology, and generalizations which have stemmed from this, have hidden the wider use of the smock. Rather than concentrating on rural workers, this chapter therefore diversifies from traditional histories of the smock to explore the many situations in which men wore the garment as a piece of occupational workwear including the army, detectives, for 'dirty' trades such as dustmen, and criminals. It will also investigate the use of the smock in the United States and Australia, linking this to developments in the British smock trade. First, however, *The Hidden History* will turn to examine different varieties of smocks, aside from their broad categories,[15] as well as considering the lifecycle of the garment and how they were cared for, including waterproofing.

Types of smock

Surviving examples and the 'picturesque' images in genre painting, primarily produced for middle-class audiences, strongly influence how we think about smock frocks today. Many rural and urban working men favoured varieties of smocks or 'slops', including plainer versions, which have all but disappeared from view. However, they do survive in photographs of prisoners. The Prevention of Crimes Act in 1870 made the photographing of criminals compulsory and these images provide a sample of the dress worn by provincial, usually working people, in the early 1870s.[16] Prisoners were typically photographed in their own dress, by local photographers, generally as they arrived in gaol.[17] As such, they were taken without foreknowledge, the photographer, rather than the subject, determining how they should be portrayed and their sartorial impact.[18] It was no longer a privilege to be photographed but was part of surveillance and a new means of control. Pretrial prisoners were only given prison uniform if their own dress was inadequate, infested or needed to be confiscated as part of their trial.[19] The rigid frontality of the prisoner's pose within an isolated narrow space, often with a number board or alternative method of identification such as showing hands, enforced the power of the institution, whether prison, asylums or charity schools, who also photographed individuals in this way. It reinforced the sitter's social inferiority as a supervised and scrutinized object.[20] Produced to obtain proof, to measure and analyse, the prisoner photographs are a record of otherwise visually unrecorded people and the clothing that they wore at a particular moment in time.[21] Where caches of these photographs survive, Buckinghamshire, Oxfordshire and Bedfordshire for example, men wore the honeycombed and embroidered smock into the 1870s (see Figures 5.1 and 5.2).

The photographs also reveal other types of smocks worn by working men. Historically, short smocks were identified with northern England and particularly associated with navvies, although their use now seems to have been more widespread.[24] These have little gathering or fullness, perhaps with

FIGURE 5.1 *Edward Varney of Westcott, 1872. An agricultural labourer, aged thirty-six, convicted of stealing a pocketbook, he is wearing perhaps a coloured smock with darker embroidery. There are local surviving examples,[22] and in the Luton collection there are also olive green smocks with black or brown embroidery, presenting similar colouring when photographed in black and white. These were bought ready-made from shops in Chesham Bois and Polluxhill, Bedfordshire, suggesting that the garment photographed here might have had a similar origin.[23] Victorian Prisoner Photographs © Centre for Buckinghamshire Studies, Buckinghamshire Council, reference: Q/AG/23–26 Prisoner 4984.*

some smocking on the sleeves and embroidery around the neck, and either a roll collar or open neck, thus like a robust contemporary shirt[25] (see Figures 5.3 and 5.4). Like shirts, these smocks often had shoulder straps as reinforcement in an area of weakness and used the selvedge to both save time for seamstresses and to add strength and durability to the garment for wear and washing.[26] A photograph dating from the late nineteenth century shows Job Green, a west Dorset shepherd, born in 1814, in a short smock made by his wife, a comparable style to Figure 5.3.[27] Another very similar one survives in Dagenham, Essex, likewise smocked at the cuffs, decoratively embroidered with Prince of Wales

FIGURE 5.2 *Joseph Collier of Haddenham, 1872. Aged sixteen, with two convictions for obtaining goods by false pretences, he wears a typical round smock, with honeycomb smocking and basic embroidery, probably ready-made. It was most likely used for work as it appears damaged on the right sleeve cuff. Victorian Prisoner Photographs © Centre for Buckinghamshire Studies, Buckinghamshire Council, reference: Q/AG/23–26 Prisoner 5059.*

FIGURE 5.3 *A short linen smock, MERL, 52/151. © Museum of English Rural Life, University of Reading. This is hand stitched, made from coarse linen, formed from a width of fabric, with re-enforcement panels/straps on each shoulder.*

feathers and the motto 'Ich Dien', as is the Dorset example, possibly the reason that it has been preserved.[28]

An unfitted jacket or coat, without smocking or embroidery, is also photographed. These light-coloured linen 'slops' as they were confusingly often called, perhaps partly derived from the open smock and/or the fustian jacket, were usually ready-made.[29] For Joe Swinford in Filkins, in late-nineteenth-century rural Oxfordshire, they were seen as more up-to-date as well as being useful, warm and looking nice when washed and ironed.[30] It is difficult to distinguish these from any other type of smock or slop in the written records of manufacturers and sellers (see Figure 5.5). An example of an unworn duck jacket survives in Australia, made as part of a convict uniform, stamped with the date 1865. With a roll collar, it is also stamped with the maker's mark, Robert Thomas Tait & Co., who operated out of the Strand as an army and navy contractor.[31] In the United States, the 'sack' was very similar, a coat without a lining or waist seam, unfitted and made of linen or cotton blends in natural colours. They were inexpensive and sold ready-made

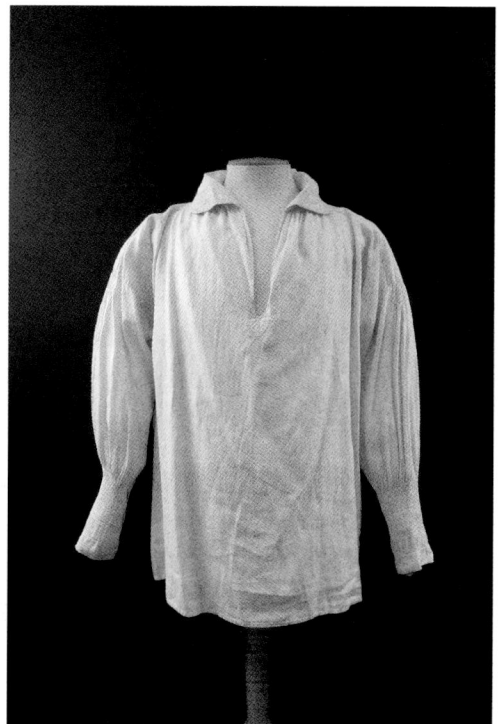

FIGURE 5.4 *A short smock. © Image used with kind permission of Oxfordshire County Museum Service, Slop; OXCMS: 1982.213.3. Embellished with feather stitch including a heart at the neck opening, a traditional re-enforcement for front openings, this is hand-sewn, formed from a width of linen, with smocking at the top of the arm and above the cuff.*

from at least the 1840s.[32] The round frock increasingly became the dress of youths whereas men wore the 'slop' jacket alongside it, perhaps as it resembled a more fashionable suit jacket, as photographed by Joseph Gale in *The Shepherd and his Boy* exhibited at the Crystal Palace Exhibition in 1898.[33] Many varieties of 'smock' were thus worn alongside each other and, as we will see, were embedded into the daily life of working men across the country.

Colour and care

As investigated in Chapter 4, opportunities for acquiring clothing were multifarious, with local retail markets, to a degree, determining what men wore. In the highly visually literate society of the time, identifying different types of

FIGURE 5.5 *Joseph Hazell of Amersham, 1871. A labourer, aged forty-three, convicted of stealing wine, he is wearing a 'slop'. Victorian Prisoner Photographs © Centre for Buckinghamshire Studies, Buckinghamshire Council, reference: Q/AG/23–26 Prisoner 4232.*

smocks was key to understanding a man's sartorial coding. Observers readily absorbed details such as whether it was short or long, as well as associations with particular occupations and how the garment's appearance changed over its life cycle, recalling, if necessary, even the type of textile used for the smock. Smocks were usually made of linen or linen mixed with cotton. Names for the different types of linen are confusing to modern readers but they helped to determine the quality of the smock. Dowlas, for example, was a coarse commonly used linen for smocks, but regarded as superior to canvas, which was often made from hemp.[34] Drabbet was a mixed fabric, with a cotton weft and linen warp, so it was off-white in colour and associated with later smocks. Stiff and coarse, it was suitable for plainer coat-like smocks and also bought by a manufacturer in London to use for waterproofs.[35]

Whiteness seems incongruous for both country and workwear, but the bleaching process for many types of linen, using lye, was commonplace.[36] Although white smocks were most common, surviving in the greatest numbers, from the late eighteenth century onwards many were coloured, which may have added to their attractiveness for purchasers. Hop pickers in Kent wore green smocks, as did a man in 1851, who borrowed one to commit a robbery in Leighton Buzzard, Bedfordshire.[37] William Howitt, in 1848, suggests that the locality determined the colour of a smock, blue 'Newark' ones being popular in the Midlands, for example.[38] As with embroidery patterns, small clusters of similar garments, along with personal preferences, may have skewed the surviving evidence which overall does not have such a logical pattern. Blue smocks appear from the beginning of the nineteenth century in prints depicting the garment so, although they became associated with the Midlands, this was not always necessarily so.[39] Buff and light brown ones were also worn, their colour, as with blue and green smocks, practical for working in, an example of a brown one also described as 'deal coloured', after the wood, in a court report of its theft in 1824.[40] In the 'Dorsetshire Labourer', an essay of 1883, Thomas Hardy notes that the colour of clothing was one of the biggest changes in the previous twenty years. Whereas before on a fair day white or 'whitey brown' was prominent with very little black, by the 1880s 'the crowd is dark as a London crowd', as labourers moved away from wearing smocks.[41]

To make them waterproof, smocks were steeped in boiled linseed oil which also made them darker and shiny.[42] While in this state, they could be cleaned just by wiping down like an oilcloth, although the fabric wore out faster.[43] The idea of specific waterproof clothing gradually developed from the early nineteenth century, The Royal Patent Water-proof Cloth Warehouse, at 2 Haymarket, advertising waterproof cloth including canvas for smock frocks, all stamped 'Ackermann and Co.'s as warranted genuine', in 1802.[44] By the 1820s, specific garments like the mackintosh, rather than just cloth, were developed. Rubber coats needed to have a loose fit to be wearable.[45] India rubber was not just watertight but airtight as well, leading to its own problems, including smell, and this type of waterproof clothing remained expensive particularly for manual labourers who could use linseed oil instead. C. B. Reynolds operated a Waterproofing Establishment in Devizes, Wiltshire, taking two days to waterproof a garment, including smock frocks for 2 shillings each.[46] Of course, this was expensive, costing more than some smocks, so using linseed oil was a cheaper option. With the invention of vulcanization in 1844, which improved flexibility to some extent, along with the stimulus of the Crimean War, there was a surge in patented waterproof garments during the 1850s, led by the India Rubber Waterproof Works in East London and the Mandleburgs in Manchester from 1856.[47] These designs were increasingly sophisticated, relying on scientific and manufacturing progress, so subsequently were patented, something the smock was not able to compete with.

Smocks were certainly thought of as weatherproof. In a murder case in 1860, a witness wore a smock frock to the inquest, 'because it was a wet evening'.[48] Similarly, the defence of a man accused of stealing a smock from a cider mill was that he had only borrowed it to put on as it was raining.[49] In 1884, a report about a rural harvest festival in Sidlow, Surrey, records an old man wearing a black smock frock to the church service: 'A garment now, alas! becoming rarer and rarer, but by the means of which, nevertheless, he was probably the only one who got home with a dry skin in the evening'.[50] Richard Jefferies notes that older shepherds in Wiltshire in the 1870s still preferred blue smock frocks: 'But the rising generation use the greatcoat of modern make, at which their forefathers would have laughed as utterly useless in the rainstorms that blew across the open hills'.[51] Gertrude Jekyll also states that a smock 'turns an astonishing amount of wet', the round smock, with no openings, being thought of as weatherproof.[52]

White and unoiled smocks when new, started out often startlingly bright and, of course, unworn and therefore stiff and unwieldy. In a robbery in Huntingdon, near York, four burglars were wearing smocks, a witness stating that 'they seemed to be stiff and glazy as if they were new ones'.[53] Descriptions often state the condition of a smock as in the search for a man connected to horse stealing in 1823 in Tadcaster who wore 'a new Smock Frock'.[54] In a report about an accident on the Stratford and Moreton railway, a youth wore a new smock frock which got caught up in the waggon somehow, pulling him under the wheels of the train leading to his death. The report usefully tells us what a 'new' smock frock meant: 'which of course was stiff, and stood out from his person'.[55] Until worn in, whether oiled or not, the smock was an encumbrance. Although hard-wearing and durable, they could be bulky and weighty if long, the act of manoeuvring in them being difficult, from causing your gait to change, to getting in and out of them. Taking off the round frock in particular, which needed to go over the head, was likened to a snake shedding its skin.[56] When farm servants absconded in Shropshire in 1810, the report describes one as wearing a 'nearly new' smock frock, and the other a new one.[57] Apart from their age and height, this was the only description given, so must have served as a good visual indicator.

As outerwear, the fact that smock frocks made of linen or linen mixed fabrics could be washed in contrast to woollen coats, which were far more difficult to clean and indeed were generally just brushed down, perhaps helped account for their popularity.[58] In 1839, John Crockett was sending clothing, including a smock frock, shirt and stockings, for washing to the next village, when it was stolen from a cart and subsequently pawned.[59] Likewise, when a man absconded from service stealing 20 pounds, a report described him as wearing a 'newly washed' smock frock, which presumably affected its colour and texture.[60] Cleanliness had a symbiotic relationship to decency, reflected in the quest for 'white linen' shirts, chemises, other undergarments and household linens.[61] Smocks could also be made new with laundering, the sought after 'snowy whiteness' often being commented upon. It was important to keep up appearances, clothing being a very public indicator of fluctuations in prosperity and differences in income, a clean white smock signalling access to, and money available for, washing. This outward display could visually broadcast social worth and financial sufficiency, showing that an individual owned at least the two sets of outer clothes necessary for undertaking the laundering process.[62]

If economically viable, clothes were acquired either for work or best. Edwin Grey, recalling his childhood in rural Hertfordshire in the late 1860s and 1870s, remembered: 'All the smock wearers that could afford it had two of them, one for working in and the other for best, as it was termed … those worn for best were, many of them elaborately worked from the shoulder downwards to just below the breast, having blue-glass beads inserted here and there amongst the smocking work near the shoulders'.[63] Those with only one smock might reverse it or turn it inside out to make it appear clean and respectable, also hiding their poor clothing beneath.[64] There was a certain amount of pragmatism, saving the newest smock frock for Sunday wear and to show off, until another could be afforded and take its place. Sunday best was a visible emblem of industry and thrift – the absence of it suggested idleness and improvidence.[65] In Hertfordshire, a murder case turned on where the accused's working smock was and why he wore his best one to work. His working one was very worn on the sleeves and wristbands but had suspiciously disappeared.[66] Smocks might be used until no longer wearable, as James Miles did in November 1849, buying a second-hand smock informally in the summer, but he had 'only taken it into wear lately, because his other was not worn out'.[67] This slippage from the new to old was common practice in many types of clothing.[68] Labourers wore their worst clothes to actually work in, which were often dirty and in need of repair (see Figure 5.6).

As Grey notes, the addition of beads and buttons may have added to the showiness of best smocks worn for special occasions.[69] A variety of buttons are found on surviving smocks: brass, metal, bone, vegetable ivory, horn, mollusc, mother of pearl and glass, suggesting this adornment was common practice, for example, a Lincolnshire smock having a button marked with an image of a sheep.[70] The woodmen near East Grinstead were said to have worn dark grey smocks embroidered in white and finished with buttons in pairs.[71] Buttons were sold in relatively rural shops, one bankrupt draper, grocer and druggist's stock in Lambourn on the Berkshire downs including silk, pearl, horn, 'brace', metal, plated, gilt and fancy buttons.[72] A navvy employed on railway works near Aberdovey

FIGURE 5.6 *William Larner of Stokenchurch, 1872, an agricultural labourer who was convicted of stealing part of an old iron vice. The poor state of his smock, torn with loose stitching, suggests it was very much used for work or perhaps reflected poverty. Victorian Prisoner Photographs © Centre for Buckinghamshire Studies, Buckinghamshire Council, reference: Q/AG/23–26 Prisoner 4702.*

stole a smock from a farm servant in Cemmaes, near Machynlleth in mid Wales. 'The new buttons I put on lately myself, and … the patch on the shoulder', identified it for the male servant, suggesting the care taken and the value of the garment for its owner.[73] On each metal button of a smock from Nettleham, Lincolnshire, is a picture of a wagon and the name 'G. Codling'. George Codling was a tailor and draper from the village, so these occupationally related buttons may have been a way of promoting his business too.[74] Mrs Garnett recalled about navvy embroidered smocks that 'It was the fashion in some places to sew pearl buttons on slops, and I have been told of six dozen sewn on one!'[75] This was self-fashioning by men often within isolated communities, reflecting localized fashions of different sections of the workforce. Working men were actively customizing their clothing themselves, using a needle and thread to do so, challenging the accepted view of mainstream Victorian masculinity. For working men, sewing, for example as carried out by sailors and soldiers, was an industrious and productive activity, not seen as unmanly, and here used to self-fashion and further hone masculine identity through dress.[76] As with embroidery, sewing on buttons was also a relatively cheap way of indicating financial stability through excess decoration and adding to surface embellishment, as well as subverting the uniformity of the smock frock.[77]

Patching and repairs should also not automatically be seen a sign of abject poverty, but as a way to prolong a garment's life and maintain its value.[78] Such maintenance could be carried out by the wearer or a local tailor, or by local needlewomen, who were sometimes given repairs to mend in return for outdoor relief under the Old Poor Law.[79] Having invested in the garment and its decoration, maintaining and trying to preserve the longevity of the usefulness of a smock, before it became suitable only for rags, was prudent for a working man.

Smocks were bound up with an individual's personality, of feeling sartorially correct, as well as their usefulness and comfort. One man who wore them his whole farming life, and was apparently only once persuaded into a coat to go to church, on his return changed back into a smock remarking, 'now I be happy again'.[80] Edwin Grey did not wear one himself but was assured that they were 'very warm and comfortable' and 'most convenient', easy to wash and look after, their often large pockets practical and apparently convenient for poaching.[81] Their usefulness made them invaluable clothing for many men, whose occupational wear we will now turn to examine.

Navvies

Railway and canal workers or navvies (short for navigators), like agricultural workers, were engaged in downright hard manual labour. Smocks offered navvies a hard-wearing overall, easily removable when needed and with decoration that appealed to working-class flamboyance. Early canal navvies were former agricultural labourers, working for short periods on local projects to earn extra income, this practice continuing into the 1840s. Better wages and a period of consistent employment, unlike the casual work of the land, attracted local men who formed the bulk of the labour force.[82] The Manchester Statistical Society notes, in 1845, that many left railway work to return to their homes to help with the harvest between July and September. Stoked by the railway 'mania' of 1845–7, when around 200,000 men were constructing railways, more than there were in the army, 'navvy' also became a byword for uncivilized and vicious behaviour. However, after the collapse of railway building in 1847, and an influx of Irish workers, many men returned to agricultural labouring once more.[83] By the mid-century, there were also 'true' navvies who migrated, following building projects around the country and developing valued expertise. The fluidity of the two areas of employment shows how generally integrated the sectors were, men easily moving between spheres and sharing proclivities, including wearing smocks, not being 'a race apart', despite what some contemporary popular literature might suggest.[84]

From the 1830s, smocks, usually short, commonly appear as the dress of the navvy. Thus in 1840, three 'railway men, in smock frocks' robbed a 'lad' on the road near Kibworth and Great Glen.[85] The *Gloucester Chronicle* published a description of a navvy working on the Cheltenham and Great Union Railway in 1839, noting his 'peculiar' attire. This included 'a velveteen shooting jacket with white buttons, a scarlet plush waistcoat … with little black spots on it', and a bright handkerchief. Also 'His "dickey" or small smock frock, is slung when he travels at his back and tied by the arms in front: in this he carries whatever else he has in the world apart from the clothes he wears'. The description ends by remarking on navvy hairstyles, 'wearing one or more ringlets on each side of his face, on which great value is placed'.[86] Although not uncritical commentary, the report also complaining about their drinking and brawling habits among other things, the description highlighted specific dress codes not current in the mainstream. The smock, even in an attenuated form and here used partly as a haversack, was part of this. However, many working men wore brightly coloured waistcoats and handkerchiefs, so this description is not far from outlining general working-class male dress of the period.[87] David Brooke cautions against categorizing the navvy by a set of 'navvy' characteristics, including dress and eating and drinking habits, suggesting that it varied across the country, the only unifying factor being their clothing's high quality in order to stand up to wear and tear.[88] While this is undoubtedly true, the figure of the 'navvy' was nevertheless recognizable to contemporaries, identified as an occupation partly by wearing a short smock. George Elson in his autobiographical tale, imitated navvy dress in the mid-nineteenth century, wearing 'a short white slop and fustian trowsers [sic]'.[89]

With the rise of the ready-made industry, smocks were increasingly cheap for navvies to buy and also for employers, who often controlled navvy spending through the truck system.[90] Reading was known for producing 'railway' clothing, which probably included smocks from Bousfield.[91] Samuel Spencer's clothing warehouse in Chester sold men's and boys' ready-made clothing including slops for the engineer, mechanic and navvies.[92] In Crich, Derbyshire, Thomas Beardah sold smock frocks and 'navvies' slops in his shop,[93] as did Thomas Eagles, shopkeeper and clothier of Springfield Hill, with his stock of smock frocks and 'railroad clothes of every kind'.[94] These shopkeepers were able to stock diversified products, although essentially variations on the same garment, for different consumers (see Figure 5.7).

FIGURE 5.7 *John Smith of Newport Pagnell, 1871. A navvy from Dullingham, Yorkshire, aged twenty-four, convicted of stealing money, he wears a short smock. Victorian Prisoner Photographs © Centre for Buckinghamshire Studies, Buckinghamshire Council, reference: Q/AG/23–26 Prisoner 4328.*

Men who worked continuously as navvies led a transitory life, following the progress of the railways around the countryside and developing their own language and customs. The builder employed gangs of navvies, shanty towns growing close to where they worked, huts hastily constructed from available materials, whether turf or timber. These temporary encampments of huts caught the popular imagination although many navvies lived a more mundane existence by lodging in ordinary houses.[95] One newspaper report described the 'truck' shop which was part of an unspecified navvies village and from where men were forced to obtain their supplies in lieu of their wages. This consisted of groceries, tobacco and clothing including 'gay plush vests, closely studded over with mother-of-pearl buttons', moleskin trousers and 'an ample supply of smock frocks gaudily and fancifully embroidered'. One bundle of smock frocks also had a 'cross neatly worked on the breast'.[96] Encampments depended on itinerant salespeople or enterprising local tradespeople to bring goods to them.[97] With the huge amount of building work taking place in mid-nineteenth-century London, navvies were also a familiar sight in the capital's streets. A description from a newspaper in 1864 notes that there were a large number of navvies around due to the railway work going on dressed in 'smock-frocks, high-lows, and red belcher handkerchiefs'.[98] James Greenwood, a journalist, describes navvies excavating a London railway cutting in 1867 in red, blue or white smocks.[99]

Like agricultural workers, navvies also wore smocks as respectable and best dress. When men were killed while doing their job, as at Chipping Hill near Chelmsford in 1842, their co-workers donned their smocks to accompany their coffins to their final resting place.[100] Similarly in 1846, when a navvy was killed in an accident at Sutton, building the Croydon and Epsom railway, his 400 co-workers donned their white smocks and white 'ribands' to accompany his body to the grave as well as paying for his funeral.[101] In 1843, the *Sherborne Journal* commented on this 'very interesting appearance', the wearing of white smock frocks and white ribbons in hats, which 'is that usually followed by this class of men in burying their fellow labourers'.[102] For journalists, the spectacle of such funerals included the dress paraded for this display of working-class solidarity. The Ambergate Company cut the first sod in the new railway line between Boston and Ambergate in Derbyshire in 1847, with festivities in Bottesford, a large number of navvies attending in coloured caps and 'clean white smock frocks'.[103] Depicted in *The Illustrated London News*, in Grimsby in 1849, Prince Albert laid the foundation stone of the Royal Dock. Arriving at the station, the train then proceeded to the entrance of the docks under two triumphal arches. The steam engine was then unhitched and 'a whole army of navigators, some hundred strong, in white smock frocks and with blue favours' pulled the carriages to the ceremony, an accompanying band playing 'martial'

FIGURE 5.8 *William Quarterman, 'on the tramp', 1871. Aged twenty-six, he was convicted of stealing a shirt. Victorian Prisoner Photographs © Centre for Buckinghamshire Studies, Buckinghamshire Council, reference: Q/AG/23–26 Prisoner 4295.*

music.[104] The specific short white smock associated with navvies also appears in the few prisoner photographs that survive of them (see Figures 5.7, 5.8 and 5.10). A similar style of garment in the Museum of English Rural Life (MERL) collection (see Figure 5.9) uses buttons as embellishment and is comparable to one worn in the painting of labourers at rest by Briton Riviere, the men in well-worn clothing.[105] These smocks had minimal smocking, possibly to prevent stone and other dust gathering in the pleats and also so that they would be lighter to wear.[106]

By 1865, an article in the *Newcastle Chronicle* saw the heyday of the navvy as being over. However, in a detailed portrait of those 1,400 currently working in the Derwent Valley, it depicts them as a kind of noble savage, living outside the normal rules of civilization but working hard:

> They are all strong, brawny men, with sinews like iron – perfect models of strength and endurance. With their coarse woollen shirts, smock frocks, fustian trousers,

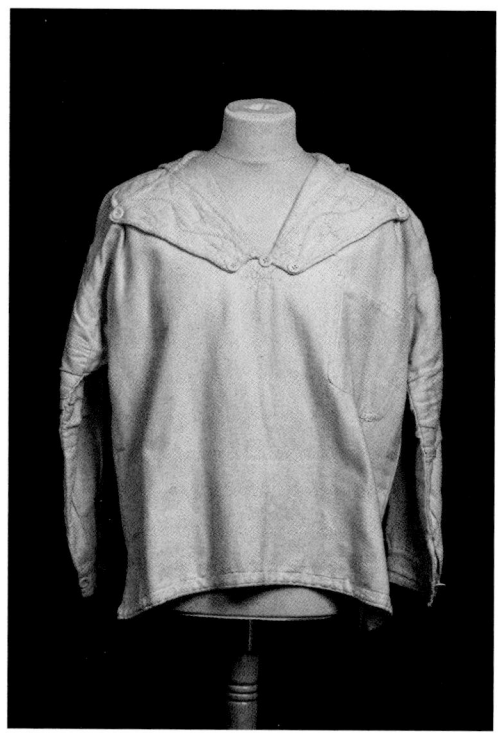

FIGURE 5.9 *A short cotton smock, MERL 81/147. © Museum of English Rural Life, University of Reading. This is relatively light weight, with both hand and machine stitching used.*

heavily mudded boots, laced with leather whangs round their thick legs, which are encased in ribbed-wove [sic] stockings, they are prepared for any work.[107]

The smock was a garment that could stand up to tough treatment, the article commenting that in cold weather the navvies' wardrobe was so limited that they would wear all their clothing at once to keep warm and this also allowed them to travel about the countryside easily. Sunday wear included a smock frock and fustian trousers for those that did not have a cloth suit.[108]

A paper given at a Farmers Club in 1869 notes that the 'long smock frock dangling about the heels of the labourer is rapidly giving way to the short slop of the navvy', suggesting a wider use of this garment in the 1870s and 1880s.[109] Being both practical and cheap, many manual labourers, including agricultural workers wore the 'navvies short smock' open at the neck. George Clausen painted *A Spring Morning: Haverstock Hill*, shown at the Royal Academy in 1881, while living in Hampstead. The men he depicted in the background mending the road are

FIGURE 5.10 *George Olney of Newport Pagnell, 1871. He was a navvy, aged thirty-nine, and convicted of stealing a ham. Victorian Prisoner Photographs © Centre for Buckinghamshire Studies, Buckinghamshire Council, reference: Q/AG/23–26 Prisoner 4194.*

wearing smocks, leading to speculation that they were rural labourers who came into the suburbs from outlying areas to find work. However, the short smocks that they wear were worn by many different labourers and navvies by this date, making them difficult to visually distinguish from each other if indeed there was actually a distinction.[110] As the workforce constructing new transport networks, buildings and other infrastructure for the country, the clothing choices of the navvy also reflected a practical modernity which appealed to other working men.[111] As Ford Madox Brown's painting *Work* (1852–65) suggests, with its classical heroic allusions, for viewers of the painting and others, navvies could be seen as contributing to civic pride and progress for the good of all, underpinning national prosperity and development, the labouring masculine body displayed in a short ready-made smock.[112]

Dustmen

Smocks were also worn widely in manufacturing work and other occupations,[113] although they were particularly useful for 'dirty' trades such as night-soil men and chimney sweeps.[114] In a comic sketch, widely reproduced in the provincial press, a chimney sweep was drinking with a tailor in the King's Arms Tavern, Camden Town. The sweep wore a smock frock, the tailor wittily calling it a 'soot-frock' as it was filthy. They swopped clothes for a joke, the sweep escaping up a chimney with the tailor's clothes, which were his holiday wear or best clothes, leaving him with the dirty smock frock.[115] However, many sweeps also advertised themselves as general carters, a trade more often associated with the smock.[116] Henry Mayhew describes the clothing of a sweep as a dark-coloured corduroy suit but when working 'a sort of blouse or short smock-frock of coarse strong calico or canvas' to protect the suit from soot.[117] Sweeps were often rivals with dustmen for business, competing out in the streets.[118] Brian Maidment details how dustmen were known for dandyish touches to their dress, such as bright colours and velvet textures, a counterpoint to the masculine assertiveness of the functional traditional short jacket necessary for their job. Ambiguity over gender roles was apparent to middle-class commentators, with feminized dandyism and pride in overt self-display ridiculed as incompatible with their role as collectors of dirt.[119] As dustmen lost their independent status and became civic employees from the

FIGURE 5.11 *George Scharf, between 6 & Seven O'Clock morning, Sumer [sic], watercolour,* circa *1834. 1862,0614.1194.* © *The Trustees of the British Museum.*

mid-nineteenth century onwards, smocks were probably a cheaper uniform to provide than jackets and seem to have replaced them within the general trade.[120] In 1859, dustmen and watering men in the City of London wore smock frocks and their typical shovel hats, as two impostors were caught dressed in this way collecting tips from householders and businesses at the end of the 'watering' season[121] (see Figure 5.11 depicting a dustman and cart). In an advertisement for a tender for street cleaning and watering for the Board of Health for the borough of Derby, the contractor needed to provide all the men employed in scavenging and watering with a blue smock frock with a metal number fixed to the collar, as well as a waterproof 'sou' wester' hat.[122] The smock was a recognizable uniform for these vital urban workers.

By the mid-nineteenth century, dustmen were increasingly seen as an essential social necessity and having an almost altruistic vocation, working for the good of the city. Those who undertook the job were thus afforded a new dignity. Commentators praised the cleanliness, neatness and uniformity of their dress, often a smock, suggesting for Maidment 'a more feminized and countrified figure than usual', no longer vulgar, violent or particularly virile. The smock softened both masculinity and the threatening dirty trade so that the dustman was part of a new polite civic order, useful, productive and successful, one of the 'labour aristocracy.'[123] When 300 dustmen and their families were invited for a charity tea in Kingsland, London, in 1866, the older ones were wearing smock frocks with a flower in their buttonhole, the younger ones, flannel jackets and a 'kingsman', a silk handkerchief fastened in a 'holiday' bow.[124] Depicted as dressed in this way in illustrated periodicals such as *The British Workman*, smocks were however just cheap, ready-made, widely available and washable.[125] Worn by many working men, the modern perception of femininity surrounding the smock is perhaps misplaced.

Military wear

During the eighteenth century, providing garments for the army and navy was a major stimuli for the ready-made clothing trade.[126] A naval ratings uniform was not established until 1857 although, by 1790, men's naval slops were 'uniformly blue'.[127] The pattern from a 'duck or white drill frock' worn on the Royal Yacht during the 1840s was the basis for the uniform and the famous sailor collar. In the late eighteenth and early nineteenth centuries, the navy used a simple short smock with a broad collar much like those worn by other working men.[128]

With manufacturers such as Hyde's, Gurteen's and Bousfield's turning out quantities of smocks, they were also a useful overall for the Victorian army, particularly during the Crimean War (1853–6). When the Scots Greys sailed out of Liverpool in August 1854 towards the Black Sea, a soldier wrote back about his experiences including the clothing he was made to wear as soon as the ship left the dock. This consisted of canvas trousers and a smock frock, which caused 'a great deal of merriment … laughing at the others comical appearance', perhaps hinting at the perceived unmanliness of this dress in a military context.[129] Another letter, from a member of the 39th Regiment, also mentioned the sea kit for soldiers voyaging to the Crimea, consisting of a blue striped shirt, smock frock, tin can, thread, needles and pocket knife.[130] An article about equipping the army before Sevastopol describes a 'sea-frock' made of canvas to be worn with light serge pantaloons. These were to be issued to every soldier and were based on frocks previously used in the West Indies, so presumably plain and relatively light.[131] Uniforms used on campaigns could be amended by the regimental commander improvising to provide practical, warm or cool, clothing for soldiers.[132] A smock frock was also described as 'regimental necessaries' supplied to the Royal Marines from the Queen's Stores in Rochester. A labourer working there stole one, his defence being that he bought it from a man in the street. Valued at 6 shillings, the magistrates suggested that such articles should be marked more clearly in order to prevent confusion with civilian clothing and so being bought by mistake.[133] In this context, there was clearly not much difference between military and civilian smock frocks, their utilitarian nature appealing to the army.

Commentary in the press revealed contemporary anxiety about the traditional army uniform and if it was fit for purpose. In 1861, after a soldier had died and many others were footsore, questions were asked about the practicality of soldiers clothing. A correspondent to *The Times* suggested that the volunteers' clothing, their 'vagaries', in essence what they already had, the working dress of labouring men, was more practical than the current soldiers' uniform. The South Kensington Engineers wore what is described as 'a sort of undress smock-frock', its advantages being its looseness, allowing ventilation in hot weather and the room to put on flannels beneath when cold.[134] Likewise, those concerned with the practicalities of army dress in the heat of India also turned to the smock frock. One officer in Kolkata complained about the dress of the 64th and 84th Regiments newly arrived wearing the same tunic as they did in England, as well as a cloak and carrying sixty rounds of ammunition, soldiers dying in the intense heat. To combat this he suggested giving them a washable white smock frock to wear in the 'cantonments' and a coloured smock in the 'field' so that a clean one was not required every day.¹³⁵ In 1858, a newspaper printed a letter from a member of the 79th Highlanders stationed in Fettehghur (Fatehpur) during the Indian Mutiny, noting that they paraded at 5 a.m. every morning in 'feather bonnets, smock frocks, kilts, arms and accoutrements'. The heat of the day was difficult to cope with but after the 6 p.m. full dress parade, they were allowed to walk in 'smock and trousers' until 8 p.m., presumably a looser fit of clothing and more suitable for the heat.¹³⁶ Where the smock proved most practical, there seems to have been less qualms about what it might represent in a different context. Thus rehabilitated as a utilitarian garment, the smock remains part of army dress.

Policing

The smock frock also became a kind of default plain-clothes disguise for the embryonic police force. Uniforms were not necessarily issued to police constables until the mid-nineteenth century, particularly in smaller towns and villages, the employer of the constables funding them through rates or subscriptions. Presumably within the community, their role to enforce law was widely known so identification by uniform was not always necessary. In 1827, police officer Davis pursued Sheen, wanted for infanticide, across the country by wearing the dress of a countryman, a smock frock, which allowed him to go into country pubs attracting less attention and seek information from Welsh drovers.¹³⁷ Rural disturbances in Sussex in 1835 were caused partly by changes in rates of pay to day labourers and the introduction of the New Poor Law. According to a report, two experienced policemen from the A division were sent down to investigate, presumably from London. They assumed various disguises including a farm servant and a sailor, both personas using smock frocks, to infiltrate the gangs who were mutilating sheep and destroying farm property by setting buildings on fire. A local patrol force was set up which succeeded in twice capturing one of the undercover policemen, 'while pursuing his nocturnal espionage'.¹³⁸ In the turbulent time of the mid-1830s, when the political atmosphere was highly charged, smock frocks offered a perfect disguise to infiltrate groups of agitators, including Chartist meetings.¹³⁹

A smock was also advantageous for tracking poachers, a policeman donning one over his uniform to apprehend a suspected poacher near Cirencester. As he was wearing a smock, he was able to approach his suspect who had stopped to eat bread, on the roadside. Not realizing that he was policeman trying to arrest him, the suspect assaulted him.[140] Indeed William Cobbett complained about such practices in a letter written to *The True Sun*, a London journal, protesting that it was 'a monstrous benefit to the poor man to get transported for seven years upon the evidence of a policeman, who, dressed in a smock frock had detected him in the act of aiming at a pheasant, or cutting and maiming a hare'.[141]

The Rural Police Act of 1839 allowed counties to establish police forces with uniformed police constables but many reverted to, or kept, ordinary clothes to investigate cases.[142] In a report into the establishment of the police constabulary force, statements were taken from offenders to determine their antisocial habits and how best to prevent them. One criminal described how he wore the smock frock as a disguise: 'a swan's-down sleeve-waistcoat and smock-frock, drab, green, or blue, according to the country'. [sic] He also borrowed a smock frock when necessary to sell goods at pubs and stole them from market stalls to sell.[143] It was a common disguise which the police too made use of.

In 1842, a detective division of the metropolitan police was set up with three inspectors, nine sergeants and a body of 'plain clothes men' to be called on when necessary. By the mid-1840s there were six policemen in each division who acted as detectives on the ground. These men blended into the crowd dressed in character, such as smock frocks at agricultural meetings or in mechanics dress, to catch offenders.[144] Wearing a smock frock, that is plain clothes, Police Constable Daniel Saunders went to investigate the selling of beer on Sundays in Bengeo near Hertford on the orders of his inspector. He was able to enter the house via the backdoor and check that beer was being drunk before moving onto the next 'beer-shop', which was doing the same.[145] To expose the illegal sale of alcohol, this method of detection became a regular occurrence.[146] In 1858, a man unknowingly assaulted a police constable, while selling oranges at Wadley fair. He was drunk and becoming rowdy and took offence at a man who told him to calm down, Police Constable Burritt, who 'was on duty there in plain clothes, in fact, wearing a smock-frock'.[147] Fairs were notorious as arenas for crime, so using the smock to blend in and to prevent incidents was logical. The inspector of the Hereford City Police undertook the smock frock disguise himself to detect pickpockets at a city fair, perfecting an awkward gait, his 'dialect the broadest that could be imagined'. No one recognized him in his persona of a country dealer, though it is not clear if he stopped any criminal activity.[148] By the mid-nineteenth century, the increasingly wealthy and respectable showmen, helped by this police intervention, encouraged the change to a more ordered profitable pleasure fair rather than a gathering outside the rule of law.[149]

Part of a large crowd who descended on Worcester for the November races and the associated criminal pickings, John Smith appeared as 'a rustic with smock-frock and Jim Crow hat, but on removal of this disguise he was found to be as well dressed as a gentleman'. He was caught picking pockets in the market using this trick 'which is well calculated for deception'. The report notes somewhat sourly that he 'is an importation from Birmingham'.[150] Pickpockets preyed on crowds, using versions of exaggerated normal behaviour to carry out the theft, from pushing, loitering and using overfamiliarity to gain trust.[151] The smock frock looked ordinary, it's capacious skirts and pockets an added bonus for pickpockets. However, the garment could also be part of 'a clever trap' as the newspaper headlines put it, an undercover policeman catching William Haywood near Wednesfield in 1860. The policeman had set out to catch him, wearing a smock frock and billycock hat to disguise himself as a drover and then 'accidentally' bumped into him outside a pub. In the dark, Haywood felt for the (police)man's smock to ascertain the veracity of his identity and then satisfied, told him of things he had done that winter to get by, the 'beaks' not having caught him. Inside the Plough beer house, the policeman unfastened the top of his smock and undid his muffler to reveal the buttons of his police uniform beneath and then arrested him.[152] Aside from being practical workwear, smocks could also be used to manipulate people and to perform a perceived role for both policemen and criminals, as well as others.[153]

United States

Relatively prosperous small-scale commercial farmers dominated the burgeoning population of the United States (over two million by 1770), representing a large market of people who needed consumer products including clothing such as the smock.[154] Linda Baumgarten speculates that 'frontier clothing' of loose frocks and smocks, worn for protection when undertaking hard manual labour, were related to the English smock, practical clothing first brought over and used by early pioneers.[155] American Indians also bought European shirts which they then decorated and wore like a smock, not tucked into the waistband.[156] From the 1760s, the homespun coarseness and frugality in dressing this way also had political connotations, a conscious opposition to elite British luxury and corruption.[157] Plain smocks were apparently used during the American Revolutionary War (1775–83), partly as disguise for those fighting the British, and entering the mythology of that conflict.[158] As in England at the same time, there are references to men wearing smocks and frocks during the 1770s, but they appear to have remained very much utilitarian workwear worn for protection.[159] Particularly on the eastern seaboard, as a purely functional garment they stood in opposition to fashion, generally not developing the flamboyance of some of the English smocks during the nineteenth century.[160]

Joan Severa notes that men wore the 'farmer's frock' to protect ordinary everyday clothing until the 1860s. These were either made at home as simple garments or bought ready-made. The examples that she has found in photographic portraits are however made from wool or tweed.[161] Short plain smocks, much like those worn by navvies, were also used by men prospecting for gold in California from 1848 into the 1850s.[162] New England farmers wore white cotton or linen smocks until the late 1880s, which seem more akin to the English examples, as illustrated by Ruby Devol Finch and her portrayal of a 'butcher' in a long white smock in 1830s Massachusetts.[163] As will be discussed in the next chapter, the smock would however be revived in New York in the early twentieth century as a garment for women.

Australia

In colonial Australia men also widely used the smock frock as a cheap utilitarian garment. From 1786, when plans were drawn up to establish a convict colony there by the Home Secretary, Lord Sydney, smocks were included as part of the necessary basic wardrobe, remaining on the list of required clothing into the 1820s.[164] In the Australian press there are descriptions of settlers wearing them from the 1820s into the 1850s, although they remained associated with farmers in these reports.[165] George Lowe advertised smocks for sale in his Hobart store in 1826, on his return with new stock from England, along with other working clothing including waterman's cord and drab jean trousers.[166] In 1848, labourers from Kensington, now a suburb of Adelaide, were charged with harbouring a sailor who had deserted his ship. They were described as having 'the appearance of countrymen. Kempster … is one of the best specimens of the true English peasant we have seen for some time; his green smock frock reminded us irresistibly of a British farm yard'.[167] Henry Capper, in 1839, stressing the utility and durability of clothing required for emigration to Australia, offered guidance for steerage passengers, the 'farm servant, mechanic, and labourer'. His list of clothing suggested for men includes fustian jackets and trousers along with round frocks costing around 2 shillings 6 pence each.[168] Thus some settlers may not have changed their dress from what they would have worn in England and initially brought their clothing with them, but the smock itself also developed independently in Australia becoming popular wear as a work shirt.

From the late 1830s 'bush' clothing evolved, derived from European workwear such as moleskin trousers and smocks. Bush clothing was casual, representing the freedom of the land, uninhibited, obscuring status and occupation, contrasting with increasingly drab urban masculine dress. Fashionable clothes were a disadvantage for frontier life and soon abandoned. The myth of the romanticized egalitarian life of the bushman quickly developed where physical prowess, 'mateship' and communality were needed to survive, hardship admired, and all classes of men wore and shared the clothing that allowed them to do this.[169] The development of the bushman corresponded to the period, during the 1840s and 1850s, when smock frocks were regularly sold both in shops, for example Hassall and Co. of Windsor near Sydney, and at auction and so onto retailers, such as in Perth in 1840.[170]

Australia represented a huge market for English slop manufacturers selling working clothing for men. Certainly pre-1850, Australian retailers who focused on practical workwear tended to do better.[171] Indeed, around 1843, George Johnson established the 'Smock Frock House', on Liverpool Street, Hobart, Tasmania, which operated throughout the 1840s and 1850s under various owners. As the name of the shop suggested, it sold everyday wear to working men, although smock frocks themselves are not mentioned in the clothing detailed in the advertisements.[172] In 1851, they advertised as outfitters for the 'Diggins', providing blue and striped Guernsey shirts along with other clothing suitable for those going to the goldfields.[173] A letter published in a newspaper in 1854 notes that whereas in England a smock frock or Guernsey was an indicator of a labourer or poor man, in Australia, those who were rich from the 'diggings', still wore 'blue guernseys', not knowing how to live in comfort, according to the correspondent.[174] A former newspaper employee, George Carr, wrote home in 1853 that he was off to follow the gold rush near Bendigo, noting that 'we intend all to be *labouring men,* and shall make our appearance in smock frocks and navvie boots – the garb of the real aristocrat of Australia'.[175] The egalitarian nature of working clothing is emphasized and the admiration of success won through hard physical labour. At this point, the smock seems to have mutated into specific goldfield wear, a 'jumper', a letter complaining about the behaviour of gold diggers also detailing that they wore 'the tartan smock frock, familiarly called [a] jumper'.[176] One report suggests that these were made from wool but concludes that: 'Jumpers are smock frocks',[177] tartan equating with a checked pattern. Philip Gosse notes that a jumper was a colonial phrase for a 'loose coarse canvas frock', which protected him when he was attacked by a kangaroo.[178] The Smock Frock House did sell 'jumpers', advertised as part of their stock to choose from to make a 'Californian Outfit', presumably to take part in the contemporary gold rush in the United States.[179]

Appearances

FIGURE 5.12 *S. T. Gill,* Prospecting, *plate 21 from* The Australian Sketchbook *1864. Colour lithograph, 17.7 × 15.2 cm (image) 28.9 × 42.6 cm (sheet), purchased, 1953, 3049.22-4. © Courtesy of National Gallery of Victoria, Melbourne.*

In illustrations by S. T. Gill of prospectors from a decade later, men wear plain short coloured smocks, a garment then widely used in Australia[180] (see Figure 5.12). These were not embroidered or even heavily smocked, but similar to the navvies' smock in England. Developing in parallel with the 'legend of the typical Australian', such workwear was worn by outback and rural men who disdained social conventions and fashionable styles, instead emphasizing their physicality and strength.[181] The gold prospector was part of this, portraying vigorous masculinity through dress and by cultivating beards. For those newly arriving in the country, it was important to immediately fit in. As Margaret Maynard notes, 'the supposed egalitarianism of rural dress … closely linked to the notion that this clothing signified colonial experience', meant that a ready-made smock frock was one item that enabled newcomers to blend in and discouraged customary ridicule from old timers.[182]

Manufacturers in London fulfilled the demand for such clothing. Mitchell & Taylor of Adelaide, who claimed to be the oldest drapery establishment in the colony, advertised in 1854 to 'Sheepfarmers and Country Settlers' that they had 'Bush Clothing' from Favell and Bousfield, London slop wholesalers.[183] So lucrative was this market that a member of the Bousfield family set up shop in Brisbane, the London Economic Outfitting Warehouse, selling the family's Axe Brand and catering specifically for bushmen as well as for categories such as mechanics and youths.[184] These city stores probably acted as wholesalers to smaller rural shops but maybe also helped to contribute to urban nostalgia for the bushman and the rural, selling the myth of a life open to anyone in the correct clothing.[185] 'Australian' smocks and hard-wearing trousers, the 'traditional' bushman's garments, originally came from London slop manufacturers, some of whom were also manufacturing English 'traditional rural' dress, the embroidered smock frock.

The smock as workwear

As the myth of the rural idyll developed, with the middle-class desire to explore the countryside in the face of urbanization, types of country people became identified, dairymaid, ganger, gleaner, yokel, almost as a handy guide for travellers into this new realm.[186] Clothing distinguished these types and these tropes have filtered into general cultural consciousness, hiding the real consumption patterns and clothing worn by agricultural and other more general workers. As we have explored, during the nineteenth century, men wore the smock for many reasons; for Sunday best, to cover poverty or to display wealth, for criminal intent or to detect this, as well as most commonly as hard-wearing practical utilitarian workwear for a variety of manual occupations including navvies, labourers and dustmen. The smock's durability and utility, and therefore it's cost effectiveness, were perhaps its most important characteristics, leading to its widespread adoption in both Britain and globally, as men took it overseas with them. In Australia, the smock was ideal wear, egalitarian and hard-wearing, gradually changing into specific bush clothing. It was also adaptable to different climates dependent on the fabric used, potentially waterproof, as well as washable.

As shown by the manufacture of ready-made clothing in Chapter 3, the construct of rural and urban is spurious. In reality these environments were porous, people moving between them easily and undefined by their dress, hence the lack of 'folk' dress in England. Working men wore types of smocks everywhere, although some particular types of the garment became associated with specific occupations. This seems partly a by-product of the development of the manufacturing industry and the need for makers and retailers to sell differentiated, but essentially the same, garments to wider male populations. Practicality was perhaps the major factor in the widespread adoption of the short smock for most working men, rather than its association with specific occupations as seized on by commentators. Men could seek to appear in a certain way, for a particular purpose, for example, for criminal activity. However, durability, comfort and affordability were probably the major factors for buying and wearing smocks. Men could also easily customize their garments, this investment in time and/or additional embellishments showing their importance to their owners. Wear, repair and personalized decoration, sometimes self-created, became a way to self-memorialize for a man, the smock instantly relaying visual public signifiers of, for example, work, experience and personal status. Disrupting mainstream notions of Victorian masculinity including the overt display of the physically fit and honed muscled body, the wearing of various types of loose smocks, and the customization of that garment through sewing, was not perceived as unmanly in the mid-nineteenth century for working men.[187] Thus essential workwear for many men, but also so much more for some as part of their visual identity, the next chapter will move onto examine why such appearances rapidly declined and what happened to the smock in the twentieth century and beyond.

6 Into the twentieth century

During the mid-nineteenth century, in popular urban imagination, smocks were linked to rural yokelism. For example, two men accused of stealing ducks and fowls were brought to court at Cambridge Town Sessions and described as having 'sun-burnt visages … attired in smock frocks and straw hats … whose appearance betokened that they belonged to that class of her Majesty's subjects known as "bumpkins".'[1] Associated as they were with the uncouth male rusticity of yokels and boors, embellished smock frocks represented all that was seen as uneducated and unmodern. The white or coloured loose-skirted embroidered garment did not fit the ideals of fashionable modern masculinity, epitomized by the sober dark-coloured suit.[2] This chapter will investigate how, by the beginning of the twentieth century, a distinctly male outer garment shifted between genders, becoming instead acceptable wear for women and children. It will trace how the status of the smock frock changed from being useful male workwear to something which was seen as impractical, old fashioned and cumbersome for men, and will also consider how nostalgia for the rural ideal led to its revival and the preservation of elements of the smock as a handicraft. Concluding with an examination of the garment's development until the present day, it will investigate the influence of the smock on recent fashions.

Decline of the male smock

During the second half of the nineteenth century, the smock frock began to fall out of favour as part of the dress of working men. They were increasingly dangerous to wear as various processes, including farming, became more mechanized. There are numerous cases of smocks being caught up in machinery, such as threshers, and causing horrific injury and even death. The problem was exacerbated as the strong fabric of many smocks was difficult to tear and thus to disentangle. In

1804, the *Ipswich Journal* highlighted this by citing an incident where a smock became snared in machinery leading to a miller being crushed death.[3] By 1835, with accidents still happening, a letter to a newspaper sounded an exasperated note: 'How often need we repeat the warning that it is dangerous for workmen to wear smock-frocks near thrashing-machines and any cog-wheels?'[4] Despite this advice, such incidents continued perhaps due to a mixture of convenience, cost and routine. Two more accidents are described in Herefordshire in 1847: 'We hope for the future, labourers will not be allowed to wear such articles of dress when working at machines, as they thus stand continually in jeopardy.'[5] Newspapers continued to report all the gory details of such misfortunes, perhaps in part as a warning, but also seemingly revelling in the macabre detail.[6] By 1860, a coroner presiding over yet another case where a boy's arm got caught in a threshing machine leading to his death, cautioned others that 'in half the inquests that were held upon persons killed in this way, death was caused by the person having on a smock frock'.[7] Accidents were increasingly portrayed as being due to the carelessness and ignorance of workers who shunned safety measures, including safe clothing, rather than the fault of employers.[8]

Coupled with the impracticalities of the garment, during the second half of the nineteenth century the growing proliferation of both the visual media including photography, and also glass, such as shop windows and mirrors, may have impacted on self-perceptions about appearance: how people regarded themselves and others. Those who could not manage to portray an orderly appearance might appear to others as neglectful and immoral, outside of social convention, rather than as lacking access to washing facilities and pecuniary help.[9] Individuals or institutions could use the smock frock as a convenient aid, a garment that if in a half-decent state could cover dishevelment and hide dirt. However, it also came to represent an otherness: of the rural, not fitting into modern urban society, backward and old-fashioned. Moreover, during the 1880s, as workhouses continued to clothe male inmates in cheap and utilitarian smock frocks, a newspaper reported that the inhabitants of one Midland's village complained that 'It [a smock] makes us all look like paupers', and so stopped wearing smocks within a year. The only person left wearing one was a poor old man who relied on the parish for support, as well as on smock cast-offs, and breaking stones for an income.[10]

Katrina Honeyman dates the popularity of the suit for all classes from the 1850s reflecting the new male image of sobriety, rising real incomes and the expansion of white-collar occupations. This stimulated the market for tailored woollen suits, although not achieving complete democratization until the 1920s.[11] A lack of manly characteristics, for example wearing a skirted garment, risked downward social mobility for the working man, especially as male fashion moved towards form fitting, body revealing styles in the last quarter of the nineteenth century.[12] In urban settings, there was a need to blend in, to become anonymous, the smock now not allowing this.[13] Men no longer wished to be associated with increasingly caricatured rusticity, summed up by this commentary in the early twentieth century:

> On market days, our visitors do not care to publish their rural origin by wearing costumes for us town-bred folk to stare at and patronisingly admire … As soon as you chatter … about a style being quaint and picturesque, sending this garment to a museum and that to a collector, country folk are scared and break for ever with the fashion.[14]

Those who wanted to get on in life abandoned smocks for cheap ready-made jackets and suits, leaving the garment to elderly men and, on stage, as visual shorthand for a simple bumbling fool.[15]

The rustic was one of a set of formulaic characters such as the Cockney, the Irishman and the costermonger, which formed the basis of music-hall entertainment. By the late nineteenth century, these characters were based on perceptions of everyday life and the attitudes of the (urban) man in the street, with the country bumpkin representing the supposed differences between town and country, highlighted for comic and dramatic effect.[16] For such a caricature to work, 'rustics' needed to be a distinct group both in appearance and lifestyle, so that the urban working-class music-hall audiences could scorn and ridicule their peculiarities.[17] Thus in 1873, Mr W. Bailey performed comic songs dressed as an 'agricultural labourer' in a smock frock, such as 'Loading the Hay' at the Canterbury Music Hall in Lambeth, London.[18]

A Phenomenon in a Smock Frock was also a hugely successful play throughout the 1850s and, taking around 50 minutes to perform, was soon popular with amateur dramatic companies too.[19] Originally developed for the Lyceum Theatre under the management of Madame Vestris and Charles Matthews, William Brough was the 'house author' in the vaudeville department and his 'droll farce' was received favourably after its premier at the theatre on 13 December 1852.[20] John Buttercup, a milkman, was the 'phenomenon' mentioned in the play's title. His costume specifications were a white smock frock, cord breeches, gaiters and thick hob-nailed boots, the actor being directed to speak with a strong Somersetshire dialect. The plot revolved around Buttercup returning a lost pocketbook, complete with 50 pounds, for which he is offered a reward that he will not take, even when the reward is upped to 2 sovereigns. Sowerby, the gentleman who had lost the pocketbook, exclaims: 'Is it possible, that beneath that lowly garb I have at length discovered the phenomenon – an honest man!' Flattery will not corrupt Buttercup so Sowerby employs him to speak the truth about his household as 'few are fools enough to do it'. Not unexpectedly, everything starts to go wrong as Buttercup accuses the housekeeper of fixing the accounts and his unvarnished frankness about Sowerby's appearance, with his ignorance of social airs and graces, is hurtful. As Sowerby cannot get rid of Buttercup for seven years, eventually a plot is hatched to teach him to lie, Sowerby concluding that 'Innocent flattery and pleasant fiction serve as oil to make the wheels [of society] run easy'. Buttercup ends the play by asking the audience to collude in liking it.[21] For middle-class and urban viewers, 'low' rustic life was where passions were seen in their purest form, without polite conventions concealing feelings and distorting relationships. Similar themes were expressed in contemporary genre paintings, depicting 'homely joys', strong, natural feelings, unchecked by the artificial refinements of 'society', the antidote to aristocratic disdain and complex social mores.[22]

The title of the play even appeared to enter popular language. In 1863, the suspect in a court case, John Jones, is called a 'phenomenon in a smock frock' and a 'simple-minded countryman' when charged with stealing eggs.[23] The smock wearer was the 'little man', divorced from the modern urban setting, unable to understand the rules but invoking the joys of simple pleasures, a 'middle-brow' understanding and representation of rural life.[24] By the 1870s, female actors began to wear smock frocks to entertain the audience, Miss Milly Howard appearing at the Cambridge, her performance 'truly comic as the bumpkin in a smock frock'.[25] Simultaneously, the smock entered the fashionable discourse for women and children, perhaps making this less shocking.

Craft

In parallel to the denigration and decline of the smock as masculine wear, the elevation of the craft of smocking began, also shifting it away from its association with outworkers. This seems to have started during the mid-nineteenth century as smock making began to be judged in village shows. Often as part of improvement societies, such shows started off as an elite enterprise working 'silently and unostentatiously' to improve working-class conditions.[26] The garment showed off the skills of respectable cottagers who spent their time engaged in worthwhile endeavour, albeit for large-scale ready-made clothes manufacturers. Comments about the Harris and Tomkins smock at the Great Exhibition of 1851 exemplify this, the exhibition itself, maybe helping to popularize the idea of such shows.[27] The annual Haresfield Horticultural Show was held in July 1848 attracting local elite society, with 1,400 tickets sold. As with all British summer events, commentary about the weather was inevitable with the threat of rain all day. The show awarded prizes for best crop of wheat, earliest swarm of bees and the best-made smock frock.[28] The eleventh annual exhibition of the Dorchester, Weymouth and Cerne District Association for the Improvement of the Condition of the Labouring Classes took place in 1857, the report noting a rise in emulation in living conditions 'induced' by the association resulting in 'a superior class of products'. Within the exhibition, prizes were awarded for needlework, including linen shirts, knitted stockings and the best smock frock, the last one being won by Mary Ann Woodland of Tincleton with a prize of 7 shillings.[29] Reflecting elite perceptions, in late-nineteenth-century village shows men won prizes for manual work, women for sewing, knitting and other aspects of domesticity, reinforcing labour divisions in a public prize-giving arena. By the 1870s, the smock category was a stalwart in village and cottagers shows, firmly associated with the countryside, craft and the handmade, even though, as previously noted, smocks were still being mass-manufactured at the same time.[30]

Dress reform

Concurrently, the smock appealed, as a supposedly traditional and handcrafted garment, with the Arts and Crafts feel of its needlework, to those in the aesthetic dress movement.[31] During the third quarter of the nineteenth century, various dress reform movements had emerged starting with pre-Raphaelite or 'artistic dress' from the 1850s and 1860s, closely associated with the circle of artists comprising George Frederick Watts, Dante Gabriel Rossetti, William Morris and James Whistler. The aesthetic dress movement developed from this during the 1870s and 1880s, influencing a broader section of the upper and middle classes. Those connected with this movement looked to the smock frock, the looseness of its form and the elasticity of smocking allowing for freedom of movement, as well as being the antithesis to machine-made embellishment. The fashion columns of the newspapers noted a novel style of dress in 1880 as mainstream fashion adopted 'the new smock shape', describing it as being the same as the countryman's smock although worn with a belt at the waist.[32] Smocking gave the feeling of flexibility to a fashionable closely fitting dress, although this was still restrictive in practice.[33] However, not everyone approved, one correspondent commenting that such styles made fashionable ladies look like 'ugly men'.[34] By 1884, the correspondent for 'Our Ladies Column' had to describe what smocking was for her readers. On a visit to Hamilton & Co. of Regent Street, who specialized in smocking, she notes:

> It is the same elastic sort of gathering one used to see on the smock frock or blouses of carters and farmers' men. It seems to have gone out of fashion with them since machinery has made everything cheap and common, but is now chiefly appropriated by artistic people who believe in the excellence and reality of genuine hand-work for decoration.[35]

Hamilton's were shirt makers, listed at 27, Mortimer Street, just off Regent Street. Described in 1881 as a 'co-operative needlework business', they appeared to have branched out into making smocks for followers of the aesthetic dress movement and were described as the first to revive smocking.[36] 'Not only philanthropic, but artistic', Miss Hamilton's workers carried out 'neat and peculiar' smocking 'beautifully', the correspondent continuing: 'The revival of an appreciation of hand needlework, as opposed to machine-made garments is satisfactory'.[37] Mortimer Street became known as a hub for women's businesses associated with both the aesthetic and rational dress movements.[38]

Smocking consequently became a popular dressmaking technique for use on items such as tea gowns and mantles during the 1880s and early 1890s.[39] It implied knowledge of the aesthetic dress movement but in a mainstream way, so that the fashionable ideal was not lost.

Children's wear

The smock also began to be perennially popular in fashionable children's wear although, of course, working-class boys had previously worn them. One of the earliest newspaper references to this dates from 1879. In a column entitled 'Feminine Foibles, Fancies and Fashions, by a Lady', the writer notes that 'The funniest little novelties for juvenile wear are pinafores made in exact imitation of the country labourer's dress, which is there known by the same name of a smock frock'.[40] A newspaper commented, in 1880, that if women wanted to study the newest fashion for children, dozens of elaborately stitched and gathered smocks were hanging in ready-made clothes shops. The illustrations of Kate Greenaway were seen as influencing the 'rusticating' of children's fashion.[41] Little smock frocks were 'all the rage' with 'bright stitchery' on the 'old milkman's elaborate yoke'.[42] By the late 1880s, 'Liberty' smock frocks for children were being sold throughout the country, for instance at Corder and Sons, high-class dressmakers in Sunderland, presumably made up with Liberty fabric.[43] The Liberty Mab Smock, a revival of the traditional garment, supposedly based on Greenaway's designs, remained popular and a stock garment for children into the twentieth century.[44] Clara

Frances Lloyd, who worked in the embroidery rooms at Liberty, recalled that they 'did more smocking than embroidery … [it] was a speciality of the house'. The popularity of the style was given royal kudos when Princess Mary dressed her sons in smocks.[45]

Smocks were thus unisex children's wear, boys' clothing during the 1880s having less emphasis on gender differentiation, the fashionable aesthetic being based on women's dress. Constance Wilde comments, in 1888, in *The Woman's World*: 'in summer both [girls and boys] could wear light smock-frocks and wide hats to protect the eyes from the glare of the sun … The smocking is perfectly elastic and the frocks are such a pretty shape, not emphasising the waist – always the largest part of a child'.[46] Smocks allowed for both freedom of movement and for growth and so became an extremely useful children's garment.[47] With elements of play and fantasy popular for boys' clothing in this period, for example, sailor suits and kilts, the smock fitted in well.[48] Their spread into everyday children's clothes with various qualities for different occasions, for instance, using silk for best or occasional wear, disguised their origin and they became a perennial in children's fashion, a situation that remains today.[49] Widely adopted and mass-produced, a constant demand kept prices low for consumers of all classes. Unfitted and so easier to manufacture ready-made, but with variations to express age, gender and social status, producers could therefore promote new lines and fashions.[50] Such working garments became an important inspiration for middle-class children's dressing practices, as with the sailor suit although this had militaristic connotations too.[51] Thus, by 1886, the juvenile department of a Worcester shop advertised 'Man O'War' suits for boys and 'fishwife dresses' and the 'Smock Frock' for girls.[52] Although the smock became part of mainstream children's wear, it also remained a fancy dress stalwart for all ages. In 'Mode of Today' in 1908, Madame Duprée suggested writing to Carter's Tested Seeds as they would supply a boy's smock, a hat band printed with the company name, packets of seeds and a 'carter's whip'. She recommended adding a 'tousled reddish wig' to give a 'more pleasing' fancy dress for this free outfit innovatively advertising the seed company (see Figure 6.1).[53]

Ellen Terry

Helping to popularize the use of smocking as a decorative feature in mainstream female fashion from the 1880s were the many publicity photographs of the actress Ellen Terry. The wide distribution and popularity of cabinet cards and carte de visite photographs from the mid-1860s onwards promoted the stars of

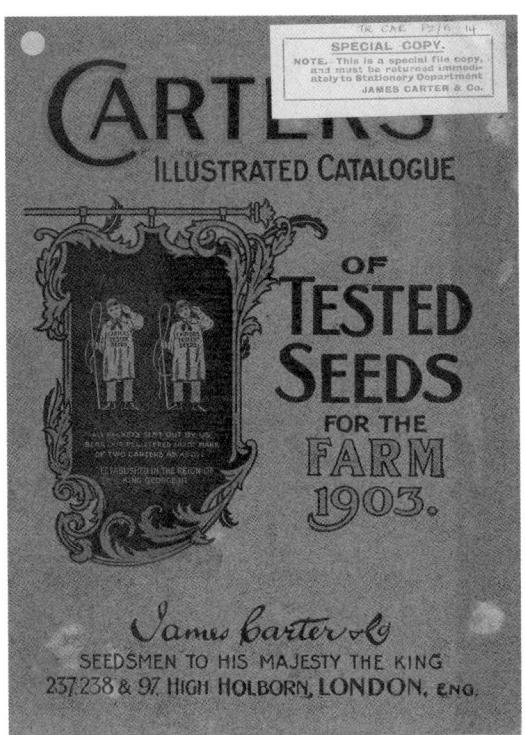

FIGURE 6.1 Carter's Illustrated Seed Catalogue of Tested Seeds for the Farm, *1903. Special Collections, MERL, TR CAR P2/A14. © Museum of English Rural Life, University of Reading.*

the stage, of which Terry was one of the most popular performers. These aided the dissemination of her artistic and aesthetic style, giving a reference point to women in the United States and England who wished to emulate her dress sense and helping it to reach the mainstream.[54] In 1884, the retail store Liberty engaged E. W. Godwin, Terry's former partner, as the director of the Historic and Artistic Studios and of a new school of dressmaking. This would essentially design and make up garments on site for their dress department to sell. It is tempting to think of how Terry may have influenced Godwin, with the way that she used and wore clothing, although they were no longer a couple.[55] Terry bought fabric for herself and her children from Liberty, even before Godwin worked there.[56]

The crossover between Terry's private persona and her public performances fascinated both her English and American audiences. The public's interest in snippets about her life may have led to a mention in 1897 in the *Hartlepool Mail*. Terry was performing in a provincial tour with the Lyceum Theatre but in September took the chance to take a driving tour of North Berkshire including the Vale of the White Horse. She came across a milkman in a 'clean white smock frock' and was anxious to purchase it from him. The milkman being 'obdurate' would not part with it, even for the famous actress, and instead directed her to the shop that he had bought it from. The newspaper reports that Terry made off 'at once' to the shop and was quickly the owner of a smock frock, which she ordered to be sent to her London address.[57] It was a rather late date to be wearing a smock frock, although milkmen did continue to wear them, partly because of their colour and their traditional associations with cowmen.[58] For Terry, the smock frock seemed to fit perfectly with aesthetics of the way that she wanted to dress. It was loose and unstructured allowing for freedom of movement as well as being naturally coloured or free from dye.[59] Terry also enjoyed sewing and embroidery herself, Lady Duff-Gordon describing how she called on her at home and found her in a circle of girls who were all sewing.[60] The smocking and embroidery may then have appealed to her from a practical as well as an aesthetic point of view.

Ellen Terry bought her country farmhouse, Smallhythe Place in Kent, in 1900, to use as a rustic retreat, a place where she could be with her daughter Edie (Edith) and both of them be at ease with their unconventional relationships, as well as where they could practise an informal way of dressing. Small Hythe, in the parish of Tenterden, was in a rural area where smocks were still worn. Terry, it seems, became slightly obsessed with the smock, ordering her visitors to wear them when they came to see her in the country[61] (see Figure 6.2). Perhaps this is not so unexpected in a bohemian artistic household and, of course, there probably was a degree of acting and artifice about living a rural life, alongside the aesthetic considerations. When living in the Hertfordshire countryside from 1868–73 with Godwin, she wore printed linen or cotton dresses, performing a role, her servant complaining that she was better clad in silk than Ellen.[62] However, her clothing does not appear to have included smock frocks at this point, only smocking as a decorative and practical embellishment.

Artists had, of course, long worn a protective overall and, during the nineteenth century as they were widely available and cheap, this might be a ready-made smock frock. Terry's former husband, George Frederick Watts, played an important role in the aesthetic dress movement, publishing an essay 'On Taste in Dress' in 1883, and was the vice president of the Healthy and Artistic Dress Union established in 1890.[63] In the later years of his life, a report described Watts as busying himself with artistic pursuits at his home, Limnerslease, near Guildford, wearing white trousers and a white smock.[64] The sculptor Hamo Thornycroft was another well-known artist wearer of the smock frock and member of the Healthy and Artistic Dress Union. As the *Pall Mall Gazette* reports in 1890: 'He invariably dons a white smock

FIGURE 6.2 *Ellen Terry and her husband, James Carew. Postcard. © Author's collection.*

frock of the pattern associated with village rustics, and his clay be-daubed hands complete the resemblance'.⁶⁵ *Vanity Fair* published a drawing of him wearing such an outfit as part of its 'Spy' series.⁶⁶ Having mixed in these artistic and intellectual circles, where the adoption of simple, utilitarian clothing displayed contempt for the whims of fashion and conspicuous consumption, and practised this mode of dressing previously herself, the smock frock was an eminently suitable garment for Terry's Kent country life.⁶⁷

Late-nineteenth-century ethnography

This artistic dressing was also bound up with elite nostalgia for an apparently rapidly disappearing 'rural idyll'. By 1888, men who wore the smock frock were seen as picturesque and harmless, part of an archaic rural past, the 'simple-minded, friendly old English labourer – smock frock included'.⁶⁸ For many, the introduction of compulsory primary education for children in 1880 changed the countryside, creating different aspirations and the desire for new jobs and working patterns. For those with no formal education, the epithet of 'simple' or 'foolish' could still be applied with impunity. The smock and its wearers became objects of curiosity. When the oldest inhabitant of Wormleighton, ironically called John Bull, died in 1887 at the age of 85, a report described him as 'a trusty and respected agricultural labourer of the old school, and a typical specimen of the smock-frock and knee-breeches man of the past generation'.[69] Amateur photographers were encouraged to take an ethnographic stance during the 1890s, Sir Benjamin Stone seeking to complete a photographic survey of contemporary Yorkshire. Change was rapidly occurring and to preserve a record, they must seize the moment before it passed, including photographing the old smock-frocked men of the villages.[70]

These photographic portraits thus captured social information as well as a physical likeness. However, the focus on elderly rural men as sitters, and as the smock's only wearers, has subsequently changed perceptions about the garment. Thomas Pitkin, described as a 'smock frock veteran' on his death in 1910, was photographed in one and was well-known for wearing the garment.[71] He was a farm labourer as well as a Primitive Methodist preacher and the first district councillor for his parish. He took part in the Royal Commission on Old Age Pensions in 1894 where Edward, Prince of Wales, questioned him about bringing up a family on 8 shillings a week.[72] Joseph Bass of Church Farm, Longwick, Buckinghamshire, was 86 years old when he died in 1916 and was well-known 'owing to his inflexible adherence to one of the most comfortable and picturesque of garments – the old fashioned smock frock'. Also 'people's warden' at Princes Risborough Parish Church for fifty years, the *Bucks Herald* interviewed him in 1898. When asked why he thought smocks went out of fashion he replied: 'Men took to jackets and coats, perhaps because they thought they looked a little better in them. That is a matter of opinion.' The interviewer then tried on a smock before leaving one of the 'most shrewd and practical farmers of the old school whom it has been my privilege to meet'.[73]

'Among Cottage People: A Rural Retrospective', an article published in *Blackwood's Magazine* in 1891 and widely reproduced in the provincial press, nostalgically discussed 'English national' dress with the demise of the red cloak for women and the smock frock as 'perfect works of art in the elaborate embroidery of the front and back yokes'. Modernity, railways, the telegraph and the post had 'extinguished the rural simplicity … the great goddess Fashion has penetrated into our villages … worshipped … as in the West End of London'. 'A restless discontent' and craving for progress had entered all classes, even

FIGURE 6.3 *Detail from a postcard, 'Rural scenes, village gossip in a quiet corner', 'EAS', circa 1908–10. © Author's collection.*

in rural districts. The youth of today did not dress like their elders and would not be capable of carrying out their 'day's work' either.[74] Postcards depicting evocative rural scenes were sold, often including a smock wearing old man (see Figure 6.3).

When *Country Life* magazine interviewed 'old' Stephen Harman, who still wore a smock in 1898, for an article entitled 'A Sussex Peasant', he said that his sons chose new fashions as they were unlikely to get a sweetheart dressed in a smock, since women did not like them.[75] Fred Gresswell, who grew up in rural Lincolnshire, suggested that suits had a better finish, along with a choice in colour and style, although they were not as strong or therefore as durable as smocks. Being bought new in the novel multiple shops, both the suit and the shop represented a modernity that the smock could not compete with.[76] The sleekness of the made-to-order suit countered the loose silhouette of the smock. The suit became a prime currency for self-fashioning an image of a modern man.[77]

Sussex smocks

As the smock's usage started to decline in the general population, as we have seen, they fed into elite society in a number of ways and their wearing also gradually became more ritualized for working men. One early example of such ritualization was for the funeral of a naval commander, T. Read, buried at Fishbourne near Chichester. He asked for his coffin to be carried by four men clad in white smock frocks, along with other particular requests which the report called 'ridiculous' obsequies.[78] Especially in rural southern England, the smock frock demonstrated authenticity and honest simple integrity, rather than the showiness of high Victorian mourning, appropriated by the middle and then working classes, accoutrements often being hired or dubiously obtained on credit. In 1873, Dr Wilberforce, the Bishop of Winchester, was buried in Lavington, West Sussex. Labourers from the estate carried his coffin, the newspaper commenting that their smock frocks were 'of such snowy whiteness that it was very difficult to distinguish them from the surplices of the clergy'.[79] By the 1880s and 1890s, workers from the local estate acting as coffin bearers wore the smock frock at many elite funerals in southern England, particularly in Sussex and Hampshire.[80] Most would no longer be wearing them on an everyday basis, so they perhaps added a picturesque element and performative aspect which linked into a perceived, socially hierarchical and specifically elite rural ideal, then seemingly fast disappearing.

The smock in the early twentieth century began to be known as the 'Sussex smock' as it was still worn there, although generally by elderly men.[81] By 1941, the smock was seen as a garment 'peculiar' to Sussex in former days,[82] perhaps partly due to William Grantham, a local landowner, who sought to revive the garment in the early twentieth century.[83] In 1913, he was set a challenge to appear at a Men of Sussex Society meeting at Arundel Castle in a smock along with Arthur Beckett, a writer on Sussex, also dressing in a smock for the occasion. Beckett needed 'some courage' to appear in a smock suggesting a struggle with the change in shape from normal men's dress. Finding women who still made them was also difficult, Beckett only having had one reply to his query from a lady who made girls' smocks. The Master of Lewes workhouse, where the smock had just been reinstated as a 'useful garment' for elderly inmates, lent him one.[84] 'John Bull', argued against this decision suggesting that making the poor wear the garment would subject them to ridicule without choice, labelling the inmates as paupers so they could be stared at, 'like ancient exhibits in an agricultural museum'.[85] Despite the original challenge apparently being set for comedic effect, Grantham took up the smock stating that he found the garment 'most useful and comfortable for shooting', wearing a black one himself, his beaters in white or khaki coloured examples.[86] *The Sussex County Magazine* reported in 1937 about the use of green smocks for shooting parties, so this trade must have provided a final flourish for men's smock makers.[87] Grantham made repeated attempts to revive smock manufacturing in the Sussex area during the 1920s and 1930s, including persuading the Royal Antediluvian Order of Buffaloes in Sussex, a fraternal organization, to wear them as their uniform and offering regular prizes for the best examples in exhibitions.[88]

Smock revival in the early twentieth century

Parallel to the development of the 'Sussex Smock' rooted in tradition, were male smock wearers connected to the rational dress movement. Along with the artists previously mentioned, free thinkers, the liberal elite, yearning for a 'simple life' in the country to improve health and well-being, much like Ellen Terry, also wore a version of this dress.[89] Letchworth was established as a Garden City in 1903 and its consultant architect from 1907 and early settler, Andrew Muir, was photographed wearing a smock and sandals.[90] Such a lifestyle was soon mocked as make-believe and all 'swank', a reimagining of 'merrie England', and not reflecting the reality of life.[91]

As professional smock makers died, revival movements grew which might supply men such as Muir. Sarah Lucy Bere, wife of the vicar of Bere Regis in Dorset, tried to interest local workers in making raffia baskets and smocks by founding the Bere Regis Arts and Crafts Association in around 1905 and starting the famed smock revival movement in Dorset. The association met regularly, several times a week, in a special room in the vicarage with fifteen to twenty workers. They copied the designs of old smocks to produce garments to sell including an order from Queen Alexandra and the presentation of a smock to Lord Baden-Powell's son.[92] A smock survives in the St Fagans collection made by Miss Amy Marsh who attended the association, the embroidery patterns identified in stitched words such as 'Essex Milkmaid' and 'Dorset Woodman'. It was made to order and cost 2 pounds 15 shillings.[93] In 1913, *The Times* reported that women in the district under the guidance of Mrs Bere made more than fifteen times what their grandmothers did, earning sufficient to pay for necessities such as artificial teeth.[94] The First World War interrupted the revival with the need for war work, the association not resuming after the end of the conflict.

The Fine Needlework Association in Beauchamp Place, London, also undertook similar work, gathering together a collection of various smocks as examples which the invalid section of the Girls' Friendly Society, in Victoria Street, copied.[95] Such societies can also be seen as part of the philanthropic craft revival movement which, from the 1880s onwards, sought to reinvigorate disappearing crafts to combat poverty, rural isolation and the encroachment of industry. With royal and aristocratic patronage, artistic and tasteful craftwork was seen as a civilizing and stabilizing influence to produce community cohesion in both rural and urban settings. Elite women 'retaught' the poor in needlework rather than do it themselves, enabling the workers to earn their own living, the produce of various societies bound for elite urban markets.[96] *Country Life* suggested that were it not for the ladies who valued smocking for children's clothes, this needlework would disappear, labourers deserting such clothing for ready-made 'slops'.[97] This 'cultural schizophrenia', as Tanya Harrod has called it, was particularly common during the interwar years. Anti-industrialism permeated upper- and middle-class tastes, excluding the machine-made and commercial from exhibitions, with industrial magnates having made all their money from what they now railed against, granting special sacralized status to the un-commodified world of craft. The pastoral, quasi-feudal vision held strong, the prosperous minority increasingly anxious about 'progress' and modernity, and mass-produced goods threatening the craftsman.[98]

Smocks in fashion

The market for revival smocks was increased as women also began to wear the garment. This seems to have been largely influenced by the sartorial practice of Ellen Terry. Terry's idea of wearing smocks as informal and practical women's wear for the country, rather than just using smocking as a decorative technique, had begun to influence the artistic and theatrical circles that her daughter Edie moved in. Also an actress, Edie toured the United States as part of the Lyceum Theatre Company in 1895, and again with Ellen in 1906–7, as well as making other trips there. At some point she must have met Claire Avery, who became an illustrator for American *Vogue,* their friendship noted in the memoirs of Edna Woolman Chase.[99] By 1914, the smock, seemingly with the help of Claire Avery and her connection to Edie Craig, found its way onto the pages of American *Vogue* as gardening wear. The article 'The Woman with a Hoe' in May 1914, told of the origin of the idea:

Some artists found them in Kent on a visit to Edith Craig's ancient Tudor farmhouse, 'Small Hythe' … all of them [the guests] wore smocks. They wore them all day long – put them on in the early morning and lived in them until dinner time, when English convention reasserted itself and everyone dressed for dinner. These artists brought the smock habit back to America to their garden-loving friends, who live in them during all of the Long Island summer, and bring them into town in winter. In town they wear them over respectable gowns as one wears an apron, but in the country each and every one of them wears her smock over a short skirt or baggy khaki trousers.[100]

Claire Avery illustrated the article and it seems fairly certain that she is the connection, the artist who went to stay with Craig and brought smocks back to Long Island. From 1910, Avery lived on Long Island in Brookhaven with Ida Haskell and Alice Broughton, a photographer and an art teacher. Edna Woolman Chase also moved there, becoming close friends with Avery and then editor of American *Vogue* from February 1914. Chase noted that Broughton wore 'Long loose smocks and … rather long skirts. She couldn't bear corsets or brassieres, and with this system it didn't matter; one couldn't tell where Bow ended and the fabric began'.[101] The women were linked to a set of progressive artists and writers who dressed unconventionally to signal their nonconformity, focused on Greenwich Village in New York. The unstructured smock was a popular choice, seemingly hand embroidered and unrestrictive.[102]

This American version was an adaption of the English garment. Edie Craig reportedly dyed her smocks in various colours and, from the outset, the American gardening smock was a coloured garment, blue, green, orange or rose, changed 'chameleon-wise' to fit each season. As the most talked about garment in spring 1915, American *Vogue* told their readers that 'the feminine world at large', now realized the smock's potential: 'Almost everyone has rushed into smocks and we are told that this summer we shall see them used for every conceivable purpose', not just by painters and gardeners.[103] By July 1915, a vivid red smock was on the front cover, illustrated by Helen Dryden, worn over a voluminous striped skirt.[104] 'Smock Shops' were set up to capitalize on the trend, for example, in Holyoke, Massachusetts, which offered mail-order smocks in blue, green and amber, with contrasting coloured stitching.[105] They were the perfect garment to sell ready-made and through mail order, since they did not requiring fitting.[106] Indeed, by December 1915, Madame June of Fifth Avenue was advertising the 'Skeeing', a novelty skating smock.[107] Home dress-makers could make up the garment in a style that looked very similar to the one illustrated on the front cover in 1915, American *Vogue* producing patterns by 1916.[108] One of these home dressmakers

FIGURE 6.4 *Alfred Stieglitz. Georgia O'Keeffe, 1918–1919. Gelatin silver print, 8 11/16 x 7 7/16 inches. Museum Purchase [2014.3.56], Georgia O'Keeffe Museum.*

was the artist Georgia O'Keeffe. She apparently designed her green smock herself in 1916, declaring it to be a work of art and writing about how she sewed all day to make it. She later wrote to Alfred Stieglitz about how she loved 'this garment' and he photographed her wearing it at Lake George (see Figure 6.4).[109] The smock fitted in with her favoured silhouette which hung loosely around her body, with simple decoration, although it was also fashionable, something that O'Keeffe was likewise very aware of.[110]

Picking up on the American fashion, in England the *Daily Mirror* of June 1915 entitled an article 'Eve in a Smock, How Girl Gardeners Have Solved the Problem of Work Costume'. The newspaper detailed the various hues that they came in, from orange, yellow, blue, green and pink, with or without collars, three-quarter or full length, 'a dainty, picturesque, rustic smock'.[111] In July 1915, the *Sunday Mirror* reported specifically about this fashion which came from the United States, the 'rather quaint mode for the old-fashioned smock … This garment, which is very similar to the smock worn by the country rustic, is being introduced into fashion for the woman who loves her garden.'[112] The suggestion was to wear it with a smart striped skirt, as it appeared on the American *Vogue* cover, and hold it in with a belt if needed. Suitable also for tennis and seaside wear, the British male smock, via America, had become a high fashion feminine garment, suiting the current female aesthetic for hip-length tunics and jackets. A report in October 1915 mollified any doubts readers might have had about the style noting that 'it is all criss-crossed with English smocking and flares out most alluringly'.[113] The colours and the variety of materials used elevated the smock into a garment women wanted to own and wear everyday, not just for gardening.[114] In 1916, Liberty advertised very similar smocks for gardening and country wear, and also to use as a kind of housecoat.[115] The smock was increasingly seen as both fashionable and practical.[116]

The First World War

Of course, this was during the First World War and, between 1915 and 1916, the smock's adoption as general gardening wear paved its way for use as an item of workwear for women war workers, particularly those who worked on the land. Lady Londonderry, Colonel-in-Chief of the Women's Volunteer Reserve, who took a special interest in agricultural work, recommended a smock similar to that which she wore in her garden for war work, 'an exact replica of the old time labourer's smock in quaint chintz patterned cretonne'.[117] Contemporary elite female motoring coats were also made in the style of 'old-fashioned' smock frocks.[118]

Perhaps influenced by this high society take up, female munition overalls advertised from September 1916, after universal male conscription was introduced, look remarkably similar to outfits featured in *Vogue* although only available in navy, brown, green, grey or the more feminine rose.[119] From 1916, the Board of Agriculture put forward an approved costume for land work but it was expensive, at around 30 shillings, so women usually procured clothes locally at the most economical rate, with enterprising outfitters supplying them unofficially.[120] The uniform of the Women's Land Army (WLA), introduced from January 1917 and given to women for free if they signed up for a year, although called a smock did not resemble the traditional smock or its fashionable counterpart. However, in this general area of workwear and overalls there are some obvious parallels in general shape and detailing. It is not clear if the WLA used the term 'smock' because the garment was currently fashionable. Horace Nicholls, the first Ministry of Information official photographer on the Home Front, took a series of photographs of women at work during the First World War, including those who worked on the land in 1914. These show fruit pickers wearing white smock frocks, with necktie and belt, plus breeches and gaiters.[121] The WLA uniform may

FIGURE 6.5 The Landswoman: The Journal of Land Army 1, no. 8 (1 August 1918). © The British Library Board, Lou.Lon.596.

have been a later variation of what women were wearing anyway to complete agricultural work. It seems likely that, throughout the war, some women preferred to use the male smock frock or buy their own versions from department stores, which set up rooms specifically for 'Practical Dress for Working Women'[122] (see Figure 6.5).

The WLA uniform was not seen as attractive with Peter Jones, the department store, instead advertising in 1917 the 'popular Farmer Giles smock' as an overall suitable for ladies engaged in any outdoor employment, supplied in the traditional colours of the smock frock in buff, green, blue and brown.'[123] *The Tatler* published a portrait photograph of Miss Angel Archdale, only daughter of Brigadier-General Archdale, in August 1917, when she was undertaking farmwork in the Cotswolds.[124] On first glance, what she is wearing seems to be a male embroidered smock but may also be a new 'Farmer Giles' type smock then in vogue. In isolated rural Norfolk, where there was no contact with official organizations for war work, Dorothea Cross stated that 'I wore a smock for most of the war', and was photographed wearing a modern version then available for sale in the shops.[125] During the horrors of the First World War, the symbolism of using a garment associated with tranquil unchanging rural landscapes was also important.[126]

The smock and 'leggings' enabled women 'to go about their work in a way that any man would not be ashamed of', and was fashionable too.[127] As Susan Grayzel notes, the Land Girl movement was about patriotism not feminism, which included the preservation of femininity and womanliness. Propaganda for recruiting Land Girls portrayed an idealized and sanitized version of the English countryside, an idea that the smock played on, both as a survivor from a romanticized rural past and now as a 'feminine' embroidered garment.[128] Newspaper articles disseminating the latest fashions emphasized this need for continued femininity, even if Land Girls found it difficult to obtain or impractical to wear such clothing.[129] Women officials at the Board of Agriculture started a shopping and sewing club offering proxy shopping in London for those stationed away from the city. They provided items such as *Vogue* patterns for smocks so that local dressmakers could make them up in chintz's or Hollands in the latest fashions.[130]

There was also a debate about whether women found the smock entirely practical for heavier work. A *Country Life* correspondent reported in 1917 that 'A big discussion raged round me recently on the practicality and the reverse of smocks for such work as digging, ploughing and the like', with the complaint that if the smock fell only from the shoulders, not being held in at the waist, it was 'apt' to get in the way. Nevertheless, the large variety of smocks that were available meant that all women could find a suitable style and they offered 'splendid' protection and a practical solution to clothing needs.[131] The idea that smocks ensured comfort 'that our mothers and grandmothers never had', especially in comparison to female dress in the nineteenth century, was also important.[132] The smock furthermore began to be equated with a 'jumper', pulled over the head, with no fastenings and worn over other clothes as a simple piece of everyday workwear.[133]

Women continued to wear such smocks in the interwar period, an article in *Country Life* in 1926 illustrated with a smock of butcher blue colour, very similar in design to those seen a decade earlier, for wear on the land whether gardening or farming. The correspondent suggests that although it was extremely practical it was also picturesque and 'hallowed by tradition'. It was furthermore suitable for all figures whereas only the 'slim, hipless form can really carry off successfully breeches and a shirt'.[134] The link with the nineteenth-century male smock frock was thus once more re-established. Such 'picturesque, yet practical' clothing remained part of informal dressing, the House of Lilla, who advertised in *Country Life* throughout the 1920s and 1930s, producing various smocked garments to wear as house coats for domestic tasks, a 'sheer inducement to becoming house-fanatic', for painting as a pastime, flower arranging or gardening.[135] The smock shape was also periodically featured in American fashion pages, an article in *Harper's Bazaar* in 1943 entitled 'Teach Yourself to Smock', suggesting that it was an easy pastime for nights 'after dinner-at-home'. The article advised beginners to use striped, checked or spotted material to make matching pleats easier and emphasized the comfort of smocking as well as its history and connection to the countryside.[136] As a casual piece of dress for wear at home or on the beach, smocks continued to be a popular garment in the United States.[137]

The Women's Institute

In England, the Women's Institute (WI) popularized smocking as a handicraft from the 1920s. The WI had strong connections to the Arts and Crafts Movement, for example, May Morris, daughter of William Morris, was the secretary of her local WI.[138] The WI was initially a movement specifically aimed at women in rural villages.[139] In 1921, K. S. Woods urged the WI to develop a scheme for rural needlework and use the skills of remaining outworkers who could no longer work commercially for clothing factories.[140] Some saw the WI as taking a significant part in preserving a vision of rural Englishness by revitalizing village life. Appropriating wartime rhetoric, this would celebrate cottage industry and draw on a reconstructed rural past, where the 'peasantry' were custodians of indigenous craft trades.[141] Alice Armes was the craft advisor for the National Federation of the WI between 1923 and 1939 and wrote one of the first histories of the smock. She also helped to stimulate an interest in North Country quilting. It was part of her remit that craft should be utilitarian and useful, to help women become self-sufficient.[142] The Guild of Learners, set up in January 1920, aimed 'to assist in bringing the best instruction in handicrafts within the reach of villages', including smocking and quilting. Some WI's set up local 'industries', for example, Ticehurst WI in Sussex sold smocked dresses and jumpers for children, advertised in *The Lady* and sold to Liberty and other London stores until the Second World War.[143] Described in the 1920s as applying revival decorative smocking to 'garments for modern wear', the WI were seen as protecting an ancient craft, but updating it to be useful once more.[144] The early ideals of the movement included redefining as skilled work the unpaid unaccounted for domestic labour of women. Craftwork was part of this, offering non-exploitative paid jobs to working-class women within the home in localized and specialized industries, the WI ensuring a uniformity of standard and consistency of supply for buyers.[145]

In her 1928 book, Armes includes instructions for making a smock, expressing her hope that 'our embroiderers, spinners, weavers, potters and other craftspeople, by producing and wearing smocks, might revive one of the most beautiful of old English crafts'.[146] Although smocking was an 'acceptable' craft for the National Federation WI craft movement leadership, in reality, for rural working women, the WI represented a chance for leisure time. Preferred craft activities which fitted this remit were much simpler, such as decorating boxes. Therefore within the WI there were skilled undertakings such as smocking, either sold commercially or exhibited and under middle-class control, whereas ordinary members favoured leisure pursuits or creating something decorative for their own home.[147]

The WI continued to promote this handicraft element during the interwar period and beyond. The Barton WI, for example, held a competition for a 'smocked frock' in 1948, when one member was awarded 100 per cent marks.[148] In 1950, the newly opened Denman College also held smocking courses open to any member, the college being situated in an eighteenth-century country house thus linking to a certain notion of the past.[149] Olivia Pass, chairman of the Dorset federation of the WI, developed and popularized feather stitch embroidery during the 1950s, which had been commonly used on smocks.[150] Her embellished stitch became known as Dorset Feather Stitchery, 'old stitches in modern form'. Published in 1957, her book includes details for sending off for transfers for patterns to work up, including cushions, tablecloths and clothing, as well as practical instructions.[151] Margaret Jones, another WI member, wrote about the history of smocks for *Country Life* in 1957, relating their construction to a recent WI competition to make a piece of 'clothing' from one newspaper and a dozen pins. The organization also produced a pamphlet about 'Smocking, Traditional and Modern', priced at 6 pence, with coloured diagrams showing how to smock.[152] Later into the twentieth century, the WI movement had become less outwardly ideological and more social, with a greater middle-class membership supporting an idealized image of both motherhood and ruralism, the countryside now a site of recreation and leisure, the rural a commodity and amenity to be marketed and consumed, to which smocking leant itself well.[153] Beverley Marshall, in 1980, still recognized the role of the WI for keeping alive the tradition of smocking, with instructions for making smocked clothing included in her book.[154]

Smocks in the late twentieth and twenty-first centuries

Smocks increasingly became seen as 'the last relics of a vanished peasant costume', made by amateur needlewomen, whose 'hands [were] more accustomed to heavy toil'.¹⁵⁵ The emphasis on the amateur sewer, women making smocks for their families, suggested that in the late twentieth century, those who had time to undertake handicrafts under the watchful eye of the WI and other sewing teachers, could replicate this. The revival of interest in the history of smocks around this date, coincided with the fashion for them in women's wear in both the UK and the United States, encompassing 1960s hippy styles and the country look of Laura Ashley.¹⁵⁶ Laura Ashley traded on a nostalgic view of the past, an exhibition of WI handicrafts at the Victorian and Albert Museum in 1952 famously inspiring her, one of the company's early lines in the 1950s being gardening smocks. Around 1975, in a departure from her usual style, Laura Ashley designed a dress based specifically on a combination of the smock and kaftan, with full sleeves and pleating across the bodice.¹⁵⁷

During the 1960s and 1970s, the smock as a loose dress falling from a shoulder yoke, without smocking, but perhaps showing off a large-scale print, was periodically reworked by couturiers such as Yves Saint Laurent and Givenchy.¹⁵⁸ The looseness also appealed to Japanese designers, for instance Kenzo during the 1970s, and Comme des Garçons used the shape, photographed by Peter Lindbergh in the 1982.¹⁵⁹ The opposite to 'body con', for those outside the mainstream, the smock speaks of otherness and the unconventional. John Galliano thus produced a knitted silk smock dress for his 'Fallen Angels' collection in Spring/Summer 1986, shaped like a smock, the knitted design simulating both smocking and embroidery, suggesting 'purity', and highlighting the broad influence of the smock frock¹⁶⁰ (see Figure 6.6).

The shape of the smock, and its needlework, continues to inspire fashion designers into the twenty-first century. Sarah Burton at Alexander McQueen used honeycomb smocking to exquisitely shape a dress in the Spring/Summer 2013 bee-influenced Ready-to-Wear collection.¹⁶¹ Since 2014, London designer Molly Goddard has made tulle versions of the smock shape, ruched and pleated to give volume and texture.¹⁶² Her dresses are known for their handcrafting and homespun feel, recalling dressing up and childhood smocks but remaining both grown-up and feisty.¹⁶³ Goddard states that *Tess of the d'Urbervilles* was her inspiration for her Autumn/Winter 2019 show which re-envisioned a green smock frock¹⁶⁴ (see Figure 6.7). Her most famous dress thus far is an exaggerated shocking pink tulle version worn by perhaps a truly, if fictional, unconventional outsider, the assassin Villanelle in the BBC TV series *Killing Eve*.¹⁶⁵

The influence of this dress in particular has perhaps helped to lead to a concurrent revival of the 'tent' dress, also chiming with feminist ideas in the late 2010s.¹⁶⁶ Goddard's dresses are seen as feminine, flamboyant and daring but

FIGURE 6.6 *John Galliano, knitted silk smock dress, 'Fallen Angels' collection, Spring/Summer 1986. Lot 155, Sale 18 June 2019. © Courtesy of Kerry Taylor Auctions.*

wearable, the often exaggerated scale and visual impact, including the heft and bulk, giving dominance to women, the antithesis of masculine power dressing.[167] In periods of political anxiety, the smock shape and the associated embellishment has become an important reference point for contemporary designers reflecting a desire to seek solace in the nostalgic and the homespun, as well as the remembrance of a simpler childhood time. The smock is also a talisman for the 'slow fashion' movement with its timeless feel and referencing of the handmade. As 'anti-fashion' it is seen as less ecologically damaging, with the increasing realization that fast fashion is one of the biggest causes of environmental destruction. Much as Ellen Terry used it, the smock continues to be the choice for women seeking to dress outside mainstream popular fashion, for the unconventional musician, model, actor, artist or assassin, who wants to stand out and create her own unique identity. As the smock has become part of female clothing, the shape and decorative elements of the garment are suggestive of particular ideas. No longer just a representation of an 'English peasant', the smock is also now part of the language of high fashion, a long way from its origins as cheap workwear for men.

FIGURE 6.7 *Molly Goddard, green smock, Autumn/Winter 2019. © Ben Broomfield (photograph), Molly Goddard.*

Full circle

The male desire for modernity in dress prevailed over the smock's benefits of durability and cheapness during the latter half of the nineteenth century. Increasingly mocked as a sign of backwardness and stupidity, the smock displayed as cumbersome and awkward, and a characteristic of comic yokels on the popular music hall stages, becoming a garment that working men did not want to be associated with. It was unmanly and old-fashioned, not appropriate attributes of dress for the modern man. Rather than disappearing as a footnote in dress history, the smock however became entwined with late Victorian and Edwardian nostalgia for a rapidly disappearing and changing countryside. This was manifest in several ways; for example, its adoption by the artistic elite; the link between an idealized country childhood and its perennial use as fashionable children's wear; and the study and recording of the 'last' wearers, including the veneration of the 'Sussex' smock. The surge in the middle-class love of handicrafts led to the preservation of the needlework techniques used to make smocks, initially during the 1880s.

Alongside the handicraft element of smocking, the smock shape and smocking detail also became fashionable through the conduit of artistic and aesthetic dress. The sartorial practice of Ellen Terry and Edie Craig crossed the Atlantic influencing American relaxed dressing and leisurewear to reach the pages of American *Vogue*. As female fashion from America, the smock morphed once more back in England into specific wear for the house and garden favoured initially by aristocratic ladies, then followed more broadly by other fashion page readers, including those working during the First World War. Fashion designers have sporadically used the smock as inspiration for the last 100 years, often when needing to evoke nostalgia for a rural past or a bohemian feel or, ironically in terms of male labourers, leisure and freedom.

Thanks to the work of contemporary designers such as Molly Goddard, the smock has lost its associations with tweeness and to a lesser degree, rural nostalgia, to become part of the current vocabulary of modern fashion. Today it perhaps suggests care in making, longevity and sustainability.[168] The craftsmanship needed is outwardly visible, the shape and associations give comfort in an increasingly anxious world. Indeed, Gucci Autumn/Winter 2020 collection, put male models in smocks once more, bringing the garment full circle. Gucci's designer, Alessandro Michele, sought inspiration from childhood for his collection, but also wanted to deconstruct modern masculinity and highlight the 'positivity of being strange'. His collection strove to harness the idea of different visual elements in a diverse definition of 'boundarylessness' masculinity, rather than one imposed by expected traditions.[169] By linking the many facets of the smock's history together over the last 150 years, this chapter has revealed how the smock moved from being disdained and rejected by men to come to the forefront of fashion, currently for both men and women. While the use of the smock once more in conventional menswear remains uncertain, the fact that the designers are using it as a reference point for questioning contemporary masculinity and to move past the silhouette of the suit, actually evokes its hidden history as male utilitarian workwear outside the fashionable mainstream.

Conclusion

While it has origins in the seventeenth and eighteenth centuries, the male smock frock came to the fore in the nineteenth century. The development of the garment also reflects alterations to living conditions and the clothing industry, revealing wider cultural and social change.[1] Differentiated forms of the smock, including shorter and plainer versions, gave it longevity as general occupational workwear for many different working men. The increasing pace of development in manufacturing ready-made clothing was, at least in part, due to the innovations of the ready-made smock producers in the 1840s and 1850s, many of whom later became men's clothing manufacturers fulfilling a continuing demand for cheap ready-made clothing.[2]

Despite what was said in commentaries around the turn of the twentieth century, the smock was never historically English peasant or folk dress – a signifier of national identity. Instead, from the eighteenth century onwards, the national dress of the English could be seen as the popularization and preoccupation with fashion throughout all strata of society and across both genders. Perhaps surprisingly, the smock played a role in this as part of male working-class fashions, chosen and bought by men for themselves.[3]

In addition, the smock makes us consider ideas about working-class masculinity. The smock frock masks the figure, hiding signs of disease, malnutrition and even starvation, in contrast to the modern ideal masculine body shown off using form-fitting clothing. The embroidered smock frock also questions our assumptions about Victorian male sartorial display, certainly for working men. Over the course of the century, 'modernity' won out with the increasing predominance of variants of the suit, the sometimes flamboyant and/or coloured smock frock, gradually relegated to the realms of the archaic or the comic, where it became shorthand for uncouth, uneducated rusticity. However, overalls are still required both in agriculture and other occupations. As museum curator Bridget Yates noted in the 1970s:

Nowadays, of course, the equivalent is the polythene fertiliser bag worn by the tractor drivers and tied round the waist with red binder twine. One day I shall have the nerve to insist that Strangers' Hall [Norwich Museum] acquires one, accessioned perhaps as 'Smock, polythene, blue, printed ICI in black letters'.[4]

Today it is 'the ubiquitous boiler suit' which protects and gives warmth to those who work the fields,[5] the workwear descendent of the smock as overall, which was its primary function.[6] The white protective coat is still associated with laboratories, perfume sellers, livestock auctioneers and, ironically, museum curators, with connections to hygiene and smartness, food and health.[7]

The evocation of childhood, for collectors and writers about smocks in the early twentieth century, turned the garment into an emotional object, generating feelings of nostalgia, cherishment and sentimentality for the golden age of their rural childhood, some years earlier, an idea to which we are still, to some extent, enthralled. Figures wearing smocks were produced as lead farm toys, including carters, shepherds and dairymen, to perpetuate the rural myth through generations.[8] No longer suitable for the modern man to wear, from the late nineteenth century, the embellished male smock continued to evolve to become part of both children's and women's fashion, associated with domesticity and femininity, including home-sewing and craft.

The smock frock has a complex history of diverse representations in different eras and as a cypher for perceptions and nostalgia about a particular imagined rural past, becoming mired as the dress of the 'picturesque' English agricultural labourer of yesteryear, who led a simple 'honest' life. The elite at both ends of the political spectrum used representations of the smock; the right to illustrate the conservative and traditional, rigidly hierarchical, countryside, the left, also seeking a pre-industrial arcadia but where there was more equality. The many constructions that swirl around the smock frock have overridden its essential usefulness and mundanity as a piece of utilitarian mass-produced workwear and then as a practical child's garment, both key parts of modern sartorial practices.

As academic attention increasingly focuses on 'everyday' clothing and more mundane dress practices, different ways of exploring the clothing needs of the mass of the population, the working people, and particularly men, prior to the twentieth century need to be uncovered. *The Hidden History* has sought a way to build a fuller analysis of the ordinary clothing of working people across various periods and geographical areas, especially menswear, exploiting underused sources such as here newspapers, trade directories and prisoner photographs. This research includes the necessity of understanding how clothing was made, particularly by female outworkers, and bought by and sold to working people, also offering evidence as to how working people felt about their clothing and the value that they placed on particular garments. Challenging assumptions about the false division between functional and fashionable clothing for working people, this research also shows how the representation of the smock has impacted across all social classes.

Clothing was, and still remains, a very public signifier of social and economic status for all classes and the dress of working people should not be brushed over as unchanging, unexciting or unimportant, or dismissed as a research area through lack of evidence. As this research has shown, the choices that working people made could drive the direction of the clothing industry as a whole. With examples of smocks surviving in museum collections, the material object has provided another way into this field and, in particular, the emotional and sensory responses to smocks, as they shift across historical and social contexts. By considering the smock's heft, it's decoration, it's patching and repairs, the way it was made, what feeling it provokes in the wearer or the viewer – and we have noted everything from pride, indifference, disdain, disgust, sentimentality, pragmatism and amusement – this research has analysed how various people actually used smocks as an everyday sartorial practice, as well as examining their abstract form, their representation. Embodying characteristics which juxtapose the rural, the mass-manufactured, craft, innovation, nostalgia, subversion of masculine tropes, and an imagined past, the smock is both a sometime radical garment and a representation of collective and/or personal memories, occasionally both at the same time.

By connecting visual, material and written cultures within shifting contexts, *The Hidden History* has shown that the experience of wearing a smock can no longer be seen as static but is nuanced, complex and dependent on placing within a specific social and cultural locale. Investigating the clothing cultures of nineteenth-century working people can disrupt the dominant fashion history narrative and recalibrate our ideas around everyday clothing practices, as revealed here by this research into the smock frock.

Notes

Introduction: Form and definition

1 B. Yates, 'Rural Dress in Norfolk', *Strata of Society, Proceedings of the Seventh Annual Conference of the Costume Society, April 6–8, 1973* (London: V & A, 1974), 8, © reproduced with permission of The Licensor through PLSclear.

2 Joseph Strutt compares the round frock, well established by 1799, to the medieval sequannie or tuin, in his *Dress and Habits of the English People*, see A. Buck, 'The Countryman's Smock', *Folk Life* (1963): 18. The decoration of Roman and Anglo-Saxon tunics at the neckline and wrists have also been compared to the smock frock, see B. Marshall, *Smocks and Smocking* (Sherborne: Alphabooks, 1980), 59.

3 A. Armes, *English Smocks with Directions for Making Them* (Leicester: Dryad Press, 1928), 5.

4 See Marshall, *Smocks and Smocking*, 39, for a plan to cut a smock from one piece of fabric.

5 Ibid., 8, 42. The French 'blouse' was appropriated from rural clothing, worn and associated with all French workers from the 1830s onwards. It became a garment connected with being an insurgent on the barricades and so a disruptive worker. The blouse became more generally worn, in factories for example, because it was cheap. It thus became both a marker of poverty and displayed pride in being a 'worker', see A. Faure, 'The Working Man's Blouse in 19th Century Paris, The Norms of Dignity', *Modes Pratiques, Journal of Clothes and Fashion History*, Special Issue in English (January 2018): 89–94. Boilly paints a man wearing a blue smock embroidered in red in 'The Movings' of 1822, available online: https://www.artic.edu/artworks/97681/the-movings?q=boilly (accessed 19 June 2020).

6 Marshall, *Smocks and Smocking*, 72, notes that this is not actually a very comfortable garment to wear.

7 Buck, 'The Countryman's Smock', 16, for further details and measurements that Miss Buck took from different types of smocks. Also 32–3, for the overcoat style, plus Marshall, *Smocks and Smocking*, 30–3.

8 *Buckingham Advertiser and Free Press*, 6 May 1905, 6.

9 See B. Reay, *Rural Englands* (Basingstoke: Palgrave Macmillan, 2004), 205, for variations in terminology in other areas of rural life. See also Yates, 'Rural Dress', 8.

10 My thanks to Sarah Thursfield for pointing out the origin of the term. See oed.com for early references. See also B. Lemire, *Fashion's Favourite: The Cotton Trade and the Consumer in Britain 1660–1800* (Oxford: Oxford University Press, 1991), 85, and S. Chapman, 'The "Revolution" in the Manufacture of Ready-made Clothing 1840–60', *London Journal*, 29, no. 1 (2004): 54–5, who notes that the firm of Moses was repeatedly called a slopseller in their insurance records. See online http://findit.library.yale.edu/catalog/digcoll:550590 (accessed 15 June 2020), for an illustration of sailor's slop trousers and a smock from 1793.

11 *Leicester Chronicle*, 6 March 1875. A theft case in Peterborough refers to both a slop frock and smock frock allegedly stolen by Francis Welby, see *Stamford Mercury*, 23 January 1863.

12 *Leicester Chronicle*, 21 December 1839.

13 *Sheffield Independent*, 7 September 1874.

14 G. Holman, *Made in East Anglia: A History of the Region's Textile and Menswear Industries* (Pasold Resource, no. 1, 2015), http://www.pasold.co.uk/resource-page, 121; F. Thompson, *Lark Rise to Candleford* (1945; London: Penguin Books, 2000), 48.

15 *Grantham Journal*, 22 August 1857. See *Grantham Journal*, 17 October 1857, for the account of the Quarter Sessions trial where he was found not guilty. Similar use of terminology also appeared in a trial in Hillmorton, Leicestershire, where the case is theft of a smock frock, although it is called a 'slop' by the prisoner, see *Leicestershire Mercury*, 1 September 1855, and also a case in the nearby Lindsey Sessions with the theft of smock frock or slop by William Sills, *Stamford Mercury*, 25 April 1851. Both terms are used in court cases into the 1860s.

16 *Stamford Mercury*, 11 December 1807.

17 *Taunton Courier, and Western Advertiser*, 23 February 1859. William Howitt also uses slop and frock see W. Howitt, *The Hall and the Hamlet: Or Scenes and Characters of Country Life* (London: Henry Colburn Publisher, 1848), vol. 2, 258–61.

18 *Hereford Times*, 19 February 1842.

19 *Silurian, Cardiff, Merthyr, and Brecon Mercury, and South Wales General Advertiser*, 15 May 1852; this is also the case in Frome, see *Sherborne Mercury*, 15 November 1864.

20 'He had on a short smock that the navvies wear', see 'The Frome Libel', *Salisbury and Winchester Journal*, 10 March 1855. See Chapter 5, 91–7, for details about navvy smocks.

21 *Hertford Mercury and Reformer*, 29 February 1840.

22 *Hertford Mercury and Reformer*, 7 March 1840.

23 Ibid.

24 Ibid. An overall was still known as a slop in Herefordshire in the late twentieth century, see M. Hall, *Smocks* (Princes Risborough: Shire Publications, 1979), 3.

25 For example, see T. Palmer, 'slops (brown and white), Engineers, railway and smock frocks', in Crewkerne, *Bridport News*, 14 March 1868; Thomas Jones, four dozen slops and smock frocks, Hereford, *Hereford Times*, 31 July 1858; James Smallbones, slops and smock frocks, Devizes, *Wiltshire Independent*, 18 June 1868; with others similar dating from the late 1850s and 1860s.

26 *Exeter Flying Post*, 27 December 1876. See also 105 for Australian usage.

27 *The Ipswich Journal*, 8 October 1842.

28 See Reay, *Rural Englands*, 163, for examples. See *Bedfordshire Times and Independent*, 24 September 1943, 8, for a comparison of the smock and surplice.

29 *Somerset County Gazette*, 17 August 1839.

30 *The Evening Chronicle*, 12 August 1846.

31 *Exeter and Plymouth Gazette*, 15 September 1908, 3.

32 *Sussex Agricultural Express*, 3 October 1941, 4.

33 See Chapter 3, for the ready-made trade.

34 Buck, 'The Countryman's Smock', 16.

35 See B. Reay, *Microhistories, Demography, Society and Culture in Rural England, 1800–1930* (Cambridge: Cambridge University Press, 2002), 259–61, for more about the methodology of microhistory.

36 For example, Marshall, *Smocks and Smocking*.

37 J. Styles, *The Dress of the People, Everyday Fashion in Eighteenth-Century England* (London: Yale University Press, 2007), 45.

38 Ibid.

39 L. Baumgarten, *What Clothes Reveal: The Language of Clothing in Colonial and Federal America* (Williamsburg: Colonial Williamsburg Foundation, 2002), 56.

40 For a discussion about this type of history see J. Sharpe, 'History from Below', in *New Perspectives on Historical Writing*, ed. P. Burke (Cambridge: Polity Press, 1992), 24–41. For a recent summary see http://www.historyworkshop.org.uk/history-from-below-a-reading-list-with-marcus-rediker/ (accessed 15 June 2020).

41 P. K. Andersson, *Streetlife in Late Victorian London: The Constable and the Crowd* (Basingstoke: Palgrave Macmillan, 2013), 2, 5–9, 220. See also V. Richmond, *Clothing the Poor in Nineteenth-Century England* (Cambridge: Cambridge University Press, 2013), 15, who notes that the voices of the 'poor' were filtered through their social superiors.

42 P. Hudson, 'Industry, Working Lives, Nation and Empire, Viewed through Some Key Welsh Woollen Objects', in *History Matters: History after Hobsbawm: Writing the Past in the Twenty-first Century*, ed. J. Arnold and M. Hilton (Oxford: Oxford University Press, 2017), 163–5, 183.

43 B. Burman and A. Fennetaux, *The Pocket: A Hidden History of Women's Lives* (New Haven: Yale University Press, 2020), especially 16–20, 34.

44 Andersson, *Streetlife*, 132–3. B. Lemire, *The Business of Everyday Life: Gender, Practice and Social Politics in England, c. 1600–1900* (Manchester: Manchester University Press, 2006), 126–8, for a summary of male generational dressing in eighteenth-century London.

45 See, for example, Baumgarten, *What Clothes Reveal*, 212; P. Bailey, '"Will the Real Bill Banks Please Stand Up?" Towards a Role Analysis of Mid-Victorian Working-Class Respectability', *Journal of Social History* 3, 12 (1979): especially 341–3, on how respectability could be assumed as a role for gain in some form.

1 The smock and rural England

1 See Chapter 6 for a discussion about the smock entering the female fashion vocabulary and children's wear during the late nineteenth century.

2 See, for example, Norman Thelwell's cartoon from 1960, an illustration for *Punch*, see http://www.reading.ac.uk/adlib/Details/collect/7114 (accessed 30 April 2020).

3 A. Howkins, 'The Discovery of Rural England', in *Englishness: Politics and Culture, 1880–1920*, ed. R. Colls and P. Dodds (London: Croom Helm, 1986), 64.

4 See B. Reay, *Rural Englands* (Basingstoke: Palgrave Macmillan, 2004), 10.

5   Howkins, 'The Discovery of Rural England', 66, 69.

6   See Reay, *Rural Englands,* 1–3, 137, for the collecting of folk songs by middle-class enthusiasts and the editing process to get rid of innuendo and coarseness.

7   Reay, *Rural Englands*, 6–7.

8   R. Worth, 'Rural Working-Class Dress, 1850–1900: A Peculiarly English Tradition?', in *The Englishness of English Dress*, ed. C. Breward, B. Conekin and C. Cox (Oxford: Berg, 2002), 102. Also A. Bermingham, *Landscape and Ideology: The English Rustic Tradition, 1740–1860* (Berkeley: University of California Press, 1989), 10–11. R. Worth, *Clothing and Landscape in Victorian England: Working-Class Dress and Rural Life* (London: I. B. Tauris, 2018), 86, 100. D. Matless, *Landscape and Englishness* (London: Reaktion Books, 2016), 82, who notes that the interwar preservationists regarded the late eighteenth/early nineteenth century as the point when England was most beautiful, and also in general for interwar views and nuances of traditional and pictorial pastoral conventions.

9   See the socialist connections of artists such as William Morris and Walter Crane, for example, as well as the right-wing sympathies and nationalism of the early organic movement, with the Springhead Ring in Dorset, T. Harrod, *The Crafts in Britain in the Twentieth Century* (London: Yale University Press, 1999), 160, 162, and Matless, *Landscape and Englishness,* particularly chapter 3.

10 *Gloucestershire Chronicle,* 17 March 1906, 5.

11 *Taunton Courier, and Western Advertiser,* 23 December 1903, 3.

12 C. Payne, *Toil and Plenty: Images of the Agricultural Landscape in England 1780–1890* (London: Yale University Press, 1993), 1. Bermingham, *Landscape and Ideology*, 158–62.

13 T. Barringer, *Men at Work: Art and Labour in Victorian Britain* (New Haven: Yale University Press, 2005), 103–6, and chapter 2 in general.

14 See Xan Brooks, 'Rural Retreat', *The Guardian* Review, 3 March 2018, 7–11, for new 'rural' writers and the reality they portray in comparison to the urban myth of the timeless countryside.

15 Payne, *Toil and Plenty*, 26.

16 Ibid., 28. W. Howitt, *Rural Life in England* (London: Longman Orme Brown Green & Longmans, 1838), vol. 1, 157–8.

17 R. Worth, 'Clothing the Landscape: Change and the Rural Vision in the Work of Thomas Hardy (1840–1928)', *Rural History* 24, no. 2 (2013): 203, 206–8. Hardy's father, a stone mason, wore smocks which were lent, in 1918, for an amateur dramatic production of *Under the Greenwood Tree* and subsequently lost.

18 T. Hardy, *Far from the Madding Crowd* (1874; Ware: Wordsworth Editions, 2000), 113. Other 'picturesque' working dress went through a similar process of traditionalization in the Victorian period, for example, dustmen seen as a 'real cockney aborigine', heroic and ancient, see B. Maidment, *Dusty Bob & A Cultural History of Dustmen, 1780–1870* (Manchester: Manchester University Press, 2007), 176–8.

19 K. Snell, *Annals of the Labouring Poor: Social Change and Agrarian England, 1660–1900* (Cambridge: Cambridge University Press, 1987), 387–92, 397–8.

20 Worth, 'Clothing the Landscape', 211, 213.

21 See H. Metcalfe, 'Recalling the Comforts of Home: Bachelor Soldiers' Narratives of Nostalgia and the Re-creation of the Domestic Interior', in *Martial Masculinities. Experiencing and*

Imagining the Military in the Long Nineteenth Century, ed. M. Brown, A. M. Barry and J. Begiato (Manchester: Manchester University Press, 2019), 63–5, for a useful summary about the definition of nostalgia, which could be temporal and spatial.

22 See M. Lambert and E. Marx, *English Popular Art* (London: B. T. Batsford, 1951), v, who note that 'the innocent eye' was disappearing, country craftsmen and individuality in design dying out with changing social habits such as consumers buying from chain stores.

23 Lambert and Marx, *English Popular Art,* 62. See also M. Jones, 'The Vanished Smock-Frock', *Country Life,* 11 April 1957, 719, for similar comments.

24 R. Kenny, J. McMillan and M. Myrone, *British Folk Art* (London: Tate Publishing, 2014), 12, 126. See also O. Douglas (2018), 'Why the Folk?', https://merl.reading.ac.uk/news-and-views/2018/09/why-folk/ (accessed 16 June 2020).

25 Kenny, McMillan, Myrone, *British Folk Art,* 129, note the revivals of interest in folk art at such times.

26 *Cornishman,* 23 January 1896.

27 A. Armes, *English Smocks with Directions for Making Them* (Leicester: Dryad Press, 1928), 3.

28 *The Magazine of the Fine Arts,* 1821, cited S. Smiles, 'Defying Comprehension: Resistance to Uniform Appearance in Depicting the Poor, 1770s to 1830s', *Textile History* 33, no. 1 (2002): 28.

29 Worth, 'Rural Working-Class Dress', 103–4. A similar process occurred with Welsh costume, promoted by the literary and artistic elite of Wales as they saw 'Welsh culture' vanishing. The 'costume' was actually Welsh rural dress which became fossilized during the nineteenth century, see C. Stevens, 'Welsh Costume: The Survival of Tradition or National Icon?', *Folk Life,* 43 (2004–5): 56, 64, 66, 69. See also the research on the history of emotions, particularly nostalgia, and the way that objects provoke different emotions as they interact with people and travel across time, see J. Begiato, 'Moving Objects: Emotional Transformation, Tangibility, and Time-Travel' in *Feeling Things: Objects and Emotions through History*, ed. S. Downes, S. Holloway and S. Randles (Oxford: Oxford University Press, 2018), 232, 238.

30 Harrod, *The Crafts in Britain,* 20, 27, who points out that they were concerned with artistic fulfilment not social matters.

31 Harrod, *The Crafts in Britain,* 144–5. Industrial designers also turned to the 'non design' of everyday objects displaying scythes with modernist sensibilities in the Dorland Hall Exhibition, Lower Regent's Street, in 1933, 120–1. Also Matless, *Landscape,* 196.

32 Armes, *English Smocks.*

33 Kenny, McMillan, Myrone, *British Folk Art,* 130–1, for other similar examples including ship's figureheads and 'God in a bottle'. See also Worth, 'Rural Working-Class Dress', 98–100, who mentions Helen Allingham, Myles Birket Foster and Henry Peach Robinson as artists and photographers who promoted this way of thinking.

34 See letter from H. Lumley Ellis, *Country Life,* 5 June 1942, 1094–5.

35 J. Begiato, *Manliness in Britain, 1760–1900* (Manchester: Manchester University Press, 2020), 17.

36 Reay, *Rural Englands,* 9. J. Lewis-Stempel, *The Running Hare, The Secret Life of Farmland* (London: Doubleday, 2016), 124, 185.

37 Harrod, *The Crafts in Britain*, 136–7, also 172, 174, for the reinvention of the Cotswolds from a depressed industrial area to Arcadian idyll.

38 H. Tanner, 'Smocks and Smocking', *Countryman* 48, no. 1 (1953): 82; Maidment, *Dusty Bob*, 35, for similar misrepresentations about dustmen.

39 R. Worth, 'Rural Labouring Dress, 1850–1900: Some Problems of Representation', *Fashion Theory, The Journal of Dress, Body & Culture* 3, no. 3 (1999): 339. Worth, *Clothing and Landscape*, 142, 150. See also V. Elson and R. Shirley, *Creating the Countryside, The Rural Idyll Past and Present* (London: Paul Holberton Publishing, 2017), for comments about the urban reconstruction of the countryside, especially 8, 37, 41, 58.

40 Payne, *Toil and Plenty*, 1–2.

41 Bermingham, *Landscape and Ideology*, 193.

42 https://www.nationaltrust.org.uk/documents/50-things-activity-list.pdf (accessed 15 June 2020). For contemporary outbursts of nostalgia and its connection to the political upheavals of 2016, see I. Jack, 'A Generation Hooked on Nostalgia Is Trying to Return Britain to the Past', *The Guardian*, 1 April 2017, 39. See also Elson and Shirley, *Creating the Countryside*, 51, who note that National Trust members now outnumber farm workers seven to one.

43 See Lewis-Stempel, *The Running Hare*, 279, who notes the loss of country workers living in the countryside. See also J. Kennedy, *Authentocrats: Culture, Politics and the New Seriousness* (London: Repeater Books, 2018), 142–3, 153–6, for the view that a made-up rural southern English idea has become a synecdoche of national identity.

44 Lewis-Stempel, *The Running Hare*, 118.

45 Worth, 'Rural Labouring Dress', 339. Worth, *Clothing and Landscape*, 150, 155.

46 S. Carden, 'Cable Crossings: The Aran Jumper as Myth and Merchandise', *Costume* 48, no. 2 (2014): 264.

47 A. Hood, 'Material Culture and Textiles: An Overview', *Material History Bulletin* 31 (Spring 1990): 6–7, who notes that descriptive analyses of surviving textiles, while necessary and providing a valuable foundation, are biased by the availability of the surviving objects, the historical context often unevenly researched, perpetuating myths, as in the case of smock collections. There is a similar situation with ready-made quilted petticoats, see C. Rose, 'Bought, Stolen, Bequeathed, Preserved: Sources for the Study of 18th-century Petticoats', in *Textiles and Text, Re-establishing the Links between Archival and Object-Based Research*, ed. M. Hayward and E. Kramer (London: Archetype Publications Ltd., 2007), 115–16, 118.

48 Worth, 'Rural Working-Class Dress', 110.

49 *Bucks Herald*, 16 April 1910, 9, donated by W. Bradbrook, ARCS, worn by the late John Loke of Ledburn, Mentmore. N. Tarrant, *Smocks in the Buckinghamshire County Museum* (Aylesbury: Buckinghamshire County Council, 1976), 8–9 plus illustration.

50 *Bucks Herald*, 16 April 1910, 9.

51 A. L. J. Gosset, *Shepherds of Britain, Scenes from Shepherd Life* (London: Constable, 1911), 249.

52 *Western Gazette*, 19 January 1923, 9.

53 *Western Gazette*, 10 October 1930, 16.

54 Tarrant, *Smocks*, 3.

55 I. Mida and A. Kim, *The Dress Detective: A Practical Guide to Object-Based Research in Fashion* (London: Bloomsbury, 2015), 16.

56 Mida and Kim, *The Dress Detective*, 8, 62.

57 See the recent exhibition at the Fashion Institute of Technology, New York, 'Fashion Unravelled', brochure available online: http://www.fitnyc.edu/museum/documents/fashion-unraveled-brochure.pdf (accessed 15 June 2020).

58 C. Steedman, 'Englishness, Clothes and Little Things', in *The Englishness of English Dress*, ed. C. Breward, B. Conekin and C. Cox (Oxford: Berg, 2002), 35–6.

59 See 109–12 for reasons for the smock's decline and the connection to music hall comedy.

60 See 114–15 for the development of the smock as children's wear.

61 M. Spufford and S. Mee, *The Clothing of the Common Sort, 1570–1700* (Oxford: Oxford University Press, 2017), 16.

2 Histories of the smock frock

1 A. Buck, 'The Countryman's Smock', *Folk Life* (1963): 16.

2 Cited *Shrewsbury Chronicle*, 24 July 1857; see also *Wellington Journal*, 17 October 1863, where the smock was said to have been worn by Anglo-Saxon peasants.

3 *Sheffield Evening Telegraph*, 27 October 1893, and *London Daily News*, 26 October 1893, 5, the theory of Mr Bentall, an Essex archaeologist. The frock, as an outer tunic, has had associations with priests since the fourteenth century, see oed.com.

4 *Nottingham Evening Post*, 25 January 1894; see also *Nottingham Evening Post*, 26 October 1893, for a similar discussion. Both A. Strutt and Mrs Ashdown, both nineteenth-century writers about the history of dress, related the smock to the Anglo-Saxon tunica, ultimately of Roman origin, see O. Cave, *Traditional Smocks and Smocking* (London: Mills and Boon, 1979), 10, for a summary, and 12–19 for a history of the tunic. This argument was aired once more as the garment died out, see *Derby Daily Telegraph*, 28 September 1922, 2.

5 *Wells Journal*, 10 November 1855, and *Reynolds's Newspaper*, 17 January 1886. See the *Cornishman*, 12 May 1898, where it was called a 'little altered descendant of the Saxon frock', and now 'a curio'. See also a 'Lady's Letter', *Lichfield Mercury*, 20 July 1888, and *Hemel Hempstead Gazette and West Herts Advertiser*, 24 April 1886, where it was stated to be 'a genuine survival of Saxon attire', although then only worn by older labourers. Also A. Armes, *English Smocks with Directions for Making Them* (Leicester: Dryad Press, 1928), 3, and A. L. J. Gosset, *Shepherds of Britain, Scenes from Shepherd Life* (London: Constable, 1911), 245.

6 M. Brown, *Somerset Smocks*. Reprint from *Notes & Queries for Somerset & Dorset*, 30, part 305 (March 1977): 1, and E. Finney, N. Hely-Hutchinson and A. Mackenzie, *Smocks from the Hereford Museum Collection* (Hereford: Herefordshire Heritage Services, 2005), 5.

7 See J. Arnold, *Patterns of Fashion 4: The Cut and Construction of Linen Shirts, Smocks, Neckwear, Headwear and Accessories for Men and Women, c. 1540–1660* (London: Macmillan, 2008), 13, for examples of surviving female smocks from this period, 54–64. Also J. Arnold, 'Smocks, Shirts, Falling Bands and Mantuas: Evidence of Loosely-Fitting Garments and

Neckwear produced for the Ready-to-Wear Market, c. 1560–1700', in *Per Una Storia della Moda Pronta, Problemi e Ricerche* (Milan: Pitt Immagine, 1990), 19, for the silk-women who carried out the embroidery.

8 Arnold, 'Smocks, Shirts, Falling Bands and Mantuas', 21, who notes that Shakespeare's pedlar Autolycus in *A Winter's Tale* sells smocks, although Arnold cautions that some of these may have been stolen as well as probably ready-made. Queen Elizabeth I, however, distributed ready-made linen smocks to poor women as part of the Maundy Thursday ceremony.

9 Buck, 'The Countryman's Smock', 18. See Brown, *Somerset Smocks*, 1, and M. Nichols, *Smocks in Luton Museum* (Luton: Borough of Luton Museum and Art Gallery, 1980), 1, where she notes that Dr Johnson equated a smock with a woman's undergarment or shift.

10 *Leamington Spa Courier*, 25 November 1843.

11 M. Spufford and S. Mee, *The Clothing of the Common Sort, 1570–1700* (Oxford: Oxford University Press, 2017), 35.

12 See also W. Shakespeare, *Hamlet*, Act 3, scene iv, where 'frock' is equated with livery.

13 D. de Marly, *Working Dress: A History of Occupational Clothing* (London: B. T. Batsford, 1986), 26, although she does not provide a source for her suggestion. Likewise, see J. Shrimpton, *British Working Dress: Occupational Clothing 1750–1950* (Oxford: Shire Publications, 2012), 8.

14 D. Tankard, '"They Tell Me They Were in Fashion Last Year": Samuel and Elizabeth Jeake and Clothing Fashions in Late Seventeenth-Century London and Rye', *Costume* 50, no. 1 (2016): 26, 28. She has also found that home-made linen was bought to make up shirts and smocks, although the smocks made in 1667 appear to be for a woman, see D. Tankard, 'Giles Moore's Clothes: The Clothing of a Sussex Rector, 1656–1679', *Costume* 49, no. 1 (2015): 46.

15 D. Tankard, *Clothing in 17th-century Provincial England* (London: Bloomsbury Visual Arts, 2019), ebook, chapter 7 and chapter 3 for mercers' inventories.

16 N. W. Alcock and N. Cox, *Living and Working in Seventeenth Century England: An Encyclopedia of Drawings and Descriptions from Randle Holme's Original Manuscripts for the Academy of Armory (1688)* (London: British Library, 2000), CD ROM.

17 Dryden's poem available online: http://www.bartleby.com/204/181.html (accessed 15 June 2020).

18 P. Sykas, 'Fustians in Englishmen's Dress, From Cloth to Emblem', *Costume* 43 (2009): 4. Fustian was a coarse textile with a linen warp and a cotton weft.

19 Spufford and Mee, *The Clothing of the Common Sort*, 36. See also M. Spufford, 'The Cost of Apparel in Seventeenth Century England, and the Accuracy of Gregory King', *Economic History Review* 53, no. 4 (2000): 677–705, for further details, especially, 700.

20 M. Spufford, *The Great Re-clothing of Rural England: Petty Chapmen and Their Wares in the Seventeenth Century* (London: Hambledon, 1984), 107–8, for details of the publication, also 118–19, 121.

21 J. Styles, 'Product Innovation in Early Modern London', *Past and Present* 168, no. 1 (2000): 136–7.

22 For example, 'Lett some of the coursest sort for Seamens and ordinary peoples use be strong blew Cloath, and some white for the like ordinary use', see Styles, 'Product Innovation', 138.

23 Styles, 'Product Innovation', 138–40. S. North, *Sweet and Clean? Bodies and Clothes in Early Modern England* (Oxford: Oxford University Press, 2020), 203–5.

24 See B. Lemire, *Dress, Culture and Commerce: The English Clothing Trade before the Factory, 1660–1800* (Basingstoke: Macmillan Press, 1997), 36, who notes that between 1684 and 1694, the stock for export included 4,000 shirts for the Hudson's Bay Company.

25 Spufford, *The Great Re-clothing*, 210, 229–30. Also B. Lemire, 'Developing Consumerism and the Ready-made Clothing Trade in Britain, 1750–1800', *Textile History* 15, no. 1 (1984): 33.

26 Available online: https://archive.org/details/universaletymolo00bailuoft for entries (accessed 15 June 2020).

27 Sykas, 'Fustians', 5, 8.

28 B. Lemire, *Fashion's Favourite: The Cotton Trade and the Consumer in Britain 1660–1800* (Oxford: Oxford University Press, 1991), 90, 93. See also figure 24, for the Hogarth sister's 'Frock-shop' trade card which sold ready-made frock suits, and Sykas, 'Fustians', 4, for a similar example from 1706 also with large 'Plate buttons'.

29 Buck, 'The Countryman's Smock', 18.

30 S. Levitt, 'Cheap Mass-Produced Men's Clothing in the Nineteenth and Early Twentieth Centuries', *Textile History* 22, no. 2 (1991): 179.

31 Sykas, 'Fustians', 6, 8–9.

32 *Stamford Mercury*, 4 December 1746.

33 See Chapter 3, 41–6, for the history of the trade in Abingdon.

34 Lemire, *Dress, Culture and Commerce*, 19–22.

35 M. Ginsberg, 'The Tailoring and Dressmaking Trades, 1700–1850', *Costume* 6, no. 1 (1972): 67.

36 Buck, 'The Countryman's Smock', 18. The Foundling Hospital in London also ordered linen frocks for boys to wear as protection for their clothes when working outside, one purchased for garden work in 1755, see M. Hall, *Smocks* (Princes Risborough: Shire Publications, 1979), 5.

37 Sykas, 'Fustians', 13–14.

38 See J. Milhous, 'Gravelot and Laguerre: Playing Hob on the Eighteenth-Century English Stage', *Theatre Survey* 43, no. 2 (2002), particularly 161, where a 1744 inventory of theatre costume notes 'Hobbs frock'.

39 *Salisbury and Winchester Journal,* 1 June 1752.

40 *Caledonian Mercury*, 17 April 1756; see also *Caledonian Mercury*, 15 May 1756, for another similar reference to a 'linen smock frock'.

41 *Lincolnshire Echo,* 8 April 1932, 4.

42 *The Ipswich Journal,* 4 November 1769; see also a similar advertisement for a man from Hothfield, Kent, in the *Kentish Gazette,* 19 October 1771.

43 https://www.oldbaileyonline.org/ (accessed 15 June 2020).

44 See http://collections.vam.ac.uk/item/O316039/smock-frock-unknown/ (accessed 15 June 2020).

45 de Marly, *Working Dress*, 84, where she equates smocking with prosperity, featuring on farmers' smocks first before that of other workers.

46 See the advertisement for the washing of smock petticoats at a penny each, by John Beattie of Musselburgh Bleachfield, near Edinburgh, *Caledonian Mercury*, 28 March 1772. Various types of similar pleating appeared on fashionable dress during the 1770s, worked by dressmakers in silk, for example, see https://www.kci.or.jp/en/archives/digital_archives/1760s_1770s/KCI_024; https://www.metmuseum.org/art/collection/search/86882 (accessed 15 June 2020).

47 North, *Sweet and Clean?*, 232–3.

48 See https://www.metmuseum.org/art/collection/search/90066483 (accessed 15 June 2020).

49 See https://candicehern.com/regencyworld/morning-dress-may-1812/ for illustration from 1812. See https://books.google.co.uk/books?id=zW9OAAAAMAAJ&pg=RA1-PA162&lpg=RA1-PA162&dq=waggoners+cuffs&source=bl&ots=ss7AkAstAG&sig=ACfU3U0K0jfDhOQpxiYJOnf8U8igFYPbtg&hl=en&sa=X&ved=2ahUKEwiJnZjT6p7pAhWJI8AKHQ7nD2E4ChDoATAFegQIChAB#v=onepage&q=waggoners%20cuffs&f=false, 162, for 1809 (accessed 6 May 2020).

50 See also: http://findit.library.yale.edu/catalog/digcoll:553528; http://findit.library.yale.edu/catalog/digcoll:950635; http://findit.library.yale.edu/catalog/digcoll:976583; http://findit.library.yale.edu/catalog/digcoll:976751 and other similar prints in the Lewis Walpole Library (accessed 15 June 2020).

51 J. Barrell, *The Dark Side of the Landscape: The Rural Poor in English Painting 1730–1840* (Cambridge: Cambridge University Press, 1983), 20–1, 90–1, 99–100, 106, 128.

52 Buck, 'The Countryman's Smock', 19; In Anon., *Working Class Costume: From Sketches of Characters by William Johnstone White*, reprinted with notes, ed. P. Clabburn (1818; London: Costume Society reprint, 1971), various length of smocks are depicted, but they are plain. See plates 3 and 9 for short smocks, 25 and 27 for long examples.

53 Available online: https://digitalcollections.nypl.org/items/510d47dd-e2be-a3d9-e040-e00a18064a99 (accessed 15 June 2020).

54 See S. Smiles, 'Defying Comprehension: Resistance to Uniform Appearance in Depicting the Poor, 1770s to 1830s', *Textile History* 33, no. 1 (2002): 26–8.

55 Sykas, 'Fustians', 11–12, for the influence of jockeys' fustian frocks on fashionable young men's taste in clothing.

56 J. Styles, *The Dress of the People: Everyday Fashion in Eighteenth-Century England* (London: Yale University Press, 2007), 190, 192–3; D. Kuchta, *The Three-Piece Suit and Modern Masculinity, England 1550–1850* (London: University of California Press, 2002), 2, 5, 15. See also A. Buck, 'Clothes in Fact and Fiction, 1825–1865', *Costume* 17, no. 1 (1983): 92–3, for the sombre plain dressing of men during this period when time was too valuable to spend considering fashion; also D. Roche, *The Culture of Clothing: Dress and Fashion in the Ancien Regime* (Cambridge: Cambridge University Press, 1996), 58. This ideal of 'plainness', particularly using homespun textiles, was also developed as an ideology in the mid-eighteenth century United States, modesty, frugality, honesty and industriousness having a symbolic power represented through dress, countering the ready-made and the thoughtless emulation of fashions from the 'corrupt' British regime, see M. Zakim, *Ready-Made Democracy: A History of Men's Dress in the American Republic, 1760–1860* (London: University of Chicago Press, 2003), 2, 12, 18–19.

57 B. Lemire, 'A Question of Trousers: Seafarers, Masculinity and Empire in the Shaping of British Male Dress, c. 1600–1800', *Cultural and Social History* 13, no. 1 (2016): 13. Kuchta, *The*

Three-Piece Suit, 133. See also, C. Breward, 'The Dandy Laid Bare: Embodying Practices and Fashion for Men', in *Fashion Cultures, Theories, Explorations and Analysis*, ed. S. Bruzzi and P. Church Gibson (Abingdon: Routledge, 2000), 224–6, for discussion about Brummell's sartorial practices.

58 Kuchta, *The Three-Piece Suit*, 142, 167, 170.

59 Ibid., 171–8. See also B. Shannon, *The Cut of His Coat, Men, Dress, and Consumer Culture in Britain, 1860–1914* (Athens: Ohio University Press, 2006), who argues that middle-class men also pursued fashion in various forms, remaining consumers of male fashions throughout the nineteenth century.

60 Lemire, 'A Question of Trousers', who argues that cross-cultural and colonial practices, with the rising national status of mariners, gave a pre-eminence to trousers.

61 L. Ugolini, *Men and Menswear, Sartorial Consumption in Britain 1880–1939* (Aldershot: Ashgate Publishing, 2007), 64–7. See also Breward, 'The Dandy Laid Bare', 231, 237, for such dressing in an urban context and the virility associated with it, including boxing and gambling, rather than sexual dissonance and effeminacy, particularly surrounding Oscar Wilde, which dandyism later came to represent.

62 W. Howitt, *The Hall and the Hamlet: Or Scenes and Characters of Country Life*, Vol. 2 (London: Henry Colburn Publisher, 1848), 260–2.

63 *Hull Packet*, 14 July 1848.

64 Smiles, 'Defying Comprehension', 31–2, who notes that George Holyoake records in the 1830s that if workers dressed too well their wages might be reduced, so kept their better clothes for outside work. See C. Breward, *The Hidden Consumer: Masculinities, Fashion and City Life, 1860–1914* (Manchester: Manchester University Press, 1999), 211, who suggests that subtleties in dress details and coding were hidden from the gaze of the uninitiated observer. See also Ugolini, *Men and Menswear*, 69.

65 Breward, *The Hidden Consumer*, 212–13; also V. Richmond, *Clothing the Poor in Nineteenth-Century England* (Cambridge: Cambridge University Press, 2013), 48–50; B. Lemire, *The Business of Everyday Life: Gender, Practice and Social Politics in England, c. 1600–1900* (Manchester: Manchester University Press, 2006), 122, 126–8; C. Payne, '"Murillo-like Rags or Clean Pinafores": Artistic and Social Preferences in the Representation of the Dress of the Rural Poor', *Textile History* 33, no. 1 (2002): 49–50.

66 P. K. Andersson, *Streetlife in Late Victorian London: The Constable and the Crowd* (Basingstoke: Palgrave Macmillan, 2013), 165.

67 H. Medick, 'Plebeian Culture in the Transition to Capitalism', in *Culture, Ideology and Politics: Essays for Eric Hobsbawm*, ed. R. Samuel and G. Stedman Jones (London: Routledge and Kegan Paul, 1982), 92.

68 See C. Breward, 'The Politics of Fashion and the Pleasures of Youth, Young Men and Their Clothes, 1814–1914', in *Artist, Rebel, Dandy, Men of Fashion*, ed. K. Irvin and L. A. Brewer (New Haven: Yale University Press, 2013), 78–9, who suggests that aristocratic urban 'dandies' were doing something similar in opposition to the hegemonic puritanical culture.

69 See P. Johnson, 'Conspicuous Consumption and Working-Class Culture in Late-Victorian and Edwardian Britain', *Transactions of the Royal Historical Society* 38 (1988): 38–40, for the urban context. Also Levitt, 'Cheap Mass-Produced Men's Clothing', 181.

70 Breward, 'The Politics of Fashion', 81–4.

71 Ibid., 86.

72 Levitt, 'Cheap Mass-Produced Men's Clothing', 181.

73 A. Toplis, *The Clothing Trade in Provincial England, 1800–1850* (London: Pickering and Chatto, 2011), 129–30.

74 *Staffordshire Advertiser,* 24 August 1805.

75 See C. Steedman, *An Everyday Life of the English Working Class: Work, Self and Sociability in the Early Nineteenth Century* (Cambridge: Cambridge University Press, 2013), 194–5.

76 Styles, *The Dress*, 199; Toplis, *The Clothing Trade*, chapter 7; Breward, *The Hidden Consumer*, 202; Also Andersson, *Streetlife*, who notes the flamboyant dress of male urban gangs, particularly their colourful neckerchiefs, 162–3.

77 Lemire, *The Business*, 134.

78 *Gloucester Journal*, 12 October 1795.

79 *Derby Mercury*, 4 February 1819.

80 B. Marshall, *Smocks and Smocking* (Sherborne: Alphabooks, 1980), 42, 59.

81 C. Blackman, 'Colouring the Claddagh: A Distorted View?', *Costume* 48, no. 2 (2014): 232; Richmond, *Clothing the Poor*, 299; also Andersson, *Streetlife*, 202–3, for the disregard and indifference to respectable norms such as the use of bad language.

82 Blackman, 'Colouring the Claddagh', 232.

83 Buck, 'The Countryman's Smock', 19, 22, 32. She also notes that the sun bonnet, worn by rural working women, developed decorative versions like the smock, but was linked to a fashionable form, see Buck, 'Clothes in Fact and Fiction', 103.

84 L. Child, *The Little Girl's Own Book* (Edinburgh: Robert Martin, 1847), 212.

85 Buck, 'Clothes in Fact and Fiction', 95. See also E. Grey, *Cottage Life in a Hertfordshire Village* (St Albans: Fisher, Knight, n.d. [1935]), 31, who notes that 'some' smocks, especially those for best, were elaborately worked. See also Richmond, *Clothing the Poor*, 298, who questions how the poor felt about their possessions when cheap goods proliferated.

86 Ugolini, *Men and Menswear*, 30.

87 Hall, *Smocks*, 14.

88 Buck, 'The Countryman's Smock', 29–33. See also Marshall, *Smocks and Smocking*, 25–7. See Museum of English Rural Life, Reading, accession number 91/2 for an example of this type of smock.

89 I. E. Anthony, *The Countrymen's Smocks in the Welsh Folk Museum*, reprint from AMGUEDDFA, *Bulletin of the National Museum of Wales* 18 (Winter 1974): 6–7.

90 Richmond, *Clothing the Poor*, 94.

91 See also P. Hudson, 'Industry, Working Lives, Nation and Empire, Viewed through Some Key Welsh Woollen Objects', in *History Matters: History after Hobsbawm; Writing the Past in the Twenty-first Century,* ed. J. Arnold and M. Hilton (Oxford: Oxford University Press, 2017), especially 182–3, for a consideration of a garment's meaning in the context of the life of its wearer.

92 See J. Craik, *The Face of Fashion: Cultural Studies in Fashion* (London: Routledge, 1994), 179–80, who also includes body decoration such as tattoos.

93 Anthony, *The Countrymen's Smocks*, 4.

94 C. Rose, *Making, Selling and Wearing Boys' Clothes in Late-Victorian England* (Abingdon: Routledge, 2016), 76. In 1837, a school was proposed in Ampthill, Bedfordshire, to teach girls, aged from 6 years, how to smock, operating from 2 to 5 twice a week, girls to be recommended by committee members for admission, so under elite control, paying a penny a week which they would get back in clothing at the end of the year, presumably as smocks. There is no evidence that it became operational. See Bedfordshire and Luton Archives and Records Service, Letters of the May and Strange Families, Z699/161.

95 R. Parker, *The Subversive Stitch, Embroidery and the Making of the Feminine* (London: Women's Press, 1996), 154 and 154–73, for middle-class attitudes to embroidery and its role in the creation of femininity and domestic 'comfort'.

96 Parker, *The Subversive Stitch*, 174–5.

97 Rose, *Making*, 76.

98 For the 'inexperienced', *The Workwoman's Guide* of 1838, describes how to make a round frock 'at home', thus cheaper than buying one. Details for a 'waggoner's smock frock', includes layouts for cutting pieces and a full embroidery design, showing how the needlework should fit onto the smock. The *Guide* advises that their price at clothing warehouses, between 9 and 18 shillings, depended 'on the quantity and quality of the work in them'. Anon., By a Lady, *The Workwoman's Guide, Containing Instructions to the Inexperienced…* (1838; London: Simpkin, Marshall, and Co., 1840), 137, available online: https://archive.org/details/workwomansguide00workgoog/page/n8 (accessed 15 June 2020).

99 Marshall, *Smocks and Smocking*, 10.

100 Blackman, 'Colouring the Claddagh', 230.

101 R. Worth, 'Rural Labouring Dress, 1850–1900: Some Problems of Representation', *Fashion Theory, The Journal of Dress, Body & Culture* 3, no. 3 (1999): 336–7, 339.

102 Lincolnshire Museums, Shepherd's Smock, LCNLL: 1973/5212, a plain cream linen man's smock with no smocking or embroidery. His father, who had worn it for some time, handed down the smock to Mr Tayton, a 'shepherd boy'. A similar white embroidered smock reflected the wearer's status as the chief shepherd at Lewes sheep fair, see letter from H. Lumley Ellis, *Country Life*, 5 June 1942, 1094–5.

103 See Chapters 3 and 4.

104 Johnson, 'Conspicuous Consumption', 29.

105 Richmond, *Clothing the Poor*, 99–101, 299.

106 M. Jones, 'The Vanished Smock-Frock', *Country Life,* 11 April 1957, 720, where she relates it to patterns found on canal dress and domestic decoration.

107 See M. Howell, *The Handbook of Dress-Making; including correct rules for the pursuit of the above art, and concisely illustrating the Mode of Fitting at Sight* (London: Simpkin, Marshall and Co., 1845), 46, where she notes that it was a trimming 'worn as a stomacher in the front of silk or satin dresses, or as an embellishment to the tops and cuffs of full sleeves'. It was also a technique noted in the *Workwoman's Guide*, 35, for baby clothes. See https://www.kci.or.jp/en/archives/digital_archives/1820s_1840s/KCI_074; https://collections.mfa.org/objects/578684; https://collections.mfa.org/objects/128004 (accessed 16 June 2020), for some surviving examples.

108 Buck, 'The Countryman's Smock', 32.

3 Making

1. For example, see A. Twigger Holroyd, *Folk Fashion* (London: I. B. Tauris, 2017), 143.
2. R. Kenny, J. McMillan and M. Myrone, *British Folk Art* (London: Tate Publishing, 2014), 132, where it is noted that quilts and samplers were more usually middle-class work. See also V. Richmond, *Clothing the Poor in Nineteenth-Century England* (Cambridge: Cambridge University Press, 2013), especially chapter 4, where she mentions the long-held assumption that working-class women were expected to make underwear but not outer clothing for men, 94.
3. *Bedfordshire Times and Independent,* 12 August 1932, 8.
4. J. Thirsk, 'Popular Consumption and the Mass Market in the Sixteenth to Eighteenth Centuries', *Material History Bulletin* 31 (Spring 1990): 53–4.
5. J. Styles, *The Dress of the People: Everyday Fashion in Eighteenth-Century England* (London: Yale University Press, 2007), 28, 165.
6. For example, see, Fisk's Clothing Warehouse, Oxford, 41 above.
7. M. Ginsberg, 'The Tailoring and Dressmaking Trade, 1700–1850', *Costume* 6, no. 1 (1972): 64.
8. B. Lemire, 'Developing Consumerism and the Ready-made Clothing Trade in Britain, 1750–1800', *Textile History* 15, no. 1 (1984): 35–41, in particular. Also B. Lemire, *Fashion's Favourite: The Cotton Trade and the Consumer in Britain 1660–1800* (Oxford: Oxford University Press, 1991), 191–3, for the London trade in ready-made shirts. See S. North, *Sweet and Clean? Bodies and Clothes in Early Modern England* (Oxford: Oxford University Press, 2020), 201, for examples of sixteenth-century shirts.
9. For example, Lemire, *Fashion's Favourite,* 184–5, and chapter 1; B. Lemire, *Dress, Culture and Commerce: The English Clothing Trade before the Factory, 1660–1800* (Basingstoke: Macmillan Press, 1997); B. Lemire, '"In the Hands of Work Women". English Markets, Cheap Clothing and Female Labour, 1650–1800', *Costume* 33 (1999): 23–7, especially.
10. Lemire, *Dress, Culture and Commerce,* 56.
11. In 1812, 1,200 smock frocks were advertised for sale alongside 1,100 coats and jackets, 470 waistcoats and other items, the stock of a retiring slop seller see the *Public Ledger and Daily Advertiser*, 8 December 1812. See also 3,390 linen frocks in a navy slop sale, *Public Ledger and Daily Advertiser*, 20 September 1814. 540 'check shirts and frocks' were offered for auction for the attention of Greenland and Baltic captains in 1803, see *Hull Packet*, 15 February 1803. See A. Toplis, *The Clothing Trade in Provincial England, 1800–1850* (London: Pickering and Chatto, 2011), 152–3, and S. Chapman, 'The "Revolution" in the Manufacture of Ready-made Clothing 1840–60', *London Journal* 29, no. 1 (2004): 45.
12. See M. Charpy, 'Adjustments, Bodies and Clothing in Standard Industrial Sizes during the 19th Century', *Modes Pratiques, Journal of Clothes and Fashion History*, Special Issue in English (January 2018): 185–6, for an interesting discussion about fit in the French ready-made context.
13. S. Chapman, 'The Innovating Entrepreneurs in the British Ready-made Clothing Industry', *Textile History* 24, no. 1 (1993): 6–7, where smocks are classified as a specialist section of standardized clothing, bought in quantity by farmers from manufacturers such as Gurteen; A. Godley, 'Introduction. The Development of the Clothing Industry: Technology

and Fashion', *Textile History* 28, no. 1 (1997): 4; See also C. Rose, *Making, Selling and Wearing Boys' Clothes in Late-Victorian England* (Abingdon: Routledge, 2016), who found new clothing manufacturing firms by examining, for example, the Board of Trade Registrations. These firms were otherwise obscured, if one was just investigating retailers, 57–9, 108, 211, a similar consideration undertaken in this research.

14 A. Howkins, *Reshaping Rural England: A Social History 1850–1925* (London: HarperCollins Academic, 1991), 7–14. See also N. Verdon, *Working the Land: A History of the Farmworker in England from 1850 to the Present Day* (London: Palgrave Macmillan, 2017), 2, who notes that this equates to one in four men.

15 This was a pattern which also continued in urban areas, for example, Leeds, see A. Kershen, *Uniting the Tailors: Trade Unionism amongst the Tailoring Workers of London and Leeds, 1870–1939* (Ilford: Frank Cass, 1995), 26. P. Crouch, 'Entrepreneurs, Manufactories and Small Industrial Communities, 1850–1914' (PhD thesis, University of Leicester, 2010), 12, notes that Gurteen did not try to compete with northern woollen and cotton industries but specialized in different textiles and clothing, exploiting gaps in the market.

16 S. Levitt, 'Bristol Clothing Trades and Exports in the Georgian Period', in *Per Una Storia della Moda Pronta, Problemi e Ricerche* (Milan: Pitt Immagine, 1990): 37–40. Ransford & Co. were wholesale clothiers, shirt and frock manufacturers in Webster & Co.'s *Directory of Bristol and Glamorganshire*, 1865, suggesting that the skills needed for making both garments were transferable between the two. My thanks to Sarah Thursfield for pointing this out.

17 *Nottingham Review and General Advertiser for the Midland Counties,* 21 January 1842.

18 *Stamford Mercury,* 11 May 1838. See also William Slater and John Parkins, linen weavers and smock frock manufacturers in Grantham, who dissolved their partnership in 1832, but Slater carried on the business afterwards, *Stamford Mercury,* 1 June 1832.

19 *Stamford Mercury*, 26 April 1844.

20 *Salisbury and Winchester Journal*, 11 May 1835. 'Russia' was 'Russia duck', a linen. By the nineteenth century, the raw material for the flax and hemp industries was often imported from Russia rather than grown locally, the resulting product a popular choice for smock frocks, see R. Worth, *Dress and Textiles (Discover Dorset)* (Wimborne: Dovecote Press, 2002), 21.

21 Lemire, *Dress, Culture and Commerce*, 69, for similar situation in the quilted petticoat trade, a possible precursor to the smock trade.

22 *Worcester Journal,* 13 March 1858.

23 Advertisement, Lascelles & Co. *Directory of Worcester and Neighbourhood*, 1851.

24 *Commission on Employment of Children, Young Persons and Women in Agriculture* (1867), second report of the commissioners, with appendix part 1, Parliamentary Papers, 4202-1, vol. 13, 299. A farmer in Hanley Castle, Mr Drinkwater, complained that he found it difficult to get female fieldworkers as most were employed in gloving or slop work. See ibid., 263.

25 Examples of female smock makers working at home include: Ann Brown, aged 82, at Plumtree, made smock frocks, see *Nottingham Review and General Advertiser for the Midland Counties*, 27 March 1829; Ellen Brearey alias Moore and her grandmother made smocks for Michael Charlton of the Thursday Market, York, *Yorkshire Gazette*, 24 December 1831; Mrs Butterfield in Doncaster earned four shillings a week making smock frocks, see *Hampshire Advertiser*, 6 December 1834; Mary Bufton made an embroidered smock thought to

have been used as a sample to show customers in Hereford in around 1835. See Toplis, *The Clothing Trade*, 140, for Bufton's wedding dress of 1834. Women were often asked to identify smocks they had made in theft cases, for example, the case of Thomas Hartland, *Hereford Times,* 7 January 1837; Mr Wain, a draper of Tamworth, sold smock frocks made by Maria Knight for him, including blue ones, identified in a court case, *Staffordshire Advertiser,* 25 March 1837; Leah Cupper, Butterley, Shropshire, maker of smock frocks, *Hereford Times,* 30 March 1839; Anne Townsend, Elton, near Gloucester, who also ran the Traveller's Rest pub, *Gloucestershire Chronicle,* 22 August 1846; Maria Ann Dobbs alias White, smock maker, worked all night at it too, sometimes without a fire, to make one smock per day for which she got 4 or 6 pence, *Oxford Chronicle and Reading Gazette,* 6 November 1847; Sarah Mansell made them for clothier John Woodall in Shrewsbury, *Shrewsbury Chronicle*, 4 July 1851; Hannah Hall of Sheffield made smock frocks all her life, dying at the age of 68, see *Northampton Mercury*, 17 February 1855; Mary Whadley, who made smock frocks for two clothiers, Beard and Dike, in Cheltenham, see *Morning Chronicle,* 10 April 1857 and *Cheltenham Chronicle*, 7 April 1857; Esther Moreton, in Woolhope, Herefordshire, combined smock making with working in the fields, *Hereford Journal,* 15 July 1857; Jane Judge and Rachael Ford were smock frock makers in Bishopstone, near Swindon, in 1861 (census) and Eliza King in Bishops Cannings, Wiltshire, in 1871 (census); Mrs Shaw in Oxfordshire was still smocking in 1912, earning a few shillings a year, see B. Seebohm Rowntree and M. Kendall, *How the Labourer Lives: A Study of the Rural Labour Problem* (London: Thomas Nelson and Sons, 1913), 43.

26 *Hereford Times*, 2 August 1845; Mrs Philpotts was able to identify her husband's stolen smock as she had made it, see *Hereford Times,* 10 July 1847.

27 MERL Object number 59/25, http://www.reading.ac.uk/adlib/Details/collect/4065 (accessed 16 June 2020). See also *Burnley Express*, 26 September 1903, 3, where an article suggests that seventy years previously, women travelled to customer's houses to make up smock frocks for them, working in the same way as itinerant tailors.

28 Three smocks can be linked to a small area of Worcestershire with the same design of leaves and flowers, see M. Hall, *Smocks* (Princes Risborough: Shire Publications, 1979), 15–16, and Worcestershire County Museum, smock collection, 1965/226 and 1966/281, also 1965/320 and 1966/621. There seems to be no standard garment with construction and finishing completed in many different ways.

29 'The Exeter Bible and Domestic Mission', *Exeter and Plymouth Gazette,* 9 November 1872.

30 Toplis, *The Clothing Trade*, 98, 100. For example, on 25 November 1831, she was paid a shilling for making James Price's frock, see Worcestershire Record Office, Castlemorton Overseers' Accounts, 1831–6, 9581/20.

31 Chapman, 'The "Revolution"', 47–9.

32 Ibid., 49

33 A. Godley, 'Comparative Labour Productivity in the British and American Clothing Industries 1850–1950', *Textile History* 28, no. 1 (1997): 72.

34 P. Sharpe, '"Cheapness and Economy": Manufacturing and Retailing Ready-made Clothing in London and Essex 1830–50', *Textile History* 26, no. 2 (1995): 203–4, and figure 1, showing the selling of 'Haverhill slops', which were probably smocks.

35 The ready-made smock appeared on workhouse tenders for garments during the 1830s until the 1870s, for example: Southam Union wanted boys' smocks in three sizes, see *Leamington Spa Courier*, 8 September 1838, continuing until 1870, *Leamington Spa Courier,*

17 September 1870; Warwick Union needed Russia duck smock frocks in different sizes, see *Leamington Spa Courier*, 15 December 1838; as did Stratford-upon-Avon Union, see *Leamington Spa Courier*, 19 August 1837; Dore Union wanted 'strong' smock frocks for men, youths and boys, see *Hereford Times*, 8 March 1856.

36 K. Honeyman, *Well-suited: A History of the Leeds Clothing Industry, 1850–1990* (Oxford: Oxford University Press, 2000), 10–11; see also P. Sharpe, *Adapting to Capitalism: Working Women in the English Economy, 1700–1850* (Basingstoke: Macmillan Press, 2000), 65–7.

37 Chapman, 'The Innovating Entrepreneurs', 22–3. Chapman, 'The "Revolution"', 44–5.

38 Chapman, 'The "Revolution"', 47.

39 See, for example, J. Chartres, 'Rural Industry and Manufacturing', in *The Agrarian History of England and Wales, VII, (part II), 1850–1914*, ed. E. J. T. Collins (Cambridge: Cambridge University Press, 2000), 1115–23, who discusses rural outworking for straw plaiting, gloving, lace and later ready-made clothing but not the smock trade.

40 *The National Gazetteer of Great Britain and Ireland* (1868); the *Victoria County History for Berkshire* also noted that the spinning and weaving of flax and hemp flourished in the town during the eighteenth century, continuing as the manufacture of sacking into the 1830s, see online https://www.british-history.ac.uk/vch/berks/vol4/pp430-451#anchorn246 (accessed 16 June 2020).

41 G. Holman, *Made in East Anglia: A History of the Region's Textile and Menswear Industries* (Pasold Resource, no. 1, 2015), 43, http://www.pasold.co.uk/resource-page.

42 *Oxford Journal*, 27 September 1788.

43 *Oxford Journal*, 25 May 1816.

44 Goods including a smock frock were obtained by false pretences from Hyde & Son, drapers, see *Reading Mercury*, 6 April 1829.

45 K. S. Woods, *The Rural Industries Round Oxford: A Survey* (Oxford: Oxford University Press, 1921), 149.

46 *Robson's Commercial Directory of Berkshire* (London: William Robson, 1840); *Pigot and Co.'s National and Commercial Directory and Topography … for Berkshire* (London: James Pigot, 1844); The Oxford contributors to the Great Exhibition included, 'Class 20, No. 111, Harris and Tomkins, Abingdon, smock frocks – honourable mention'.

47 *Reading Mercury*, 8 May 1847. See also Berkshire Lent Assizes, where Sarah Pocock was convicted of stealing a white duck smock frock from J. Hyde, Reading, whom she used to work for, *Reading Mercury*, 6 March 1847.

48 Honeyman, *Well-suited*, 45.

49 *Berkshire Chronicle*, 24 April 1869, and R. Wilson, 'Trade, Industry and Domestic Activity at the Old Clothing Factory Site, Abingdon', *Oxoniensia* 54 (1989): 282–3.

50 *Reading Mercury*, 21 March 1857. After 'forty years' in the 'Retail Woollen and Ready Made Clothes Business', Hyde and Son sold it on to Mr Henry Baker, their partner since 1854, and Messrs. Badcock and Badcock of Abingdon. Baker had been their retail manager since 1848. *Berkshire Chronicle*, 22 April 1854.

51 Wilson, 'Trade, Industry and Domestic Activity', 282–3.

52 Holman, *Made in East Anglia*, 7.

53 See also ibid., 24.

54 Similarly, Nicoll's had 1,200 outworkers in 1850, see Godley 'Introduction', 6. Hyam's at the same date claimed to employ 8,000, with 30,000 dependent on their business, so Hyde's was still substantially smaller, see Sharpe, 'Cheapness', 207. 'Putting out' work was common practice by this date, especially with the collapse of the Grand National Trades Union after 1834, see Ginsberg, 'Tailoring', 66.

55 A 'tailoress' made male outer wear, see Sharpe, 'Cheapness', 208. She notes a similar increase in tailoresses in Colchester during the 1840s as Hyam's expanded, see Sharpe, *Adapting to Capitalism*, some working at home and some in 'proto-factories', 66–7.

56 In 1850, two men, a 'smock frock cutter' and a 'cutter' were accused of stealing cloth from this room, see *Berkshire Chronicle,* 20 July 1850; *Reading Mercury,* 20 July 1850.

57 Kershen, *Uniting the Tailors*, 12. See also an advertisement for a situation in Newark, where a young man had been in charge of a wholesale and retail business in clothing and smock frocks and had 'a thorough knowledge of cutting every description of Frocks', *Stamford Mercury,* 4 July 1834. Surviving short smocks were made up from fabric widths, reducing the amount of cutting out required. See 85 for an illustration of a short smock.

58 See K. Honeyman, 'Gender Divisions and Industrial Divide: The Case of the Leeds Clothing Trade, 1850–1970', *Textile History* 28, no.1 (1997): 47–8, and despite the fact that women had historically cut linen to make garments – my thanks to Sarah Thursfield for drawing my attention to this.

59 1861 Census, Abingdon, Parish of St Helen, and 'The Origin of an Industry', 3, Cuttings and News Album of J. H. Viner, 1891–1945, Abingdon Museum, accession number 1980.191.623.

60 Godley, 'Introduction', 6. See also Woods, *The Rural Industries,* 150, who notes the difficulty of maintaining standards with work being done from home.

61 *Worcester Journal,* 23 July 1846; see also *Wiltshire Independent,* 15 December 1870, for a description of a 'middle sized' one.

62 Holman, *Made in East Anglia,* 121. See the label attached to the hem of a smock sold by Henry Hyde of Polluxhill, tailor, draper and grocer, with a length of seventeen nails, M. Nichols, *Smocks in Luton Museum* (Luton: Borough of Luton Museum and Art Gallery, 1980), no. 12, illustrated. For the development of sizing during the eighteenth century see J. Styles, 'Product Innovation in Early Modern London', *Past and Present* 168, no. 1 (2000): 161–2.

63 A bundle of Hyde's unmade smock frocks was stolen from a cart in Abingdon, presumably on their way to outworkers in surrounding areas, Borough Court, *Reading Mercury*, 15 November 1862.

64 Wilson, 'Trade, Industry and Domestic Activity', 283. 'The Origin of an Industry', Abingdon Museum, accession number 1980.191.623.

65 See online: https://www.abingdon.gov.uk/history/people/john-creemer-clarke (accessed 16 June 2020), for further details about Clarke's role. Holman, *Made in East Anglia*, 4, 146. Those used to handling textiles were able to retrain as machinists. By 1866, Gurteen's were regularly buying repair supplies for Singer sewing machines.

66 Holman, *Made in East Anglia*, 5, which continued into the twentieth century, see ibid, 69.

67 Holman, *Made in East Anglia,* 134.

68 *Jackson's Oxford Journal*, 12 March 1864. Hyam had 300 hands in their Colchester factory by 1907, when it was thought to be 'the largest wholesale firm dealing exclusively in ready-made clothing', see Sharpe, 'Cheapness', 209–11.

69 Holman, *Made in East Anglia*, 42–3, 122.

70 *Jackson's Oxford Journal*, 22 July 1871.

71 Holman, *Made in East Anglia*, 152.

72 *Oxford Journal*, 24 August 1867. See also Holman, *Made in East Anglia*, 51, for George Courtauld, another similar example.

73 K. Snell, *Annals of the Labouring Poor: Social Change and Agrarian England, 1660–1900* (Cambridge: Cambridge University Press, 1987), chapter 1, especially 59.

74 *Commission* (1867), vol. 13, 406.

75 *Commission* (1867), vol. 13, 84, 353–4. See also the availability of fieldwork compared to variable slopping jobs in Wantage, 395.

76 *Commission* (1867), vol. 13, 80, 83, 350, 374, 397. Witney is also described as a place where female occupations included gloving and slopping, see 364.

77 *Oxford Journal*, 22 June 1872. Figures for ready-made manufacturers of army clothing in France suggest that 2,000 workers would produce around 60,000 pieces a year, see Charpy, 'Adjustments', 200. M. Bright Rix, *Boars Hill, Oxford* (Oxford: Hall the Printer, 1943), 21. Smock workers were still noted as living in Cowley St John, Oxford, in the 1911 census. Outworkers in Shippon, very close to Abingdon, were making 'engineer's slops' for Hyde and Clarke in 1866, perhaps an off-shoot of the original smock trade, see *Reading Mercury*, 20 January 1866.

78 'The Origin of an Industry', 3, Abingdon Museum, accession number 1980.191.623.

79 Hyde and Salkeld, round frock and clothes manufacturers, Robson's *Directory* (1839), Hyde and Leete, clothes dealer and manufacturer (and frock), Hunt's *Oxford Directory* (1846). George Frankling was his partner in the 1851 census and Thomas Bays, previously his shop manager, in 1856, see *Jackson's Oxford Journal*, 25 October 1856.

80 Hyde sold the business to his manager John Seary in 1869, whose name appears on the photograph, available online: http://pictureoxon.com/frontend.php?keywords=Ref_No_increment;EQUALS;POX0561796&pos=1&action=zoom&id=1183089 (accessed 16 June 2020), and *Jackson's Oxford Journal*, 17 April 1869.

81 1851 Census – Thomas Hyde lived in Summertown. By 1871, the employment figure, with mechanization, had fallen to '160 hands'.

82 Hall, *Smocks*, 19–20. Also A. Farwell, 'A Gathering of Smocks', *The Countryman* 70, no. 1 (1968): 83. This was also the same for the women of nearby Wheatley, see C. Bloxham, 'Oxfordshire Smocks', pamphlet, Oxfordshire Museums.

83 See advertisement, *Mathieson's Oxford Directory* (Oxford: Wheeler and Day, 1867) and *Jackson's Oxford Journal*, 16 October 1869. Grover and Baker sewing machines were used in the Abingdon factory too.

84 *Bridport News*, 14 March 1868.

85 *Hertford Mercury and Reformer*, 7 March 1840, and see 3–5 above for a court case involving Hertfordshire railway frocks.

86 *Post Office London Directory, 1841, Part 1: Street, Commercial, & Trades Directories* (London: Kelly's Directories, 1841), 128, 321. See Lemire, *Fashion's Favourite*, 72–3, for history of the clothes trade in Houndsditch.

87 For more information about Samuel Favell and his elite links in the City of London see http://benbeddome.blogspot.com/2017/07/samuel-favell-etc.html and see also https://www.oldbaileyonline.org for cases relating to Favell and Bousfield. (accessed 16 June 2020).

88 Samuel Favell died in 1830. John, Samuel's son, a 'woollen factor', appears to have changed his name from Favell to French during the 1840s and was not part of the business.

89 For example, see *Sydney Morning Herald*, 12 August 1843. The firm of Moses followed a similar business model, see Chapman, 'The Innovating Entrepreneurs', 16; Chapman, 'The "Revolution"', 45–7, 52.

90 Birmingham Record Office, Letter from John Muston, Hobart, to Messrs. Favell and Bousfield, London, 3 October 1835, MS 254/2/12. In the report about a fire at their factory in 1852, Bousfield were described as 'wholesale clothiers and exporters', *Kentish Gazette*, 4 February 1851.

91 *Geelong Advertiser*, 29 April 1851. Cases of their 'slops' were also variously advertised for sale across different Australian newspapers, including in Adelaide, Melbourne and Hobart, during the 1850s and 1860s. See, for instance, *Adelaide Times*, 6 August 1853, for a consignment comprising a variety of trousers.

92 S. Levitt, 'Cheap Mass-Produced Men's Clothing in the Nineteenth and Early Twentieth Centuries', *Textile History* 22, no. 2 (1991): 184.

93 See *The London Gazette*, 9 September 1851, 2302, and 24 November 1863, 6013.

94 'Grinding the Poor', *Lloyds Weekly London Newspaper*, 24 September 1843, 1. See also criticism by H. Mayhew and J. Binny, *The Criminal Prisons of London and Scenes of Prison Life* (1862; London: Frank Cass, 1968), 194–5, 476. Ironically, prisoners may have been making slops for Australian convicts. See also Sharpe, *Adapting to Capitalism*, 67, for Mayhew's comments about middlemen and the sub-contraction of piece work for women.

95 Worcestershire Record Office, Worcestershire Quarter Sessions Order Book, volume 10, 211b-212, 'List of prices for goods manufactured in Worcester County Prison', 1818. Similar clothing was auctioned off in 1820, see 321a, 324a.

96 *The Era*, 2 February 1851, *Lloyd's Weekly Newspaper*, 2 February 1851, *Jackson's Oxford Journal*, 1 February 1851. The size of the firm was nothing new, a London slopseller in the late eighteenth century calculating that he employed 1,000–1,200 workers each week, see Lemire, *Dress, Culture and Commerce*, 70–1.

97 *The Courier*, 24 June 1842.

98 *Reading Mercury*, 12 February 1848. It is not clear who placed the advertisement, whether it was Bousfield or somebody else.

99 *Billings Directory and Gazetteer of the Counties of Berkshire and Oxfordshire* (Birmingham: Billings, 1854); *Slater's Directory of Berkshire* (1852). In 1843, Robert Poulton was an 'extensive' manufacturer of smocks in the Market Place, Reading, *Berkshire Chronicle*, 6 May 1843.

100 *Macaulay's Reading Directory* (1865).

101 *Jackson's Oxford Journal*, 20 December 1856.

102 *Reading Mercury*, 11 November 1865, Borough Magistrates Court, Mary Wicks, a widow, and similarly Sarah Allwood/Horwood, a 'sempstress', both of whom made up Bousfield smocks before illegally pawning them, see *Reading Mercury*, 24 January 1846 for Horwood.

103 *The Hobarton Mercury*, 12 November 1855, and *The Argus*, 29 October 1855. Huge quantities of clothing were required for convicts, the contracts for which the army subcontracted to the London slop trade. Garments required during the 1850s included smocks, see L. Young, 'The Experience of Convictism: Five Pieces of Convict Clothing from Western Australia', *Costume* 22 (1988): 78–9. It seems likely that Bousfield was involved in this trade.

104 For example, Kirkcaldy in Fife was a centre of linen manufacturing, the blue variety sent to England for smock frocks, see *Fife Free Press, & Kirkcaldy Guardian*, 22 August 1903, 5.

105 *Berkshire Chronicle*, 9 August 1862.

106 Holman, *Made in East Anglia*, 43. See also Chartres 'Rural Industry', 1104, who notes the expectation of cheap labour and flexibility with rural workers.

107 Sharpe, 'Cheapness', 211. See also Ginsberg, 'The Tailoring', 68, for criticism of Nicoll and Moses; and see Chapman, 'The "Revolution"', 50, for Nicoll and Hyam.

108 Sharpe, 'Cheapness', 211.

109 See A. Toplis, 'The Manufacture and Provision of Rural Garments, 1800–1850: A Case Study of Herefordshire and Worcestershire', *Textile History* 40, no. 1 (2009): 159–60, and 65 above for further details about this advertising.

110 *Lloyds Weekly*, 21 April 1861. These were an early sewing machine which apparently looked like large fretsaws worked by treadles and could sew twenty stitches a minute, see http://www.harmer.org/norfolk2.pdf. See also https://www.fiddlebase.com/british-machines/w-f-thomas-co/ (accessed 16 June 2020).

111 See A. Buck, 'The Countryman's Smock', *Folk Life* 1 (1963): 23, who notes a smock in Norwich Museum with machine-stitched embroidery.

112 *Maidstone Telegraph,* 16 November 1861. Fifty-one Axe Brand machine-hands who had 'kept time' were rewarded with a trip to Crystal Palace by train, see *Chatham News*, 11 July 1863. The Axe Brand Sewing Factory continued into the twentieth century with a new owner.

113 *Wellington Journal*, 15 June 1861.

114 *Leeds Times*, 29 November 1851.

115 R. Schorman, *Selling Style: Clothing and Social Change at the Turn of the Century* (Philadelphia: University of Pennsylvania Press, 2003), 19, 37, and 134–8.

116 *The Sydney Morning Herald*, 7 November 1861.

117 Styles, 'Product Innovation', 157–8. See https://books.google.co.uk/books?id=4JsDAAAAQ AAJ&pg=PA35&dq=&redir_esc=y#v=onepage&q&f=false for a copy of the act (accessed 5 October 2020).

118 *Nelson Examiner and New Zealand Chronicle*, 9 May 1863, 5.

119 Styles, 'Product Innovation', 148–58, for eighteenth-century patent medicine sellers using similar strategies. Rose, *Making*, 97–9, notes that permanent labels tended to be from clothing retailers and that it was rare for manufacturers to label their clothing, although

they may have more often used card tickets which were removed when the garment was worn and so have been lost, as with the Bousfield 'ticket'.

120 For example, *Southern Reporter*, a newspaper covering the Scottish border region, 12 March 1868.

121 Advertisement, circa 1885, British Library, Evan.5828, available online: https://www.bl.uk/catalogues/evanion/Record.aspx?EvanID=024-000003780&ImageIndex=0 (accessed 16 June 2020). The company had been in existence since at least the 1840s as a cabinet and carpet warehouse, adding drapery in the 1850s. It disappeared after 1909.

122 *Man of Ross, and General Advertiser*, 22 March 1866; *Journal of Mental Science*, April 1899, v.

123 Bousfield does not appear in Cassell's *Directory* of 1868 but, as 'slopsellers', had a tender accepted for the East London Union in 1867, although it is not clear for what type of clothing, see *London City Press*, 21 December 1867. They were listed in the post office directories of the 1880s as clothiers. The firm were still trading in 1898 and 1901 from 126 Houndsditch, see bill from J. R. Bousfield & Co., author's collection. They disappear from the Australian press after 1869 although Axe Brand 'mole' trousers continue to crop up in advertisements into the 1880s, see for example, Hall & McLean advertisement, *The South Australian Advertiser*, 12 May 1880.

124 Rose, *Making*, 109.

125 Schorman, *Selling Style*, 142–3.

126 Rose, *Making*, 213–14, although, as Rose points out, this makes it very difficult to trace manufacturers, a lack of labelling making mass-produced clothes overlooked and unidentifiable in surviving collections or contemporary retailers' catalogues.

127 *The Ipswich Journal*, 15 April 1882, West Suffolk Chamber of Agriculture meeting.

128 Noted in the firm's earliest account book, see N. Evans, *The East Anglian Linen Industry: Rural Industry and Local Economy 1500–1850* (Aldershot: Gower Publishing, 1985), 159.

129 Holman, *Made in East Anglia*, 121–2; smock frocks, drabbet and hemp were stolen from their warehouse in 1844, see *The Ipswich Journal*, 7 December 1844. S. Payne, *The Gurteens of Haverhill: Two Hundred Years of Suffolk Textiles* (Cambridge: Woodhead-Faulkner, 1984), 22. The company was founded in 1784, see Crouch, 'Entrepreneurs', 37 and 82.

130 Hyam started to manufacture clothing himself in the late 1830s and 1840s. See P. Sharpe, 'De-industrialization and Re-industrialization: Women's Employment and the Changing Character of Colchester 1700–1850', *Urban History* 21, no. 1 (1994): 93–5, where the handbill is also illustrated.

131 Crouch, 'Entrepreneurs', 83, 90; Holman, *Made in East Anglia*, 167; Mr Neobard, draper and hosier of Puckeridge, Hertfordshire, had stock which included 'capital Haverill [sic] twill smock-frocks' along with other ready-made clothes, *Hertford Mercury and Reformer*, 29 August 1846. At this date, they may not have been from Gurteen's. Their men's cord trousers were advertised in the *Essex Newsman*, 21 May 1881.

132 Holman, *Made in East Anglia*, 125.

133 M. Brown, 'Somerset Smocks', reprint from *Notes & Queries for Somerset & Dorset*, 30, part 305 (March 1977): 4.

134 Crouch, 'Entrepreneurs', 82.

135 *Chelmsford Chronicle*, 14 September 1888.

136 Crouch, 'Entrepreneurs', 37–8.

137 *Morning Chronicle*, 18 October 1850. Complaints about the low wages paid to weavers also surfaced in 1845, as Gurteen reduced wages while manufacturing supposedly prospered, see letter to the editor, 'Low Wages at Haverhill', *Bury and Norwich Post*, 19 February 1845.

138 Richmond, *Clothing the Poor*, 63.

139 Buck, 'The Countryman's Smock', 23. See also Hall, *Smocks*, 20, for a similar process in Sussex. See J. Styles, 'Design for Large-Scale Production in Eighteenth-Century Britain', *Oxford Art Journal* 11, no. 2 (1988): 15, for a discussion about the process of producing standardized consumer products in the eighteenth century using outworkers. The smock exhibited at the Great Exhibition in 1851 by Abingdon firm Harris and Tomkins was apparently designed by their foreman, Thomas Watson, and worked up by Esther Stimpson in the nearby village of Radley, see *Jackson's Oxford Journal*, 18 October 1851.

140 N. Tarrant, *Smocks in the Buckinghamshire County Museum* (Aylesbury: Buckinghamshire County Council, 1976), 2, and see 56 above for the use of blocks. Women might use chalk lines to help keep gathers vertical and rows horizontal. In the twentieth century, a specific smocking board developed for this.

141 *Bury and Norwich Post*, 17 December 1867.

142 *Commission on Employment of Children, Young Persons and Women in Agriculture* (1867), First report of the commissioners, with appendix part 1, Parliamentary Papers, 4068-1, vol. 17, 108, 358–60.

143 Crouch, 'Entrepreneurs', 39, 68–9.

144 *The Ipswich Journal*, 12 October, 1872, 4.

145 *Chelmsford Chronicle*, 14 September 1888.

146 Holman, *Made in East Anglia*, 124. Crouch, 'Entrepreneurs', 154. By 1901, Gurteen's employed around half the working population of the town, showing the control that the firm had over the local labour market.

147 *Chelmsford Chronicle*, 14 September 1888. Female smock makers still appear in the 1881 Haverhill census, for example, Susan Backler.

148 Crouch, 'Entrepreneurs', 39–40.

149 *Chelmsford Chronicle*, 14 September 1888.

150 *Bury and Norwich Post*, 15 September 1891.

151 *Bury Free Press*, 11 July 1885.

152 Ibid.

153 *Bury and Norwich Post*, 27 July 1880. See also a trip to London, *Bury and Norwich Post*, 10 August 1886.

154 *Morning Post*, 16 July 1894.

155 Holman, *Made in East Anglia*, 156–7.

156 Ibid., 168. See 121–2 above for types of possible buyers in the early twentieth century.

157 Holman, *Made in East Anglia*, 227. See online https://www.gurteen.co.uk/our-story/ (accessed 14 May 2020).

158 William Steevenson, a pawnbroker and clothing salesman in Grantham, offered 'Newark Smock-frocks' as part of his stock of 10,000 male garments, see *Stamford Mercury*, 22 March 1822; and see J. Burgin, Walker Gate, Grantham, 'original house' of Newark smock frocks, *Grantham Journal*, 21 November 1857. See B. Marshall, *Smocks and Smocking* (Sherborne: Alphabooks, 1980), 16.

159 W. Howitt, *The Hall and the Hamlet: Or Scenes and Characters of Country Life* (London: Henry Colburn, 1848), vol. 2, 260. See also a similar heart on a 'slop' in the Oxfordshire County Museum Collection, OXCMS: 1982.213.3. See 85 above for an illustration of this smock.

160 Around a dozen female smock makers have been found in the 1851 census, although many women do not have a specified occupation.

161 *Pigot and Co.'s Directory of Yorkshire, Leicestershire, Nottinghamshire…* (1841), 16.

162 They are 'Smock Frock Manufacturers' in F. White, *Nottinghamshire: History, Directory and Gazetteer of the County…* (Sheffield: F. White, 1864). In the census, the Noddall's are continuously listed as tailors and drapers, in 1851, William as a Master Tailor employing thirty women, suggesting outworkers. See also the will of Stephen Noddall, 12 March 1860, where the terms of partnership with his brother are detailed, Nottinghamshire Archives, DD 1565/7/30.

163 For dissolution of the partnership see *London Evening Standard*, 21 January 1846.

164 See census 1851, 1861, 1871 and 1901, where he is described as a 'retired clothier, slop and frock merchant', before his death in 1905 at the age of 82.

165 *Stamford Mercury*, 26 May 1843. He also visited Grantham and Stamford to collect orders.

166 *Stamford Mercury*, 7 May 1852.

167 Buck, 'The Countryman's Smock', 23. See also Abingdon Museum, OXCMS: 1980.96.767, for stamps with Prince of Wales feathers, hearts and foliage.

168 Buck, 'The Countryman's Smock', 28, notes that the source of the pattern used on the Newark blocks can be traced to Warwickshire and Hampshire, so although it has become associated with the town, there was no particular regional affinity.

169 In William Shipley's reminiscences about Chesterfield, smock frock making was noted as an important industry, see *Derbyshire Courier*, 25 November 1911, 16.

170 Notice of bankruptcy, *Sheffield Independent*, 16 April 1862.

171 Obituary of Henry Clarke of Brimington, *Derbyshire Times and Chesterfield Herald*, 17 October 1891. The retail smock business of the Clarke family moved from a general drapery warehouse to a new attached premises in 1840, and was then called 'old established', see *Derbyshire Courier*, 14 March 1840.

172 See 1851 census entry for Charles Smith, at his house in Whittington, Derbyshire, aged thirty, living with his parents.

173 See 'Reminiscences of Old Chesterfield', *Derbyshire Times and Chesterfield Herald*, 25 February 1882.

174 'Reminiscences of Old Chesterfield', *Derbyshire Times and Chesterfield Herald*, 31 December 1881 and *Derbyshire Courier*, 22 February 1910, 4, 'Chesterfield'.

175 *The Derbyshire Times and Chesterfield Herald*, 12 November 1859.

176 *Derbyshire Courier*, 26 October 1861, along with £1 10s.

177 *Derbyshire Courier*, 22 June 1861; *Derbyshire Courier*, 15 November 1862; 'Reminiscences' of Old Chesterfield, *Derbyshire Times and Chesterfield Herald*, 31 December 1881.

178 The partnership of Thomas Willey, John Willey, George Collinson Willey and James Judd, manufacturers of smock frocks in the Market Place, Sheffield, was dissolved on Judd's death, see *Morning Chronicle,* 5 April 1854. They continued as Willey & Co. A smock cutter, Sarah Ann Harrison, was still living in Sheffield in the 1911 census. In 1826, John Harrison Harrall was described as a frock manufacturer, 127 Kirkgate, Leeds, see *General and Commercial Directory of Leeds* (Leeds: William Parson, 1826), 60. John Popple, a linen manufacturer from Barnsley sold his warehouse stock including 'Drabbet Coats and smock frocks, duck and linen slops and Smock Frocks &c. &c.', *Leeds Mercury*, 16 May 1840.

179 See *Leeds Mercury,* 25 April 1910, 4, 'History of Barnsley'. Joseph Elmsley was listed as a 'Frock Manufacturer', Folley Hale, Barnsley, in the 1851 census and in *Slater's Commercial Directory of Durham, Northumberland and Yorkshire* (1855), 11. In 1897, Gurteen's bought Messrs. Spencer & Co., Barnsley, for their dyeing and finishing processes, see Holman, *Made in East Anglia*, 151.

180 *Leeds Intelligencer,* 22 November 1851.

181 *Sheffield Independent,* 15 May 1858.

182 The finished goods were returned, subject to a court case, for being inferior and useless, but 'the best we can do', *Derbyshire Advertiser and Journal,* 28 September 1860.

183 In flax growing areas such as Knighton in Powys, linen was woven locally and then made into smocks, a local tailor, Mr Jones, selling them in the early nineteenth century for 5 shillings 6 pence each, with extra embroidered collars for 1 shilling, so possibly the caped versions popular in the Welsh Marches, see Hall, *Smocks*, 20.

184 See *Dundee Advertiser*, 3 April 1863, and *Dundee Advertiser*, 12 September 1867. William Keating dissolved his partnership with L. Dumon in 1869 but continued to trade for a few more years, see *The Edinburgh Gazette,* 5 October 1869, 1242.

185 For example, see *The Post Office Dundee Directory … 1869–70* (James P. Mathew & Co., Dundee, 1869), 151. Examples of smocks worn in the area include one stolen from a chest in a servant's sleeping quarters at Fraserburgh by William Sim in 1869, *Aberdeen Journal*, 21 April 1869; and, likewise, one taken from stables in the countryside near Aberdeen by John McLauchlan in 1865, *Dundee Advertiser*, 21 September 1865.

186 *Aberdeen Evening Express*, 24 November 1882.

187 Lemire, *Dress, Culture and Commerce*, 66–8. See also C. Rose, 'Bought, Stolen, Bequeathed, Preserved: Sources for the Study of 18th-century Petticoats', in *Textiles and Text: Re-establishing the Links between Archival and Object-based Research,* ed. M. Hayward and E. Kramer (London: Archetype Publications, 2007), 114, 116.

188 T. Harrod, *The Crafts in Britain in the Twentieth Century* (London: Yale University Press, 1999), 169.

189 For example, the Hyde brothers, John and Thomas, were both trustees of the Oxford and Abingdon Permanent Benefit Building Society, see Oxford Record Office, Dash. III/xliv/11, 1860. W. Gresham in Lincoln, a tailor, draper and ready-made clothes seller, was an alderman and apparently considered standing for the local parliamentary seat, 'convinced that he is as good a financier as he is a maker of smock-frocks and overalls', see *Lincolnshire Chronicle,* 9 August 1850.

190 Kershen, *Uniting the Tailors*, 30.

191 Rose, *Making*, 108, 211–12, 216; Kershen, *Uniting the Tailors*, 3; see Charpy, 'Adjustments', 200–2, for similar diversification from army to civilian clothing in France. See also the development of Thomas Burberry and his company in Basingstoke, Hampshire, available online: http://www.smockfrock.co.uk/thomas-burberry/ (accessed 16 June 2020).

192 Schorman, *Selling Style*, 21. See also T. Rudd Putman, 'Joseph Long's Slops: Ready-Made Clothing in Early America', *Winterthur Portfolio*, 49, no. 2/3 (2015), 74, 89 and note 83, who suggests that domestic ready-made clothing production in port cities dominated the trade from the 1790s onwards, including companies such as Brooks Brothers by 1818.

193 Rudd Putman, 'Joseph Long's Slops', 91.

194 A. Faure, 'The Working Man's Blouse in 19th Century Paris, The Norms of Dignity', *Modes Pratiques, Journal of Clothes and Fashion History*, Special Issue in English (January 2018): 97.

195 Rose, *Making*, 124–5, 130–1.

196 Charpy, 'Adjustments', 201–3.

197 See B. Reay, *Rural Englands* (Basingstoke: Palgrave Macmillan, 2004), 16–17, for a summary and also ibid. 30, 63. Also Chartres 'Rural Industry', 1105.

198 Chartres 'Rural Industry', 1120.

199 Chapman, 'The "Revolution"', 53.

200 Ibid., 56–7.

201 Ibid., 50–2.

4 Selling and buying

1 *Ipswich Journal*, 21 September 1765. His stock also included air jackets (life jackets).

2 Creditors' notice, *Ipswich Journal*, 30 January 1773.

3 For example, in Newport Pagnell, Mrs Powell, linen draper, hosier, haberdasher and grocer, included 'Mens' Smock Frocks ready made' in her stock, *Northampton Mercury*, 17 December 1796; James White's 'Cloaths Warehouse' [*sic*] in Gloucester also sold smock frocks and included the appeal, 'Workhouse and Parish Poor cloathed on the cheapest terms', *Gloucester Journal*, 29 September 1794.

4 A similar number of references are found in the period 1750–1810, although this quantity is also skewed by the development of the local press during the nineteenth century.

5 *Berrow's Worcester Journal*, 9 February 1815.

6 *Berrow's Worcester Journal*, 5 April 1810.

7 J. Styles, *The Dress of the People: Everyday Fashion in Eighteenth-Century England* (London: Yale University Press, 2007), 28. Also, A. Buck, 'Buying Clothes in Bedfordshire: Customers and Tradesmen, 1700–1800', *Textile History* 22, no. 2 (1991): 230–1, for the same accounts.

8 For example, runaway Samuel Perkins was wearing 'a common smock frock' when he left Stowe, leaving his family chargeable to the parish, see *Staffordshire Advertiser*, 24 July 1830.

9 For instance, three labourers accused of stealing cider appeared at Worcestershire Easter Quarter sessions, described as 'all tidy looking labourers, cleanly dressed with the invariable smock frock', see *Worcester Journal*, 11 April 1844.

10 Buck, 'Buying Clothes', 232.

11 M. Brown, *Somerset Smocks,* Reprint from *Notes & Queries for Somerset & Dorset*, 30, part 305 (March 1977): 4; N. Evans, *The East Anglian Linen Industry, Rural Industry and Local Economy 1500–1850* (Aldershot: Gower Publishing, 1985), 159. See also C. Rose, *Making, Selling and Wearing Boys' Clothes in Late-Victorian England* (Abingdon: Routledge, 2016), 113 and table 4.1 for weekly wage rates from 1860, with unskilled men earning between 4 and 20 shillings in the 1860s. Agricultural labourers' wages in the south and east were around 10 or 11 shillings a week in the 1850s and 1860s, see A. Howkins, *Reshaping Rural England: A Social History 1850–1925* (London: HarperCollins Academic, 1991), 20.

12 A. Toplis, *The Clothing Trade in Provincial England, 1800–1850* (London: Pickering and Chatto, 2011), 39.

13 Toplis, *The Clothing Trade*, 38.

14 *The Aylesbury News,* 2 March 1844.

15 Worcester Record Office(WRO), Parish of Ombersley, bill to overseers, 1828, 3572/16.

16 *Salisbury and Winchester Journal*, 11 March 1843.

17 *Reading Mercury*, 24 October 1831.

18 *Derbyshire Times and Chesterfield Herald*, 7 November 1857. D. G. Vaisey, 'A Charlbury Mercer's Shop, 1623', *Oxoniensia* 31 (1966): 108.

19 L. Ugolini, *Men and Menswear: Sartorial Consumption in Britain 1880–1939* (Aldershot: Ashgate Publishing, 2007), 204.

20 Toplis, *The Clothing Trade*, 151–2.

21 *Hereford Journal*, 30 April 1828.

22 Toplis, *The Clothing Trade*, 62; WRO, Ombersley Parish Accounts, 3572/13, bill from Edward Meates, 8 December 1832.

23 *Leicester Chronicle,* 5 October 1844.

24 *Bucks Herald*, 8 June 1839.

25 W. Ablett, *Reminiscences of an Old Draper* (London: Sampson Low, Marston, Searle and Rivington, 1876), 190–1.

26 Bodleian Library, MS Top Oxon. c 453.

27 *Stamford Mercury*, 21 March 1828.

28 See *Stamford Mercury,* 4 October 1822, for a report of a burglary at the so-called Merchant Taylor's Warehouse in Newark, where ink marked clothing was stolen. This seems to have been an appropriation of the Merchant Taylor name to promote business. Email correspondence with Stephen Freeth, Merchant Taylor Company Archivist, 2017. See *Reading Mercury*, 28 January 1865, for tickets on Hyde's clothing.

29 See the previous chapter.

30 Toplis, *The Clothing Trade*, 53; *Bucks Herald*, 10 October 1840, where he also notes that he will make clothes to order.

31 *Hereford Journal*, 19 May 1841.

32 *Hereford Journal*, 12 April 1843.

33 *Hereford Journal*, 19 April 1843.

34. *Hereford Journal*, 17 May 1843. See also T. C. Whitlock, *Crime, Gender and Consumer Culture in Nineteenth-Century England* (Aldershot: Ashgate Publishing, 2005), 73, who notes contemporary alarm about large cheap drapery establishments underselling goods and threatening the business of an entire neighbourhood from the late 1830s to the 1850s.
35. See A. Toplis, 'The Manufacture and Provision of Rural Garments, 1800–1850: A Case Study of Herefordshire and Worcestershire, *Textile History* 40, no. 1 (2009): 159–60.
36. *Hertford Mercury and Reformer*, 8 January 1870.
37. *Bucks Herald*, 8 December 1877.
38. Ugolini, *Men and Menswear,* 220.
39. See C. Walsh, 'Shop Design and the Display of Goods in Eighteenth-Century London', in *The Retailing Industry Volume I, Perspectives and the Early Modern Period*, ed. J. Benson and G. Shaw (London: I. B. Tauris, 1999), 378.
40. *Halifax Courier*, 19 February 1853.
41. *Wiltshire Independent*, 29 August 1839.
42. I. Mitchell, *Tradition and Innovation in English Retailing, 1700 to 1850: Narratives of Consumption* (Farnham: Ashgate Publishing, 2014), 148–9.
43. Bradford Record Office, 14D96/1/1 Account Book of Brown Muff Department Store, 1818–26; 14D96/1/2 Stock Book of Brown Muff Department Store, 1836. They also sold 'Gurtens' for 2s. 11d. in 1824 which may relate to Gurteen's smocks.
44. See I. Mitchell, 'The Victorian Provincial Department Store: A Category too Many?', *History of Retailing and Consumption* 1, no. 2 (2015): 155–6, for a full history, where Mitchell notes that the shop had a 'famous reputation among country people'.
45. In Penrith, in 1852, William Carruthers advertised his outfitting business, which included short smock frocks, *Carlisle Journal,* 29 October 1852.
46. D. Ryott, *John Barran of Leeds 1851–1951* (Leeds: John Barran, 1951), 2–3.
47. Ryott, *John Barran,* 4.
48. S. Chapman, 'The Innovating Entrepreneurs in the British Ready-made Clothing Industry', *Textile History* 24, no. 1 (1993): 13.
49. *Aris's Birmingham Gazette,* 11 October 1824; 'Broadsheets advertising tailoring and other trades in London, Birmingham, etc, in the mid 19th century', Edwin Witherstone, 1835–55, National Art Library, G.30.S Box III.
50. Available online: https://www.bl.uk/catalogues/evanion/Record.aspx?EvanID=024-000004054&ImageIndex=0 (accessed 16 June 2020).
51. *Yorkshire Gazette,* 23 February 1839. George Headon was Tuke's competitor.
52. *Yorkshire Gazette,* 24 December 1831. Charlton was listed as a tailor and draper, see *Pigot and Co.'s … National and Commercial Directory …York, Leicester & Rutland …* (London: J. Pigot and Co., 1841), at 1 Sampson Square, which was also the marketplace.
53. *Western Times,* 17 September 1859.
54. *Nottinghamshire Guardian,* 5 October 1854.
55. V. Richmond, *Clothing the Poor in Nineteenth-Century England* (Cambridge: Cambridge University Press, 2013), 73, who notes clothing sold at Scholes market near Wigan visited by Arthur Munby in 1860.

56 *Salisbury and Winchester Journal,* 17 December 1787.
57 Bedfordshire and Luton Archives and Records Service, Quarter Session Rolls, QSR/25/1821/291.
58 This fair was moved because it was a nuisance, see *Morning Post,* 5 July 1823.
59 W. Howitt, *The Hall and the Hamlet: Or Scenes and Characters of Country Life* (London: Henry Colburn, 1848), vol. 2, 260.
60 *Wellington Journal,* 2 January 1869.
61 S. Payne and R. Pailthorpe ed., *Barclay Wills' The Downland Shepherds* (Gloucester: Alan Sutton Publishing, 1989), 84–5.
62 *Gloucestershire Chronicle,* 3 October 1846. This was a Charter Fair.
63 *Coventry Herald,* 11 October 1839.
64 *Gloucester Journal,* 8 October 1853.
65 See M. Hall, *Smocks* (Princes Risborough: Shire Publications, 1979), 14. See 32 and 89 above for embroidered 'best' smocks.
66 J. Arch, *The Autobiography of Joseph Arch* (1898; London: MacGibbon & Kee, 1966), 25, 147.
67 See, for example: http://www.workhouses.org.uk/Brighton/ (accessed 16 June 2020). See also note 3 above.
68 WRO, Bill to the Overseers of Poor of Hindlip from John Hooper, 1812, 8669/6 iii (29).
69 Toplis, *The Clothing Trade,* 114, note 30, and WRO, Powick Parish Records, 3802/10. Burden supplied various types of smocks including a 'smock frock', 'hurden frock', 'duck frock', and 'short smock'.
70 Buck, 'Buying Clothes in Bedfordshire', 231–2.
71 WRO, Ombersley Parish Accounts, 3572/16, bill from W. Corbett, Ombersley, 1828. The Parish of St Peters, Droitwich, bought a 'long smock' for Robert Crowther in November 1814, costing thirteen shillings, WRO, St Peter's Parish Book Droitwich, 1808–1819, 5476/19.
72 WRO, Droitwich St Andrew's Parish Accounts, 839/2, bill from James Horsley, 11 November 1823.
73 Toplis, *The Clothing Trade,* 99–101. Brace's male children also claimed smocks at a similar rate. Herefordshire Record Office, Abbey Dore Parish Accounts, 1794–1849, AC16/26. Smock frocks were likewise distributed to paupers in Droitwich in 1816, see Toplis, *The Clothing Trade,* 102.
74 S. King, 'The Clothing of the Poor: A Matter of Pride or Shame?' in *Being Poor in Modern Europe: Historical Perspectives 1800–1940,* ed. A. Gestrich, S. King and L. Raphael (Oxford: Peter Lang, 2005), 379.
75 M. Spufford and S. Mee, *The Clothing of the Common Sort, 1570–1700* (Oxford: Oxford University Press, 2017), 4.
76 For example, M. Finn, 'Men's things: masculine possession in the consumer revolution', *Social History* 25, no. 2 (2000), especially 135–6, 153–4; D. Hussey,' Guns, Horses and Stylish Waistcoats? Male Consumer Activity and Domestic Shopping in Late-Eighteenth and Early-Nineteenth-Century England', in *Buying for the Home, Shopping for the Domestic from the 17th Century to the Present,* ed. D. Hussey and M. Ponsonby (Aldershot: Ashgate Publishing, 2008), 47–69.

77 See, for example, in late-nineteenth-century plebeian London, E. Ross, *Love and Toil: Motherhood in Outcast London, 1870–1918* (Oxford: Oxford University Press, 1993), chapter 2, and 76–8, although the concentration is on food, without an interrogation into how different members of the family procured clothing.

78 Finn, 'Men's things', 154, for a summary of research. See, however, B. Shannon, *The Cut of His Coat: Men, Dress, and Consumer Culture in Britain, 1860–1914* (Athens: Ohio University Press, 2006), for discussion about middle-class men as consumers of 'fashion' in the late nineteenth century, particularly 4–7, for an overview.

79 Ugolini, *Men and Menswear*, 251-17. See also K. Harvey, 'Craftsmen in Common: Objects, Skills and Masculinity in the Eighteenth and Nineteenth Centuries', in *Gender and Material Culture in Britain since 1760*, ed. H. Greig, J. Hamlett and L. Hannan (London: Palgrave 2016), 68–89, for working men as consumers of ceramics referencing their occupations.

80 Ugolini, *Men and Menswear*, 218–19.

81 See B. Reay, *Rural Englands* (Basingstoke: Palgrave Macmillan, 2004), 86–7.

82 Ugolini, *Men and Menswear*, 218.

83 See Wiltshire and Swindon History Centre, Servants Ledger Book, 1830–47, 929/28-27. This happened in 1830, 1832–9. He is described as John Grant in the 1841 census.

84 See the examples cited in A. Clark, *The Struggle for the Breeches: Gender and the Making of the British Working Class* (London: University of California Press, 1997), 257–8.

85 See Ugolini, *Men and Menswear*, 225–6, for a continuation of this practice into the twentieth century.

86 G. Ewart Evans, 'Dress and the Rural Historian', *Costume* 8, no. 1 (1974): 39.

87 Toplis, *The Clothing Trade*, 36–7, 66–7. See also C. Steedman, *An Everyday Life of the English Working Class: Work, Self and Sociability in the Early Nineteenth Century* (Cambridge: Cambridge University Press, 2013), particularly 94–6, 182–4, 187–9, for the drinking culture in pubs, and its associated pleasures, for working men.

88 *Berkshire Chronicle*, 7 March 1829.

89 *Hampshire Advertiser*, 4 March 1837.

90 *Hereford Times*, 20 May 1848; *Hereford Times*, 24 June 1848.

91 P. K. Andersson, *Streetlife in Late Victorian London: The Constable and the Crowd* (Basingstoke: Palgrave Macmillan, 2013), 70–2.

92 *Essex Standard*, 13 March 1846.

93 *Chelmsford Chronicle*, 31 March 1843.

94 *Derbyshire Courier*, 23 October 1852. He was accused of theft as he put the smock on a fictitious shop account.

95 He was thus implicated in the plot as he had wasted time, see *Oxford University and City Herald*, 15 October 1825.

96 See the case of Samuel Fowler, aged 16 and an 'up-country looking lad', who stole money to buy a smock, *Exeter Flying Post*, 13 June 1850, and *Western Times*, 15 June 1850. Also a gang of youths buying a smock and stealing from a drapers in Gloucester, see *Gloucester Journal*, 18 August 1838.

97 *Wolverhampton Chronicle and Staffordshire Advertiser*, 31 March 1847.

98 *Stamford Mercury*, 20 January 1860.
99 *Leicestershire Mercury*, 22 October 1853.
100 *Staffordshire Gazette and County Standard,* 14 March 1840.
101 *Oxford Chronicle and Reading Gazette,* 5 March 1842.
102 S. Wise, *The Italian Boy: Murder and Grave-Robbery in 1830s London* (London: Jonathan Cape, 2004), 10, 39–41.
103 *Sussex Advertiser,* 21 November 1831.
104 *Salisbury and Winchester Journal,* 21 November 1831. Wise, *The Italian Boy*, 61. They were accused of murdering a 14-year-old Italian orphan living on the streets to sell his body to King's College medical school.
105 Wise, *The Italian Boy*, 6–8, 56, 190, 240.
106 Finn, 'Men's Things', 141–2.
107 *Gloucestershire Chronicle*, 22 April 1843, Tibberton Murder Case.
108 Ugolini, *Men and Menswear*, 221–2.
109 Ibid., 16, 21–3, 39–40, 43, 45, who notes that clothing worn for leisure and days off could be smarter than old clothing kept for working in.
110 Ugolini, *Men and Menswear*, 37–8, notes an example from 1933 of Arthur Beckett who lived in Sussex and still liked to wear a smock for working in his house or garden. However, if he wore it around the village, he invited scornfulness and ridicule, especially as he was a middle-class man. See also R. Schorman, *Selling Style: Clothing and Social Change at the Turn of the Century* (Philadelphia: University of Pennsylvania Press, 2003), 29–30, for the development of the ideal American man, unadorned, square shaped and square-jawed, with no skirts on coats.
111 For the theft of clothing more generally see, for example, B. Lemire, *Dress, Culture and Commerce: The English Clothing Trade before the Factory, 1660–1800* (Basingstoke: Macmillan Press, 1997), chapter 5. See Toplis, *The Clothing Trade*, 88–90, for specific smock frock examples.
112 *Oxford Journal*, 13 November 1869. These cases continued into the twentieth century. For example, one was left in field and then stolen whilst the owner was haymaking, see 'Police Court', *Nottingham Evening Post*, 11 September 1907, 7.
113 For example, see the case of Charles Canrsh [sic], who successfully said he bought a second-hand smock from a traveller for 6 pence rather than stealing it from a stable, *Leicester Chronicle*, 1 November 1856. See also the case of George Carrington of Collingham, who unsuccessfully used the defence that he had bought it off a man on the road for 6 pence and a coat, *Nottinghamshire Guardian*, 30 May 1861.
114 *Hereford Times*, 8 July 1837.
115 *Nottingham Review and General Advertiser for the Midland Counties*, 4 January 1839.
116 *Nottingham Review and General Advertiser for the Midland Counties*, 18 March 1836; see also a similar case at the Wiltshire Lent Assizes for William Little and John Tribe, where the stolen smock was sold on at a public house, *Devizes and Wiltshire Gazette*, 9 March 1826.
117 Smock frocks stolen from a draper and grocer were offered for sale at local pub, the Hind's Head, Lambourn, see *Reading Mercury* , 4 January 1840.
118 *Nottingham Review and General Advertiser for the Midland Counties*, 16 December 1831.

119 *Hampshire Telegraph*, 13 January 1869.

120 *Hereford Times,* 13 June 1857. See a similar case, also in Hereford, where James Rowley came into the city from Canon Pyon and bought a new smock frock before his old one, now parcelled up, was stolen while he was in a cider and eating house in Eign Street, *Hereford Journal,* 5 May 1852.

121 *Worcestershire Chronicle,* 13 July 1853.

122 B. Lemire, *The Business of Everyday Life: Gender, Practice and Social Politics in England, c. 1600–1900* (Manchester: Manchester University Press, 2006), 104.

123 *Worcestershire Chronicle,* 20 December 1838. They were routinely sold as part of pawnbrokers' stock of their unredeemed pledges, for example, in Aylesbury, Buckinghamshire, *The Bucks Advertiser and Aylesbury News,* 8 May 1847.

124 Lemire uses the phrase, 'alternative currency' to describe the trading of clothes with known values, which could be later sold or pawned to obtain cash, see Lemire, *The Business of Everyday Life,* 86.

125 Toplis, *The Clothing Trade*, 90.

126 *Morning Post,* 26 December 1872, 5.

127 See also Robert Mansfield's business, where working men spent large amounts of money on buying clothing, especially if single, although, as a tailor, he sold no smocks, C. Fowler, 'Robert Mansbridge, a Rural Tailor and His Customers 1811–1815', *Textile History* 28, no. 1 (1997): 29–38.

128 Ugolini, *Men and Menswear*, 226–7.

5 Appearances

1 See, for example, J. Craik, *Uniforms Exposed: From Conformity to Transgression* (Oxford: Berg, 2005), 119–24, for the importance of dressing in appropriate uniform.

2 J. Styles, *The Dress of the People: Everyday Fashion in Eighteenth-Century England* (London: Yale University Press, 2007), 211, 305.

3 See P. Hamilton, 'The Beautiful and the Damned', in *The Beautiful and the Damned: The Creation of Identity in Nineteenth Century Photography,* ed. P. Hamilton and R. Hargreaves (Aldershot: Lund Humphries, 2001), 14.

4 M. Finn, *The Character of Credit: Personal Debt in English Culture 1740–1914* (Cambridge: Cambridge University Press, 2003), 47, 279, 288, 291, 306, 315.

5 *Hereford Journal*, 28 March 1849.

6 *Salisbury and Winchester Journal*, 22 October 1821.

7 P. K. Andersson, *Streetlife in Late Victorian London: The Constable and the Crowd* (Basingstoke: Palgrave Macmillan, 2013), 140–3, 164, and P. Bailey, '"Will the Real Bill Banks Please Stand Up?" Towards a Role Analysis of Mid-Victorian Working-Class Respectability', *Journal of Social History* 12, no. 3 (1979): 346. See also S. Smiles, 'Defying Comprehension: Resistance to Uniform Appearance in Depicting the Poor, 1770s to 1830s', *Textile History* 33, no. 1 (2002): 30–1.

8   *Dorset County Chronicle,* 21 November 1861. See also Gabriel Oak in Thomas Hardy's, *Far from the Madding Crowd* (1874; Ware: Wordsworth Editions, 2000).

9   W. Tayler, *Diary of William Tayler, Footman 1837*, ed. D. Wise (London: St. Marylebone Society, 1987), 60, 11 December 1837.

10 A. Buck, 'The Countryman's Smock', *Folk Life* (1963), 25–8. Armes was the first historian to try and categorize embroidery patterns into occupational groups in the 1920s, see A. Armes, *English Smocks with Directions for Making Them* (Leicester: Dryad Press, 1928), 7–8; See N. Thornton, 'Enigmatic Variations: The Features of British Smocks', *Textile History* 28, no. 2 (1997): 176–84, for a summary of this.

11 Hardy, *Far from the Madding Crowd*, 32.

12 In Warwickshire and the Midlands, see Buck 'The Countryman's Smock', 25.

13 Waggoners' Frock or Carter's Smock was often the name given to the garment in the early nineteenth century, maybe as these occupations were commonly the most visible wearers of this attire, see Buck, 'The Countryman's Smock', 22.

14 W. Howitt, *The Hall and the Hamlet: Or Scenes and Characters of Country Life* (London: Henry Colburn, 1848), vol. 2, 258–9.

15 See 2 above for descriptions of the broad types: round, shirt-like and open.

16 By 1873, there was a debate about the value of photographing prisoners as photographs were not found to be particularly useful for the detection of criminals relative to their cost, their use rapidly diminishing after this date, see J. Tagg, *The Burden of Representation: Essays on Photographies and Histories* (Minneapolis: University of Minnesota Press, 1988), 7, 80.

17 See, for example, C. Richmond, *Oxford Gaol: Prisoner Portraits 1870–1881, Volume One: Crimes in West Oxfordshire* (Witney: Oxfordshire Black Sheep Publications, 2005), 2. Some prisons photographed prisoners on release, taken in their own clothes for identification purposes, which as they were in storage for the duration of their sentence, could appear crumpled.

18 V. Richmond, *Clothing the Poor in Nineteenth-Century England* (Cambridge: Cambridge University Press, 2013), 182–3.

19 *A Bill for Consolidating and Amending the Laws Relating to the Building, Repairing, and Regulating of Certain Gaols, Bridewells, and Houses of Correction, in England and Wales*, Parliamentary Papers 1823, I, page 9. There are some photographs of prisoners in parti-coloured prison clothing, for example, Everard Raby, received on 21 November 1872, in Aylesbury Gaol, available online: https://www.buckscc.gov.uk/services/culture-and-leisure/buckinghamshire-archives/online-resources/victorian-prisoners/ (accessed 17 June 2020).

20 Tagg, *The Burden of Representation*, 11, 36–7, 59, 76, 85.

21 Ibid., 65, 118–19.

22 N. Tarrant, *Smocks in the Buckinghamshire County Museum* (Aylesbury: Buckinghamshire County Council, 1976), number's 10, 12, 13.

23 M. Nichols, *Smocks in Luton Museum* (Luton: Borough of Luton Museum and Art Gallery, 1980), examples 6b, 6c, 12.

24 See one from Preston, said to have been worn for the ceremonial opening of the Preston and Fleetwood (Wyre) railway in 1840, *Preston Chronicle*, 18 July 1840, and one from York, Buck, 'The Countryman's Smock', 31.

25 Armes states that smocks were worn in Durham and Yorkshire, her identified Yorkshire ones being short and set into a band around the hips, see Armes, *English Smocks*, 4–5. However, smocks of a similar description were also photographed by Joseph Gale in Sussex, see B. Coe, *A Victorian Country Album: The Photographs of Joseph Gale* (Sparkford: Oxford Illustrated Press, 1988), 146. These were also called 'ban-yans', see Thornton, 'Enigmatic Variations', 181, quoting a letter to the *Surrey County Magazine* in 1930. Thanks also to Sarah Thursfield for pointing out the connection to shirts.

26 See S. North, *Sweet and Clean? Bodies and Clothes in Early Modern England* (Oxford: Oxford University Press, 2020), for construction details for shirts and shifts, 190–3.

27 See R. Worth, *Dress and Textiles (Discover Dorset)* (Wimborne: Dovecote Press, 2002), 54–5, where the photograph is reproduced. The smock survives in the Dorset County Museum.

28 Valence House Museum, LDVAL 3556, where it is dated to the 1860s. Edward, Prince of Wales, married Alexandra of Denmark in 1863. See also Abingdon Museum, OXCMS: 1980.96.767, for a stamp with Prince of Wales feathers, although a slightly different pattern.

29 D. de Marly, *Working Dress: A History of Occupational Clothing* (London: B. T. Batsford, 1986), 109.

30 A local general store in Broadwell sold these to all the men in the area from masons to farm workers until the First World War. Evidence from the oral testimony of his son, see OXOHA/OT/56 – George Swinford, Oxfordshire Museums Service, 1979.

31 See online: http://mosaicweb.com.au/Collection/FremantlePrison/Item/1135336/JACKET_FOR_CONVICT (accessed 16 June 2020), and L. Young, 'The Experience of Convictism: Five Pieces of Convict Clothing from Western Australia', *Costume* 22 (1988): 74–5.

32 J. Severa, *Dressed for the Photographer: Ordinary Americans and Fashion, 1840–1900* (Kent: Kent State University Press, 1995), 19–20.

33 Coe, *A Victorian Country Album*, 142–3.

34 See http://www.british-history.ac.uk/no-series/traded-goods-dictionary/1550–1820/doublet-dozens, 'dowlas' (accessed 16 June 2020). See also North, *Sweet and Clean?*, 115–7, 166, for a discussion about 'linen' textile terminology, and 171 for dowlas.

35 Armes, *English Smocks*, 7. The Worcestershire Collection contains a drabbet round frock, owned by a carter, with flannel lining on the shoulder straps, 1966/542, and a later machine sewn 'coat frock', the fullness held with tucks to the waist, TC6305. Drabbet had a diagonal or herringbone weave and was sold in 20 yard lengths to tailors, dyed or undyed, see N. Evans, *The East Anglian Linen Industry: Rural Industry and Local Economy 1500–1850* (Aldershot: Gower Publishing, 1985), 155–6, 158, for drabbet manufacturing in Suffolk, especially Syleham Mills.

36 For the traditional bleaching process using lye, derived from wood ash, see North, *Sweet and Clean?*, 164–5, 212–13, 220–1.

37 See http://www.smockfrock.co.uk/tag/hop-bine/ (accessed 16 June 2020), and *Bucks Herald*, 4 January 1851. Pall bearers in Kent also wore green smocks, see *Kentish Gazette*, 12 March 1850. Green and drab are very similar colours in smock lore, one meaning the same as the other, depending on the area, see M. Hall, *Smocks* (Princes Risborough: Shire Publications, 1979), 13.

38 Howitt, *The Hall and the Hamlet*, 259–60. See Armes, *English Smocks*, 6, for the association of particular colours with specific counties or areas. See also 'Confession of a Migratory

Depredator', from the Constabulary Force Commissioners' Report, *Lincolnshire Chronicle*, 31 May 1839, who notes coloured smocks as 'Green for Wilts., Somerset, Gloster [*sic*]; blue and drab for Nottingham and midland counties; many whites and drabs in Staffordshire and Lincolnshire'.

39 See for example, http://findit.library.yale.edu/catalog/digcoll:951211 (accessed 16 June 2020), of 1800. Kirkcaldy linen manufacturers used to export blue linen to England for smock frocks until cotton superseded this in the late nineteenth century, see 'The Flax Spinning Industry', *Fife Free Press & Kirkcaldy Guardian,* 22 August 1903, 5.

40 Bedfordshire Archives, Quarter Sessions Records, QSR/26/1824/392.

41 See A. Buck, 'Clothes in Fact and Fiction, 1825–1865', *Costume* 17, no. 1 (1983): 95.

42 See one in The Museum of English Rural Life (MERL), available online: http://www.reading.ac.uk/adlib/Details/collect/6987 (accessed 17 June 2020). See also, possibly, no. 6c, illustrated in Nichols, *Smocks in Luton Museum*, a new child's olive green round frock bought from a shop in Chesham Bois. The oil made drab or grey smocks brownish black in colour.

43 This was a medieval technique also used by fishermen, see B. Marshall, *Smocks and Smocking* (Sherborne: Alphabooks, 1980), 12–13.

44 *Morning Post,* 13 September 1802.

45 S. Levitt, *Victorians Unbuttoned: Registered Designs for Clothing, Their Makers and Wearers, 1839–1900* (London: George Allen & Unwin, 1986), 180–1.

46 *Devizes and Wiltshire Gazette,* 12 September 1839.

47 S. Chapman, 'The Innovating Entrepreneurs in the British Ready-made Clothing Industry', *Textile History* 24, no. 1 (1993): 10; Levitt, *Victorians Unbuttoned*, 186–8.

48 *Devizes and Wiltshire Gazette,* 29 March 1860.

49 Ledbury Petty Sessions, *Hereford Times,* 28 November 1863.

50 *Surrey Mirror,* 6 September 1884. A correspondent to *Country Life* notes that her mother, in the early twentieth century, said that smocks 'shot' the rain completely, see letter from Cicely Nash, *Country Life,* 9 May 1957, 932.

51 R. Jefferies, *Wild Life in a Southern County* (1879), 113, available online: http://www.gutenberg.org/files/36949/36949-h/36949-h.htm (accessed 17 June 2020); de Marly, *Working Dress*, 105.

52 G. Jekyll, *Old West Surrey* (1904; East Ardsley: S. R. Publishers, 1971), 258. G. Ewart Evans, *Ask the Fellows Who Cut the Hay* (1956; London: Faber and Faber, 2018), 36.

53 *Yorkshire Gazette,* 4 February 1843.

54 *York Herald,* 26 April 1823.

55 *Leamington Spa Courier,* 6 September 1828.

56 See *The Odd Fellow,* 18 July 1840, for the gait and *Bell's New Weekly Messenger,* 6 September 1835, for the snake comparison.

57 *Chester Chronicle,* 29 June 1810.

58 See B. Lemire, *Fashion's Favourite: The Cotton Trade and the Consumer in Britain 1660–1800* (Oxford: Oxford University Press, 1991), 93, note 48, for the process of washing and reviving wool clothing. See also the comparison with boys' light-coloured sailor suits from the late nineteenth century which survive in numbers in museum collections and were the

cheapest type to buy, but are much rarer in the contemporary photographic evidence, suggesting that their maintenance, including laundering, and their seasonality when made from light-coloured cotton, made them less popular and overall not such good value to buy, see C. Rose, *Making, Selling and Wearing Boys' Clothes in Late-Victorian England* (Abingdon: Routledge, 2016), 147–8, 152, 227. Something similar may have happened in terms of coloured smocks and their survival in museum collections. See North, *Sweet and Clean?*, 210, for other methods for cleaning woollen fabrics.

59 *Bucks Herald*, 23 March 1839.

60 *Staffordshire Advertiser*, 7 March 1812.

61 See B. Lemire, *The Business of Everyday Life: Gender, Practice and Social Politics in England, c. 1600–1900* (Manchester: Manchester University Press, 2006), 155, for seventeenth-century examples. See also D. Roche, *The Culture of Clothing: Dress and Fashion in the Ancien Regime* (Cambridge: Cambridge University Press, 1996), chapter 7, 'The Invention of Linen', especially 174–8, 180. Also North, *Sweet and Clean?*, for the key quality of whiteness, for example, 166.

62 See P. Johnson, 'Conspicuous Consumption and Working-Class Culture in Late-Victorian and Edwardian Britain', *Transactions of the Royal Historical Society* 38 (1988): 39–41; J. Styles, 'Custom or Consumption? Plebeian Fashion in Eighteenth-Century England', in *Luxury in the Eighteenth Century,* ed. M. Berg and E. Eger (Basingstoke: Palgrave Macmillan, 2003), 112–3.

63 E. Grey, *Cottage Life in a Hertfordshire Village* (St Albans: Fisher, Knight, n.d. [1935]), 30–1. The term 'best' refers to 'Sunday best' clothing as well as dress for other special occasions such as weddings. Coloured glass buttons sewn into the smock's embroidery were also recalled by Mr Shields of Norwich, see G. Holman, *Made in East Anglia: A History of the Region's Textile and Menswear Industries* (Pasold Resource, no. 1, 2015), 25, http://www.pasold.co.uk/resource-page.

64 Grey, *Cottage Life,* 30. de Marly, *Working Dress*, 107. Buck, 'Clothes in Fact and Fiction', 95. See L. Ugolini, *Men and Menswear: Sartorial Consumption in Britain 1880–1939* (Aldershot: Ashgate Publishing, 2007), 41, for coats also concealing poverty in a similar way.

65 Richmond, *Clothing the Poor*, 131.

66 *Morning Chronicle,* 20 November 1857.

67 *Hertford Mercury and Reformer,* 24 November 1849.

68 Particularly for everyday linens, see B. Burman and A. Fennetaux, *The Pocket: A Hidden History of Women's Lives* (New Haven: Yale University Press, 2020), 86.

69 For a smock with button embellishment on the collar and front, believed to have been worn in Great Horton, Bradford, see smock 437/1966, Bradford Arts, Museums and Heritage.

70 Lincolnshire Museums, Shepherd's Smock (LCNLL: 1977/655.1), a grey cotton twill smock worn by George Potter, a shepherd at Greetwell, Lincoln. Mr Potter was born in 1856. See also a smock in the Worcestershire Museum Collection, the collar buttoned down with small mother of pearl buttons, the embroidery in Newark block design, 1969/1191. Marshall, *Smocks and Smocking*, 85–6.

71 See letter from H. Lumley Ellis, *Country Life,* 5 June 1942, 1094–5.

72 *Berkshire Chronicle*, 13 June 1829. See A. Toplis, *The Clothing Trade in Provincial England, 1800–1850* (London: Pickering and Chatto, 2011), 132, for cheap male fashions using buttons.

73 *Shrewsbury Chronicle,* 18 July 1862.

74 Lincolnshire Museums (LCNLL: 1967/116). Census 1851, 1861, 1871. In 1861, Codling is described as employing four men and two apprentices, working from a tailor and draper's shop, so may have been making ready-made garments.

75 Available online: http://www.victorianweb.org/history/work/sullivan/4.html (accessed 17 June 2020). Note the parallels with coster dress, the 'pearly kings'.

76 See J. Begiato, *Manliness in Britain, 1760–1900* (Manchester: Manchester University Press, 2020), particularly 118–19, for further discussion.

77 See also P. Davies, 'Clothing and textiles at the Hyde Park Barracks Destitute Asylum, Sydney, Australia', *Post-Medieval Archaeology* 41, no. 1 (2013): 2, for the use of buttons in subverting uniform codes.

78 See C. Blackman, 'Colouring the Claddagh: A Distorted View?', *Costume* 48, no. 2 (2014): 230. See also Davies, 'Clothing and textiles', 13, for clothing emphasizing thrift and modesty.

79 For example, Herefordshire Record Office, Tailor's Accounts, Brampton Bryam, E61/2/1, page 119, where a smock frock was mended in June 1843. See Toplis, *The Clothing Trade*, 35, for the context of the tailor. Also Worcestershire Record Office, St Peter's Parish Book, Droitwich, 1808–1819, 5476/19, 16 February 1809 and 16 August 1811, when three pence was paid to a local woman for mending different men's smocks.

80 *Western Gazette,* 7 August 1903, 4.

81 Grey, *Cottage Life*, 30. Ewart Evans, *Ask the Fellows*, 35.

82 D. Brooke, *The Railway Navvy: 'That Despicable Race of Men'* (Newton Abbot: David & Charles, 1983), 14–15, 17–18, 20, 25. The pay was much better as a navvy being 3 to 5 shillings a day, compared to 9 to 10 shillings a week as a labourer in Northamptonshire in the mid-1830s, ibid., 21, and D. Brooke, 'The Railway Navvy – A Reassessment', *Construction History* 5 (1989): 38, 43. See also R. Jefferies, *The Toilers of the Field* (London: Longmans Green, 1907), 226.

83 Brooke, *The Railway Navvy, 'That Despicable Race'*, 10–11, 20.

84 Brooke, *The Railway Navvy, 'That Despicable Race'*, 49, and D. W. Barrett, *Life and Work among the Navvies* (1880; Kettering: Silver Link Book, reprint, n.d.), 33–4.

85 *Leicester Chronicle*, 26 December 1840.

86 *Gloucestershire Chronicle*, 21 September 1839. See James Collinson's painting, *A Son of the Soil, circa* 1856, for similar clothing and use of smock, available online: https://artuk.org/discover/artworks/a-son-of-the-soil-204699 (accessed 17 June 2020).

87 Navvies were also described as wearing fustian pea-jackets, canvas trousers, rainbow-coloured neckties, smock-frocks and hob nailed boots, which is also the attire of male manual labourers, see Barrett, *Life and Work*, 33.

88 Brooke, *The Railway Navvy, 'That Despicable Race'*, 52.

89 G. Elson, *The Last of the Climbing Boys* (London: John Long, 1900), 159.

90 The house of William England in Hartlebury, Worcestershire, a railway contractor, was burgled and 'a large quantity of new smock-frocks, shirts, trowsers [sic], and shoes, such as are worn by navvies' were stolen, *Worcestershire Chronicle*, 23 February 1848. Employers controlled their employees spending through the truck system, offering goods sold in special shops, often at inflated prices, instead of wages.

91 See 47–8 above for details about the Bousfield companies.

92 *Chester Chronicle,* 28 November 1868.

93 *Derby Mercury,* 17 January 1849.

94 *Essex Standard*, 18 June 1841.

95 See Brooke, *The Railway Navvy*, 'That Despicable Race', 39–42, 47.

96 *Glasgow Herald*, 15 May 1846.

97 Brooke, *The Railway Navvy*, 'That Despicable Race', 41–2, 49. It was calculated that one temporary encampment for the Kettering and Manton Railway spent around £100,000 a year on food in the late 1870s, see Barrett, *Life and Work*, 19, and chapter 3 generally.

98 *Dundee Courier*, 24 February 1864.

99 Richmond, *Clothing the Poor*, 24.

100 *Essex Standard*, 22 April 1842.

101 *Dundee, Perth, and Cupar Advertiser*, 27 March 1846. There are other similar references across England and south Wales during the 1840s and 1850s.

102 Quoted in the *Exeter and Plymouth Gazette*, 14 January 1843; see also *Bath Chronicle and Weekly Gazette,* 25 March 1847, for another similar.

103 *Nottingham Review and General Advertiser for the Midland Counties*, 26 February 1847. See also similarly, a procession of navvies in white smocks for the opening of the Somerset Central Railway in Glastonbury, Brooke, *The Railway Navvy*, 162–3, and for the turning of the first sod for the Wellington and Severn Junction Railway, *Wellington Journal,* 25 August 1855.

104 *West Kent Guardian,* 21 April 1849.

105 Available online: https://www.tate.org.uk/art/artworks/riviere-giants-at-play-n01516 (accessed 17 June 2020). A letter in 1968 appealed for information about the MERL smock, where it was from and what it was used for, to no avail. See *Country Life*, 29 February 1968, 479.

106 Hall, *Smocks*, 23.

107 *Newcastle Chronicle,* 9 September 1865.

108 Ibid.

109 *Western Times,* 22 December 1868.

110 Available online: https://artuk.org/discover/artworks/spring-morning-haverstock-hill-164085 (accessed 11 June 2020). K. McConkey, *George Clausen and the Picture of English Rural Life* (Edinburgh: Atelier Books, 2012), 7 and 14.

111 Y. S. Lee, *Masculinity and the English Working Class: Studies in Victorian Autobiography and Fiction* (Abingdon: Routledge, 2007), 84.

112 Available online: https://manchesterartgallery.org/collections/title/?mag-object-82 (accessed 17 June 2020) for the painting. Brown sketched the navvies from life, see T.

Barringer, *Men at Work: Art and Labour in Victorian Britain* (New Haven: Yale University Press, 2005), 46, 51. See also ibid., 37–41, for further discussion on the context of 'Work'.

113 See online: www.smockfrock.co.uk (accessed 17 June 2020), for blogs about other occupations including highwaymen, executioners, butchers and fishmongers.

114 Night soil men wore new ones for a May-day procession in Liverpool, *Liverpool Courier and Commercial Advertiser*, 13 May 1870.

115 *Exeter and Plymouth Gazette*, 26 January 1828.

116 B. Maidment, *Dusty Bob: A Cultural History of Dustmen, 1780–1870* (Manchester: Manchester University Press, 2007), 221, note 37.

117 H. Mayhew, *London Labour and the London Poor* (1861), Vol. II, 367, available online: https://archive.org/details/in.ernet.dli.2015.38652/page/n415 (accessed 17 June 2020).

118 Maidment, *Dusty Bob*, 172–4.

119 B. Maidment, '101 Things to Do with a Fantail Hat: Dustmen, Dirt and Dandyism, 1820–1860', *Textile History* 33, no. 1 (2002): 90.

120 Maidment, '101 Things to Do with a Fantail Hat', 86. Maidment, *Dusty Bob,* 92–3.

121 *London Daily News*, 15 October 1859.

122 *Derby Mercury*, 11 June 1862.

123 Maidment, *Dusty Bob*, 182–3.

124 See the illustration, in the *Penny Illustrated Paper,* 5 May 1866, 273.

125 See, for example, 'Dust oh!', depicting a dustman, *The British Workman*, March 1871, a temperance publication.

126 See 38 above for further discussion about the military stimulation of the ready-made clothing trade. See also, for example, online: https://www.metmuseum.org/art/collection/search/399824 (accessed 17 June 2020), for Hogarth's illustration of sailor's plain frock from 1747.

127 *Edinburgh Evening News*, 13 November 1890.

128 A. Miller, *Dressed to Kill: British Naval Uniform, Masculinity and Contemporary Fashions 1748–1857* (London: National Maritime Museum, 2007), 84–90.

129 *Dumfries and Galloway Standard*, 6 September 1854. See also Begiato, *Manliness*, chapter 3, for discussion about manliness embodied by soldiers.

130 *Nottinghamshire Guardian*, 29 March 1855. Navvies sent to build a railway in Balaklava were also given smocks for warm weather wear, see Brooke, *The Railway Navvy, 'That Despicable Race'*, 125–6, including illustration figure 14. The 'fearnought slop' was included in the list of navvy clothing printed in the *Illustrated London News*, 30 December 1854, 14, sent with navvies to the Crimea. 'Fearnought' was a stout woollen cloth thought to be wind and waterproof.

131 *London Evening Standard*, 14 May 1855.

132 This practice was officially discontinued in 1855 but still carried out after this date. The National Army Museum hold a woollen Guernsey Smock (1951-7-3-1) used on the Persian Campaign of 1857. Email correspondence with Belinda Day, Senior Curator, National Army Museum, 2019.

133 *Maidstone Telegraph*, 28 September 1861.
134 *Glasgow Herald*, 1 July 1861.
135 *Dundee Courier*, 12 August 1857.
136 *Perthshire Advertiser*, 26 August 1858.
137 *Staffordshire Advertiser*, 26 May 1827.
138 *Devizes and Wiltshire Gazette*, 18 June 1835.
139 Report about a gathering at Harper's Fields, Paddington, *The Charter*, 25 August 1839.
140 *Cheltenham Chronicle*, 5 December 1844. The assault of policemen undertaking arrests was not uncommon as they had no means of identifying themselves until the 1860s. See R. Griffin, 'Beating up Bobbies', online: https://victoriandetectives.wordpress.com/2013/05/08/beating-up-bobbies-2/ (accessed 17 June 2020).
141 *Westmorland Gazette*, 20 July 1833. See also *Cobbett's Weekly Political Register*, 13 July 1833.
142 A smock frock and handkerchief was stolen from a constable in 1829, *Stamford Mercury*, 6 November 1829.
143 'Confession of a Migratory Depredator', from the Constabulary Force Commissioners' Report, *Lincolnshire Chronicle*, 31 May 1839. See 87 above for coloured smocks.
144 *Newcastle Courant*, 22 August 1856; also *Lloyd's Weekly Newspaper*, 24 July 1864.
145 *Hertford Mercury and Reformer*, 18 February 1843.
146 A policeman dressed up like a carter in a smock frock and billycock hat, with a cart, to catch a man selling beer without a licence through his tea and tobacco shop, see *Bradford Observer*, 10 June 1852. See other similar cases in *Exeter and Plymouth Gazette*, 26 March 1859, *Gloucester Journal*, 23 September 1876, *Cheltenham Chronicle*, 28 July 1857, *Exeter and Plymouth Gazette*, 30 April 1853, *Bristol Mercury*, 19 February 1870.
147 *Berkshire Chronicle*, 17 April 1858.
148 *Hereford Times*, 3 May 1851.
149 H. Cunningham, 'The Metropolitan Fairs: A Case Study in the Social Control of Leisure', in *Social Control in Nineteenth Century Britain*, ed. A. Donajgrodzki (London: Croom Helm, 1977), 163.
150 *Worcestershire Chronicle*, 7 November 1849.
151 See Andersson, *Streetlife*, 116–18, for urban pickpockets in crowds. There are many examples of pickpockets using smocks as a disguise, for instance, at Mansfield statute and hiring fair, to imitate 'country bumpkins' and to circulate in the crowd to 'deceive the unwary', *Nottingham Review and General Advertiser for the Midland Counties*, 8 November 1850.
152 *Wolverhampton Chronicle and Staffordshire Advertiser*, 14 March 1860.
153 Andersson, *Streetlife*, 8, 66.
154 J. Styles, 'Design for Large-Scale Production in Eighteenth-Century Britain', *Oxford Art Journal* 11, no. 2 (1988): 10.
155 L. Baumgarten, *What Clothes Reveal: The Language of Clothing in Colonial and Federal America* (Williamsburg: Colonial Williamsburg Foundation, 2002), 72. See also C.

Shine, 'Scalping Knives and Silk Stockings: Clothing the Frontier, 1780–1795', *Dress* 14 (1988): 40–1, 46.

156 See Baumgarten, *What Clothes Reveal*, 66, 69–75, for the development of the 'hunting shirt'.

157 See M. Zakim, 'Sartorial Ideologies: From Homespun to Ready-made', *American Historical Review* 106, no. 5 (2001): especially 1555, where he notes that in 1767 linen weaving was resuscitated throughout the colony.

158 According to a letter from Captain John Chester, 22 July 1775, his Connecticut regiment responded to the Battle of Bunker Hill by marching out of Cambridge with 'frocks and trousers on over our other clothes (for our company is in uniform wholly blue turned up with red,) for we were loth to expose ourselves by our dress', cited in A. R. Cain, 'An Analysis of the Use of Farmer's Smocks by Massachusetts Militia on April 19, 1775', available online: https://web.archive.org/web/20110713202807/http://www.lexingtonminutemen.com/index.php?option=com_content&view=section&layout=blog&id=12&Itemid=68 note 1 (accessed 17 June 2020).

159 See ibid., letter from John Adams to Abigail Adams, 7 July 1774, stating, 'a frock and trowsers [sic], spade and hoe, will do for my remaining days'.

160 See also M. Wright, *Everyday Dress of Rural America, 1783–1800: With Instructions and Patterns* (Mineola: Dover Publications, 1992), 79–80, for further references to the frock from around the turn of the nineteenth century. Blue was apparently a popular colour for everyday smocks.

161 Severa, *Dressed for the Photographer*, 209. See 20–1, and 131 and 170, for home-made woollen examples which differed in detail and in construction method to the English shirt-style smock frock. See also Genesee Country Village and Museum, accession number G2019.029, for a brown checked surviving example.

162 See L. Lebart, *Gold and Silver, Daguerreotypes, Ambrotypes and Tintypes from the Gold Rush* (Paris: RVB Books, 2018), for many images of men in working smocks.

163 Severa, *Dressed for the Photographer*, 105–6. She notes that not many smocks were photographed, but also that men would choose not to be photographed in their working clothing although there is a possible advertisement for them from 1849, see ibid., 20–1. See online: http://collection.folkartmuseum.org/objects/4010/ (accessed 17 June 2020), for Finch's work. See online: https://collections.osv.org/object-26-48-32 (accessed 17 June 2020), for nineteenth-century surviving examples.

164 Young, 'The Experience of Convictism', 75–6. Initially in 1786, the suggestion was for two jackets and three smocks for a year, a generous sum, although not fulfilled. By 1820, the bi-annual supply was a jacket or a smock for winter, a canvas smock for summer.

165 Of the prisoners in Western Australia in 1856, 20 per cent were still issued with duck or dowlas smocks, see Young, 'The Experience of Convictism', 78.

166 *Colonial Times and Tasmanian Advertiser*, 12 May 1826.

167 *South Australian*, 9 May 1848.

168 H. Capper, *Capper's South Australia: Containing the History of the Rise, Progress and Present State of the Colony, Hints to Emigrants … Embellished with Three Maps Showing the Maritime Portion of the Located Districts, the … Districts of Adelaide and Encounter Bay, and the City of Adelaide* (London: H. Capper, 1839), 129, 156–7.

169   M. Maynard, *Fashioned from Penury: Dress as Cultural Practice in Colonial Australia* (Cambridge: Cambridge University Press, 1994), 166–7, 170–1.

170   *The Sydney Morning Herald*, 18 November 1847, and *Perth Gazette and Western Australian Journal*, 11 July 1840. Sometimes smocks were divided into occupational types, such as for carters, drovers or railway workers, see *The Sydney Morning Herald*, 15 September 1859 and 30 March 1858, and *Tasmanian Daily News*, 29 April 1857.

171   See R. Wuchatsch, *John Muston: Draper, Squatter, Speculator in Colonial Australia* (Pirron Yallock: Stony Rises Run, 2017), particularly 28.

172   See, for example, *Colonial Times*, 17 October 1848.

173   *Colonial Times*, 11 July 1851.

174   Letter from C. M. Pearson, *Chelmsford Chronicle,* 16 June 1854.

175   *Newcastle Guardian and Tyne Mercury,* 26 November 1853 (italics in the original).

176   Letter to the Editor, *The Argus*, 16 December 1851. See also 5 above for another reference to 'jumpers'. See online https://viewer.slv.vic.gov.au/?entity=IE1442059&mode=browse (accessed 18 June 2020), for an illustration of a 'tartan jumper'.

177   Miles Foxcroft writing home from Melbourne, Australia, about 'diggers', *Kendal Mercury*, 27 August 1853. The Parramatta Asylum for the infirm and destitute asked for samples to supply a hundred 'jumpers' or smock frocks in 1862, see *The Sydney Morning Herald*, 15 September 1862.

178   P. H. Gosse, *The Romance of Natural History* (London: James Nisbet, 1860), 255.

179   *Hobarton Guardian*, 10 April 1850.

180   They seem to have later been also called 'Crimean shirts', possibly indicating the original source of some as ready-made army clothing. See, for example, L. Cramer, 'Diggers Dress and Identity on the Victorian Goldfields, Australia, 1851–1870', *Fashion Theory, The Journal of Dress, Body & Culture*, 22, no. 1 (2018), 94. See also Maynard, *Fashioned from Penury*, 168–9.

181   Maynard, *Fashioned from Penury,* 172–6, 179.

182   Ibid., 173.

183   *Adelaide Observer*, 8 April 1854. See 47–8 and 50–1 above for details about Favell and Bousfield.

184   *The Brisbane Courier*, 13 October 1864. The Axe Brand became synonymous with moleskin trousers.

185   This has parallels with English late-nineteenth-century urban nostalgia for the smock and vanishing rural life.

186   K. Sayer, *Women of the Fields: Representations of Rural Women in the Nineteenth Century* (Manchester: Manchester University Press, 1995), 61.

187   Note that in the idealised portrayal of a labourer by George Elgar Hicks, 'The Sinews of Old England', 1857, available online https://collections.britishart.yale.edu/vufind/Record/3659731 (accessed 7 May 2020), he has a smock tied around his shoulders although a muscled forearm is displayed by the artist for the viewer.

6 Into the twentieth century

Parts of this chapter first appeared in the article, A. Toplis, 'The Smock Frock: the Journey from Fieldwork to the Pages of *Vogue*', *Textile History* 49, no. 1 (2018): 71–91, copyright © Pasold Research Fund Ltd., reprinted by permission of Taylor & Francis Ltd., http://www.tandfonline.com on behalf of Pasold Research Fund Ltd.

1   *Cambridge Independent Press,* 10 April 1847. See 25–6 above for similar mid-eighteenth century perceptions.

2   See J. Tosh, 'Masculinities in an Industrializing Society: Britain, 1800–1914', *Journal of British Studies*, 44, no. 2 (2005): 331, for a discussion about the difficulties with this term, and also 336 and 342, where he notes how little research has been completed on the masculinity of the labouring poor, especially the rural poor.

3   *The Ipswich Journal*, 5 May 1804. A similar accident was noted in 1812, when a boy's smock frock became ensnared in the spindle of a threshing machine at Grantham, Lincolnshire, and he was 'dashed to pieces', a cover recommended for the spindle to stop this happening again, see *Norfolk Chronicle*, 13 June 1812.

4   *Shrewsbury Chronicle*, 24 April 1835. Similarly the *Windsor and Eton Express*, 11 October 1828, after reporting another accident warned: 'Persons working machines should have no *loose* garments on them.'

5   *Hereford Times,* 13 November 1847.

6   See, for example, the case of Robert Galley, *Essex Standard*, 17 April 1846. See also J. L. Bronstein, *Caught in the Machinery: Workplace Accidents and Injured Workers in Nineteenth-century Britain* (Stanford: Stanford University Press, 2008), 67–73.

7   *Brighton Gazette*, 4 October 1860.

8   Bronstein, *Caught in the Machinery,* 115. See also chapter 1, ibid., for a discussion about accidents, although he does not interrogate the role of clothing in such cases.

9   V. Richmond, *Clothing the Poor in Nineteenth-Century England* (Cambridge: Cambridge University Press, 2013), 181–2.

10 *Derby Daily Telegraph,* 9 July 1914, 2.

11 K. Honeyman, *Well-suited: A History of the Leeds Clothing Industry, 1850–1990* (Oxford: Oxford University Press, 2000), 2, 20–1.

12 B. Shannon, *The Cut of His Coat: Men, Dress, and Consumer Culture in Britain, 1860–1914* (Athens: Ohio University Press, 2006), 82. See also J. Begiato, *Manliness in Britain, 1760–1900* (Manchester: Manchester University Press, 2020), for an exploration of the penalties for perceived unmanliness, particularly 83.

13 Contrary to earlier in the century, when the smock had allowed men to become anonymous, see 79 above.

14 *Hull Daily Mail*, 18 June 1912, 3; also *Sussex Agricultural Express,* 17 May 1912, 6.

15 For perceived changes in dress see 'Recent Changes in Rural Costume', *Bath Chronicle and Weekly Gazette,* 17 December 1891.

16 P. K. Andersson, *Streetlife in Late Victorian London: The Constable and the Crowd* (Basingstoke: Palgrave Macmillan, 2013), 156–7.

17 Ibid., 163.

18 *The Era*, 3 August 1873.

19 See *Caledonian Mercury*, 4 April 1853, for an early performance. See *Bath Chronicle and Weekly Gazette,* 21 April 1853, for an early amateur performance in Bath. By 1865, it was noted as 'an old favourite with the amateurs', see *Cheltenham Chronicle*, 5 December 1865. It was still performed in the 1870s, see the performance by the Nottingham Private Dramatic Club at Arnold, *Nottingham Evening Post*, 25 January 1879, and into the twentieth century by amateur companies, including performances in Australia.

20 For one of the first advertisements of the performance, see *London Evening Standard*, 14 December 1852. See *The Graphic*, 19 March 1870, for an obituary of Brough. See A. E. Wilson, *The Lyceum* (London: Dennis Yates, 1952), 67–73, for the Vestris Matthews management.

21 W. Brough, *A Phenomenon in a Smock Frock* (London: Thomas Hailes Lacy, 1852).

22 See C. Payne, *Rustic Simplicity: Scenes of Cottage Life in Nineteenth-Century British Art* (London: Lund Humphries Publishers, 1998), 23.

23 *Hereford Journal*, 4 April 1863.

24 Maidment, *Dusty Bob*, 215. See also the performance of *Truth and Honesty in a Smock Frock*, *Cambridge Independent Press,* 16 March 1878, and *He Wears a Smock Frock*, *Western Times*, 12 February 1875.

25 *The Era*, 4 October 1874, 4, 'Music Hall at the Cambridge'. See also online: http://www.smockfrock.co.uk/tag/lily-langtry/ (accessed 18 June 2020), for Lily Langtry.

26 *Dorset County Chronicle,* 11 September 1856.

27 Their contribution won an 'honourable mention' for being 'exceedingly well-made by two cottagers'. See online: http://www.smockfrock.co.uk/smocks-at-the-great-exhibition-of-1851/ (accessed 18 June 2020), for further details.

28 *Gloucester Journal*, 22 July 1848, the smock category won by Elizabeth Rodway. A similar show was held the previous year, see *Gloucester Journal,* 21 August 1847, the smock prize won by Susannah Rodway.

29 *Dorset County Chronicle,* 10 September 1857; see also *Dorset County Chronicle,* 16 September 1854 for that year's exhibition with a smock frock class, and *Bridport News,* 9 September 1865, where the prize was still 7 shillings and 'a goodly company of the gentry from the neighbourhood' attended.

30 For example, see the fifteenth annual Hanley Castle and District Cottagers' Show, with a prize in the needlework section for a smock frock, *Worcestershire Chronicle,* 4 August 1877; and similarly the 'making a smock frock' section in the Cleobury Mortimer Cottagers' Floral and Horticultural Society annual show see *Worcester Journal,* 10 August 1872.

31 K. Wahl, *Dressed as in a Painting: Women and British Aestheticism in an Age of Reform* (Durham: University of New Hampshire Press, 2013), 26–7.

32 *Dundee Evening Telegraph,* 4 October 1880. See *Nottingham Evening Post,* 25 September 1880, for the use of smocking on mantles and over-dresses, which were also given the more 'euphonious title' surplice mantles. See also S. Wilson, 'Away with the Corsets, on with the Shifts', in *Simply Stunning, The Pre-Raphaelite Art of Dressing*, exhibition catalogue (Cheltenham: Cheltenham Art Gallery and Museums, 1996), 28.

33 See Wahl, *Dressed as in a Painting*, 117–21, for more about the hybridization of artistic and fashionable dress using smocking.

34 *The Graphic*, 2 October 1880; *Dundee Courier*, 27 September 1880.

35 *Aberdeen Evening Express*, 19 December 1884; *Leicester Chronicle*, 20 December 1884; The *Post Office London Directory for 1882, comprising, amongst other information, official, street, commercial, trades, law, court, parliamentary, postal, city & clerical, conveyance & banking directories*. [Part 1: Official & Street Directories] (London: Frederick Kelly, 1882), 480.

36 *Leicester Chronicle,* 29 October 1881. See also *Bristol Mercury,* 5 February 1881.

37 *Staffordshire Sentinel and Commercial & General Advertiser*, 5 February 1881.

38 1881 Census, 1891 Census. See 'Personal Freedom and Public Space', online: https://historicengland.org.uk/research/inclusive-heritage/womens-history/visible-in-stone/personal-freedom-public-space/ (accessed 18 June 2020). For a report about an embroidered school girl's smock designed by former Hamilton's manageress, Sarah Franks, in the Hygienic Depôt, see 'Our Ladies Column', *Leicester Chronicle*, 21 December 1889. The rational dress movement was based on health and comfort, followers railing against clothing which impeded movement or harmed and deformed the body. This contrasted with the aesthetic dress movement, which developed from artistic dress and was influenced by medieval and Renaissance art, although also popularizing loose fitting dresses worn without tight lacing.

39 For example, *Weldon's Practical Needlework* books included smocking from 1887, available by mail order, see, for instance, the *Morning Post,* 29 April 1889. *The Ladies' Monthly Magazine* provided a full page of instructions, with diagrams, at the request of readers, 1 June 1888, 86, while Briggs & Co. supplied transfer designs for 'Smocking or Honey-combing made easy', see *Myra's Journal of Dress and Fashion*, 1 November 1887, 600. By 1892, gauging was said to be more popular, 'people … growing weary of smocking', see '"Liberty" and Comfort in Dress', by Fanny Douglas, *Hearth and Home*, 18 August 1892, 460.

40 *Dundee, Perth, Forfar, and Fife's People's Journal*, 8 March 1879. Also *Nottingham Evening Post*, 8 March 1879. One was for sale in a Gentlewomen's Self Help Institution in Baker Street for 12 shillings.

41 *Nottingham Evening Post*, 14 August 1880. Greenaway's drawings from the 1870s and 1880s adapted a style of dress that she saw as a child growing up in Rolleston, Nottinghamshire, close to Newark, a centre for smock frock manufacture, see M. H. Spielman and G. S. Layard, *The Life and Work of Kate Greenaway* (London: Bracken Books, 1986), 50. Lady Harberton of the Rational Dress Society criticized her for children's clothes that were 'unsuited to the practical needs and comforts of boys' and girls'. See S. M. Newton, *Health, Art and Reason: Dress Reformers of the Nineteenth Century* (London: John Murray, 1974), 124.

42 *Lancaster Gazette,* 26 January 1881.

43 *Sunderland Daily Echo and Shipping Gazette,* 9 March 1887, in the new 'Queen Mab' design.

44 See B. Marshall, *Smocks and Smocking* (Sherborne: Alphabooks, 1980), 93. Lady Elizabeth Bowes-Lyon was photographed wearing one in 1907 and Clara Frances Lloyd recalled making them into the 1920s, see C. F. Lloyd, 'Liberty's Embroidery Workrooms', *Costume* 10, no. 1 (1976): 89. *Aberdeen Journal*, 22 April 1919, 2, noted a vogue for smocks in children's wear that year.

45 Lloyd, 'Liberty's Embroidery Workrooms', 90. She also notes repairing museum pieces, incuding a shepherd's smock.

46 *Manchester Courier and Lancashire General Advertiser*, 7 July 1888.

47   See E. Ewing, *History of Children's Clothing* (Tiptree: Anchor Press, 1977), 104–9, for health benefits, including the advantages of wearing white, and connections to the Rational Dress Society founded in 1881. The Children's Dress Association in Wigmore Street sold so-called Yorkshire Smocks for children in 1891, see *Newcastle Courant*, 16 May 1891. A report commented in 1889 about the 'stretch and give' smocking gave children's clothes, *Derby Daily Telegraph*, 13 September 1889.

48   C. Rose, *Making, Selling and Wearing Boys' Clothes in Late-Victorian England* (Abingdon: Routledge, 2016), 207, 209, who notes that this 'undermines any attempt at a simple interpretation of masculinity'.

49   Rose, *Making*, 208. The royal family still dress their young children in smocks.

50   Rose, *Making*, 209, 222, 228–9, for comparison with other boys' wear.

51   Rose, *Making*, 228.

52   *Worcester Journal,* 10 April 1886.

53   *Penny Illustrated Paper and Illustrated Times*, 5 December 1908, 382. See also Mr Lasenby Liberty appearing at a fancy dress ball in 1909 as an 'old-fashioned farmer', in a smock frock with a red handkerchief tied around his neck, *Luton Times and Advertiser*, 1 January 1909, 7.

54   Toplis, 'The Smock Frock', 75–6. See K. Gawade, 'Fashioning Aestheticism: Ellen Terry, Photography and Fashion', in *Ellen Terry, the Painter's Actress,* ed. V. F. Gould and K. Gawade (Guildford: Watts Gallery, 2014), 51, 57–65, 72, for photography aiding this developing celebrity culture. Also R. Hargreaves, 'Putting Faces to the Names: Social and Celebrity Portrait Photography', in *The Beautiful and the Damned: The Creation of Identity in Nineteenth Century Photography,* ed. P. Hamilton and R. Hargreaves (Aldershot: Lund Humphries, 2001), 44–5.

55   G. Squire, 'E. W. Godwin and the House of Liberty', *Costume* 34, no. 1 (2000): 96.

56   A. Rachlin, *Edy was a Lady* (Kibworth Beauchamp: Matador, 2011), 47–8.

57   *Hartlepool Mail*, 14 September 1897.

58   See online: http://www.smockfrock.co.uk/the-white-of-the-milkman/ (accessed 18 June 2020).

59   See Newton, *Health, Art and Reason*, 102, 108, who notes the importance of natural colour for the aesthetic and rational dress movements.

60   Lady Duff-Gordon, *Discretions and Indiscretions* (London: Jarrolds Publishers, 1932), 32–3.

61   Email with Susannah Mayor, Ellen Terry Memorial Museum, Smallhythe Place, Tenterden, Kent, 2015. See also an undated letter (after 1907) From Gandy (Ellen Terry) to Sweet wee Paulette (Pauline Chase), an invitation for Nicko and Pauline to visit Ellen and James Carew at Smallhythe Place with advice on appropriate clothes to bring – 'smocks not fine dresses', ET Z 2,076, ET OUT, C (BL) Loan 125/31/2, British Library, London.

62   Squire, 'E. W. Godwin', 88.

63   R. Addison, 'Liberating Fashion: The Aesthetic Portraits of George Frederick Watts', in *Liberating Fashion: Aesthetic Dress in Victorian Portraits,* ed. R. Addison and H. Underwood (Guildford: Watts Gallery, 2015), 51. See also Newton, *Health, Art and Reason*, 80–3, for discussion about Watts's theories.

64   *Aberdeen People's Journal*, 9 July 1904, 5. Part of his house is now the Watts Studios museum. Mary Watts, his second wife, was photographed wearing a smock frock while plastering ceiling panels for Limnerslease in 1890–3.

65 *Pall Mall Gazette,* 2 April 1890.

66 Dated 20 February 1892 and entitled 'Bronze Statuary', in the 'Men of the Day' series, published by Vincent Brooks Day & Sons, the artist was Leslie Ward. Thornycroft also designed a white silk dress for his wife, with smocked and ruched panels, now in the Victoria and Albert Museum see online: http://collections.vam.ac.uk/item/O13850/dress-unknown/ (accessed 18 June 2020).

67 See Wahl, *Dressed as in a Painting,* 29–30, for Walter Crane's comments about the simple, useful and picturesque dress of labourers, and Toplis, 'The Smock Frock', 75, for Oscar Wilde's similar thoughts linking simplicity and beauty.

68 *Pall Mall Gazette,* 22 June 1888.

69 *Leamington Spa Courier,* 31 December 1887.

70 *Yorkshire Post and Leeds Intelligencer,* 30 August 1893.

71 See N. Tarrant, *Smocks in the Buckinghamshire County Museum* (Aylesbury: Buckinghamshire County Council, 1976), illustration 10.

72 *Luton Times and Advertiser,* 8 July 1910, 7, and *Bedfordshire Mercury,* 8 July 1910, 3.

73 *Bucks Herald,* 29 January 1916, 7.

74 *Newcastle Courant,* 19 December 1891. *Blackwood's* was seen as a Tory magazine.

75 J. H. MacDonald, 'A Sussex Peasant', *Country Life,* 10 September 1898, 313.

76 L. Ugolini, *Men and Menswear: Sartorial Consumption in Britain 1880–1939* (Aldershot: Ashgate Publishing, 2007), 115–16.

77 C. Breward, 'The Dandy Laid Bare, Embodying Practices and Fashion for Men', in *Fashion Cultures, Theories, Explorations and Analysis,* ed. S. Bruzzi and P. Church Gibson (Abingdon: Routledge, 2000), 233.

78 *Hereford Times,* 25 May 1850. See also William Evans of Twyneth House, Chertsey, who died in 1856 in Belgravia. Twelve estate employees wearing white smock frocks and black crape hatbands escorted his coffin back to the country, *Windsor and Eton Express,* 31 May 1856.

79 *Bucks Herald,* 2 August 1873.

80 See, for example, the funeral of Colonel Harcourt, Buxted, East Sussex, *Kent & Sussex Courier,* 7 May 1880, and Charles Powell, a magistrate, at Speldhurst, *Kent & Sussex Courier,* 27 March 1885; also the funeral of John Smith, Bishopstone, Swindon, where six old servants in white smock frocks carried his coffin, *Swindon Advertiser and North Wilts Chronicle,* 17 July 1880; in 1916, the coffin of Rear-Admiral, the Hon. T. S. Brand was buried at Glynde, Sussex, his coffin borne on a farm wagon, the drivers wearing smocks, *Daily Mirror,* 17 November 1916, including a photograph. These funerals stop after 1919.

81 See the death of Mr Rague Kemp, *Kent & Sussex Courier,* 17 June 1927, 19.

82 *Sussex Agricultural Express,* 3 October 1941, 4.

83 See *Sussex Agricultural Express,* 9 July 1914, 5, for a photograph.

84 *Liverpool Echo,* 6 July 1914, 5; *Leicester Chronicle,* 11 July 1914, 3. *Nottingham Evening Post,* 6 July 1914, 5. In the workhouse they were to be of a dark colour, worn in preference to overcoats by inmates on their day's leave each month. The master also wore one, but of a lighter colour, presumably to distinguish him from the inmates, see *Sussex Agricultural Express,* 4 December 1913, 5, and 25 December 1913, 8–9. Also see *Portsmouth Evening*

News, 29 November 1913, 10, and 4 February 1914, 4, where the Lewes smock frocks were thought to be 'handsome and hygienic garments' too.

85 *Sussex Agricultural Express,* 18 December 1913, 7. The *Daily Mirror* and the *Daily Graphic* sent letters to the Board of Guardians, asking if they could come and photograph the inmates on their day's outing, 'Have[ing] a smock parade'. The guardians thus agreed with the letter writer that the smocks were generating too much attention and they were quietly 'condemned'.

86 For example, *Chelmsford Chronicle,* 14 November 1930, 7. Beaters in white smocks were photographed at the Balneath Shoot, see *Sussex Agricultural Express,* 10 November 1933, 18.

87 M. Hall, *Smocks* (Princes Risborough: Shire Publications, 1979), 13.

88 *Sussex Agricultural Express,* 18 July 1924; 2, *Sussex Agricultural Express,* 12 December 1930, 12; *Sussex Agricultural Express,* 7 October 1938, 14. He also wore his Grenfell cloth smock frock, made in Lewes, to play stoolball, see online: https://www.stoolball.org.uk/history/story/major-w-w-grantham/biography/ (accessed 18 June 2020).

89 They continued to be worn by elite men into the 1930s for menial duties, see 169 above, note 110 for the experiences of Arthur Beckett, who overcame his earlier reservations; also The Museum of English Rural Life (MERL) smock 93/90, worn by a solicitor in Wiltshire in around 1914.

90 Available online: http://www.gardencitycollection.com/object-lbm2217 (accessed 18 June 2020).

91 See Y. Gradley, 'Life in a Garden City', *Penny Illustrated Paper.* Issue 2701, 1 March 1913: 15.

92 *Western Gazette,* 20 February 1914, 12; R. Worth, *Dress and Textiles (Discover Dorset)* (Wimborne: Dovecote Press, 2002), 73–4; and Hall, *Smocks,* 30. See R. Bere, 'Old English Smocking Patterns', *Country Life,* 11 August 1966, 351, who was her son and wore smock frocks as a child which he comments were probably more comfortable than sailor suits.

93 M. G. Rees and C. Stevens, 'Smocks in the Welsh Folk Museum Collection', *Medel* 3 (Cardiff: National Museum of Wales, 1986): 34, smock no. 14.159. See also green and blue ones in MERL 63/286 and 63/283 and items associated with Mrs Bere, 63/280–6.

94 *The Times,* 27 June 1913, 39. See also A. H. Baverstock, *The English Agricultural Labourer* (London: Vineyard Press, 1912), 44, for similar comments, who notes that it brought new social connections in the village.

95 *The Times,* 27 June 1913, 39. The Girls' Friendly Society was established in 1875 and, run by middle- and upper-class women, aimed to befriend and protect young, rural, working-class women who had moved to the city, see V. Richmond, 'Stitching Women: Unpicking Histories of Victorian Clothes', in *Gender and Material Culture in Britain since 1760,* ed. H. Greig, J. Hamlett and L. Hannan (London: Palgrave 2016), 92.

96 Richmond, *Clothing the Poor,* 108–9, 223; see J. Helland, 'Rural Women and Urban Extravagance in Late Nineteenth-Century Britain', *Rural History* 13, no. 2 (2002): 179–97, for parallels with the Scottish Home Industries and Donegal Industrial Fund.

97 *Country Life,* 29 August 1903, 319.

98 T. Harrod, *The Crafts in Britain in the Twentieth Century* (London: Yale University Press, 1999), 123–4, 137, 144, 156, theories essential to both the Arts and Crafts Movement and later craft movements in the twentieth century.

99   E. Woolman Chase and I. Chase, *Always in Vogue* (London: Victor Gollancz, 1954), 77. See also C. Barwick, *A Century of Style* (London: George Allen & Unwin, 1984), 102–4, and J. Ashelford, *The Art of Dress* (London: National Trust, 1996), 303, who first alerted me to these connections.

100 *Vogue* 43, no. 9 (1 May 1914): 49. *Vogue* hereafter refers to the American edition, British *Vogue* not being founded until 1916.

101 Chase and Chase, *Always in Vogue*, 77.

102 W. M. Corn, *Georgia O'Keeffe: Living Modern* (New York: DelMonico Books 2017), 57–9, including a *Vanity Fair* cartoon of a smock wearer.

103 'Seen in the Shops', *Vogue* 45, no. 11 (1 June 1915): 56.

104 See Toplis, 'The Smock Frock', 80–1, for illustration and further details.

105 *Vogue* 46, no. 6 (15 September 1915): 137.

106 See cartoon about the perils of buying smocks unseen and finding that they had already been worn, *Women's Wear* 15, no. 34 (10 August 1917): 53.

107 *Vogue* 46, no. 12 (15 December 1915): 104.

108 *Vogue* 47, no. 7 (1 April 1916): 103.

109 Corn, *Georgia O'Keeffe*, 61, for letters. See also ibid., figures 83, 89.

110 Corn, *Georgia O'Keeffe*, 45.

111 *Daily Mirror*, 17 June 1915. See surviving smock of cornflower blue cotton made under the tutelage of Lady Wilson of Herefordshire, possibly for gardening, E. Finney, N. Hely-Hutchinson and A. Mackenzie, *Smocks from the Hereford Museum Collection* (Hereford: Herefordshire Heritage Services, 2005), 40–1, for drawing and photograph. See also Buckinghamshire County Museum, AYBCM: 1967.345.1, for a female smock used to milk cows, available online: https://www.buckscountymuseum.org/museum/about-the-museum/collections/item-details/?modes_query=%7Bsearch%7D%3D%2A%7Bsmock%7D&start_collections=7 (accessed 18 June 2020). Female gardeners in England did not traditionally wear the smock before this point, see Toplis, 'The Smock Frock', 82, for further details.

112 *Sunday Mirror*, 18 July 1915. See also *Daily Mirror*, 12 July 1915, and *Daily Record*, 10 August 1915, for similar reports. The earliest reference to fashions for smocks in England is from the *Daily Mirror*, 11 January 1915, which reports 'Farmer Giles's old smock made from pretty material and with a broad 'nursery' belt worn in child-like fashion below the hips is one of the fancies of the moment for grown ups', the American trend seemingly influencing this fashion.

113 *Sunday Mirror*, 3 October 1915.

114 *Sunday Mirror*, 15 August 1915.

115 See sketch of a house smock of pale mauve, 'honeycombed', and worn over a black satin skirt, *Daily Record*, 16 May 1917.

116 An article in the *Daily Record* pointed out that smocking was originally an idea for children's frocks before being appropriated for women's fashions, see *Daily Record*, 27 January 1916.

117 *Daily Mirror*, 11 November 1915. Her daughter also wore a smock of 'blue crash' to look after her pets.

118 *Kent & Sussex Courier,* 24 March 1916, 7, for motoring coats displayed at Lady Wilson's 'Economy in Wartime Exhibition' in Tunbridge Wells. See also the Duchess of Sutherland wearing 'one of the new smocked coat-frocks', *Daily Mirror,* 27 May 1916.

119 *Daily Mirror,* 18 September 1916.

120 C. Twinch, *Women on the Land: Their Story During Two World Wars* (Cambridge: Lutterworth Press, 1990), 35–8.

121 Available online: http://www.iwm.org.uk/collections/item/object/205214437 (accessed 18 June 2020).

122 For example, Barker's of Kensington, *Daily Mirror,* 18 July 1917, and Derry and Tom's section for 'Land Suits, Smocks and Overalls', see the *Daily Mirror,* 21 May 1917. Copland & Lye of Sauchiehall Street, Glasgow, also provided a large selection of ladies overalls including hand smocked overalls, fastening at the front, in fadeless casement cloth, costing 22 shillings 6 pence, see *Daily Record,* 4 February 1918. Elizabeth Ltd, South Moulton Street, London, advertised the 'Olva outfit', a smock in shower proof khaki drill with coloured embroidery, see *The Landswoman: The Journal of Land Army*,1, no. 10, 1 October 1918, 225.

123 See interview with Helen Beatrice Poulter who worked for the Land Army in the Forestry Corps in 1918 and did not like the uniform. Available online: http://www.iwm.org.uk/collections/item/object/80000723, reel 6 (accessed 18 June 2020). See *Daily Mirror,* 21 July 1917, for advertisement.

124 *The Tatler,* 15 August 1917.

125 Twinch, *Women on the Land,* 42.

126 S. R. Grayzel, 'Nostalgia, Gender, and the Countryside; Placing the "Land Girl" in First World War Britain', *Rural History* 10, no. 2 (1999): 156.

127 *Daily Mirror,* 3 September 1917.

128 Grayzel, 'Nostalgia', 159–60. See also *Cornishman,* 29 March 1917, where the WLA uniform was called 'serviceable and picturesque', marking them out as 'soldiers'.

129 Ornamental smocks were detailed and sketched on the fashion pages of newspapers, for example, a gown of pewter grey cashmere for afternoon wear, smocked in blue floss silk, see *Daily Record,* 18 April 1917.

130 *Daily Mirror,* 22 July 1918, and also similarly, 'Our Club Page', *The Landswoman: Journal of the Land Army* 1, no. 6, 1 June 1918, 119. 'Chintz' is a glazed cotton printed with brightly coloured, usually floral, patterns, 'Holland' a plain linen or cotton fabric.

131 *Country Life,* 5 May 1917, 16. Coloured smocks were worn, but for ordinary farm work, women demanded brown or khaki so as not to show mud or dirt, see the *Daily Record,* 17 April 1917.

132 'The Blouse will be always with us', *Daily Record,* 24 May 1917, which included the smock in this category. See also 'When I First Put This Uniform on', a poem from *The Landswoman: The Journal of Land Army*,1, no. 12, 1 December 1918, 305, which describes the freedom felt and the practical benefits of the smock and breeches.

133 This term seems to date to 1917, developing from the 'jumper blouse' of 1916. See L. Whitmore, 'Blouse, Jumper, Jumper-blouse: the Everyday Fashions of Convenience from the First World War', paper given at the Everyday Fashion: Extraordinary Stories of Ordinary

Clothes Conference, 27 June 2019, University of Huddersfield. See above 5 and 105 for earlier usage of this term.

134 *Country Life*, 25 September 1926, lx, lxii.

135 For example, see *Country Life*, 3 March 1923, lxxiii, advertisement; *Country Life*, 29 January 1938, xlii, 'Smocks for the Busy Woman'; *Country Life*, 5 August 1939, xxx, 'Fashion Fair, Working Clothes'.

136 'Teach Yourself to Smock', *Harper's Bazaar*, New York, June 1943, 50–1.

137 See 'New Nursery Looks: Yoked and Smocked', *Harper's Bazaar*, New York, June 1957, 64–7, and 'Mainbocher's Workman Smocks on the Beach', illustrated in *Harper's Bazaar*, 67, 2660, June 1934, 51.

138 W. R. Lethaby was also a frequent contributor to *Home and Country*, the WI magazine, see M. Andrews, *The Acceptable Face of Feminism: The Women's Institute as a Social Movement* (London: Lawrence & Wishart, 1997), 68.

139 Andrews, *The Acceptable Face*, 25–7. A village was defined as having no more than 5,000 inhabitants.

140 K. S. Woods, *The Rural Industries Round Oxford: A Survey* (Oxford: Oxford University Press, 1921), 154, 171–3.

141 Andrews, *The Acceptable Face*, 31–2.

142 Ibid., 73. A. Armes, *English Smocks with Directions for Making Them* (Leicester: Dryad Press, 1928).

143 See Andrews, *The Acceptable Face*, 67–9, 72–4, who notes that members of the Guild of Learners were mainly middle-class women, with time and money, looking for a creative outlet which could be aligned with a culture of work, similar to the Arts and Crafts Movement. There were twenty-four smockers in the guild, see ibid., 174, and smocks made by WI members were also advertised in the *Home and Country* magazine for sale in London stores.

144 H. Fitzrandolph and M. Hay, *The Rural Industries of England and Wales, Decorative Crafts and Rural Potteries* (Oxford: Oxford University Press, 1927), Vol. III, 75, 79.

145 M. Morgan, 'Jam Making, Cuthbert Rabbit and Cakes. Redefining Domestic Labour in the Women's Institute 1915–60', *Rural History* 7, no. 2 (1996): 209, 211, 213–14. See also A. Jones, *The Rural Industries of England and Wales, Wales* (Oxford: Oxford University Press, 1927), Vol. IV, 119, for early debates within the WI about selling crafts for profit and how this could be developed. Andrews, *The Acceptable Face*, 71–2. A smock made in Berkshire, probably in the early days of the WI, is deposited at MERL, accession no. 83/20, see online: http://www.reading.ac.uk/adlib/Details/collect/6371 (accessed 18 June 2020).

146 Armes, *English Smocks*, 14.

147 Andrews, *The Acceptable Face*, 68, 75; Morgan, 'Jam Making', 214–15.

148 *Torbay Express and South Devon Echo*, 14 May 1948, 4.

149 Andrews, *The Acceptable Face*, 129, 131. Armes's collection of smocks, probably lent out to members and teachers to learn from, are still held here.

150 See Worth, *Dress and Textiles*, 74.

151 O. Pass, *Dorset Feather Stitchery* (London: Mills & Boon, 1957).

152 M. Jones, 'The Vanished Smock-Frock', *Country Life*, 11 April 1857, 720. Anon., *Smocking, Traditional and Modern* (1955; Ipswich: National Federation of Women's Institutes, 1959).

153 Andrews, *The Acceptable Face of Feminism*, 151, 153–4, 158–9.

154 Marshall, *Smocks and Smocking*, 19. See, for example, Margaret Thom, *Smocking in Embroidery* (London: B. T. Batsford, 1972), for smocking as a handicraft. Other techniques such as American, Italian and counterchange direct smocking stitches, have been popular since the inter-war period.

155 O. Cave, *Traditional Smocks and Smocking* (London: Mills and Boon, 1979), 28 and 34.

156 For example, Cave, *Traditional Smocks*, see plates 4 and 5, 20–1. See *Country Life*, 19 September 1985, 836-7, for a 1980s revival.

157 R. Harden and J. Hashagen, *Laura Ashley: The Romantic Heroine* (Bath: Fashion Museum and North East Somerset Council, 2013), 5–6, 22, illustrated 31.

158 For example, see 'St. Laurent – The Smock for the Day', American *Vogue*, 15 April 1965, 92–7; 'Paris Couture … Splendour, Seduction, the Pleasure Principle', American *Vogue*, 1 October 1977, 272–3, for Givenchy.

159 American *Vogue*, March 1982, where it is used for an advertisement by Macy's California to advertise contemporary Japanese designers, no page number.

160 He continued to use the design the following season, Spring/Summer 1987, see Kerry Taylor Auctions, 'Passion for Fashion' sale catalogue, London, 14 June 2016, lot 279.

161 See online, https://www.vogue.co.uk/shows/spring-summer-2013-ready-to-wear/alexander-mcqueen (accessed 11 May 2020) Look 25.

162 See video interview with Molly Goddard, Balenciaga Exhibition, Victoria and Albert Museum, 2018; also L. Cochrane, 'Dressed to Frill', *The Observer*, 19 February 2017, available online: https://www.theguardian.com/fashion/2017/feb/19/molly-goddard-london-fashion-week (accessed 18 June 2020); T. Blanchard, 'Designer Molly Goddard: The Frill Seeker', *The Observer*, 21 February 2016, available online: https://www.theguardian.com/fashion/2016/feb/21/designer-molly-goddard-the-frill-seeker-dover-street-market (accessed 18 June 2020); T. Blanchard, 'Why We Love … Molly Goddard', *The Telegraph*, 18 September 2015, available online: https://www.telegraph.co.uk/fashion/brands/Molly-Goddard-the-queen-of-smock-dresses/ (accessed 18 June 2020).

163 E. Pithers, 'Inside the Maximalist World of Molly Goddard', British *Vogue*, 15 September 2018, available online: https://www.vogue.co.uk/article/molly-goddard-spring-summer-2019 (accessed 18 June 2020).

164 E. Pithers, 'Autumn/Winter 2019, Ready-to-Wear, Molly Goddard', British *Vogue*, 16 February 2019, available online: https://www.vogue.co.uk/shows/autumn-winter-2019-ready-to-wear/molly-goddard (accessed 18 June 2020).

165 E. V. Bramley, 'Killing Eve: Six Looks to Die for from the BBC Thriller', *The Guardian*, 17 October 2018, available online: https://www.theguardian.com/fashion/2018/oct/17/killing-eve-six-looks-to-die-for-from-the-bbc-thriller (accessed 18 June 2020). This has also mutated into Halloween costume.

166 M. Ferrier, 'The Tent Dress: New Trend Aiming to Capitalise on Warm Weather', *The Guardian*, 10 May 2019, available online: https://www.theguardian.com/fashion/2019/may/10/tent-dress-new-trend-aiming-capitalise-warm-weather-empowering (accessed 18 June 2020); M. Ferrier, 'The Thrills Are Alive! The Unexpected Return of the Laura Ashley Look', *The Guardian*, 2 May 2019, available online: https://www.theguardian.

com/fashion/2019/may/02/laura-ashley-look-1970s-style-frills-flowers (accessed 18 June 2020).

167 See also podcast, 'Dress: Fancy', Episode 42, 'Thoroughly Modern Molly', available online: https://podcasts.apple.com/gb/podcast/episode-42-thoroughly-modern-molly/id1436021370?i=1000474648589 (accessed 15 May 2020).

168 Goddard sometimes posts on her Instagram account the number of hours it has taken to make a garment, for example, her Skye Dress, with eighteen hand-smocked panels, took five days to make, 24 April 2020 @mollygoddard.

169 See Gucci Fall 2020, Menswear, available online: https://www.vogue.com/fashion-shows/fall-2020-menswear/gucci (accessed 28 April 2020).

Conclusion

1 R. Worth, 'Clothing the Landscape: Change and the Rural Vision in the Work of Thomas Hardy (1840–1928)', *Rural History* 24, no. 2 (2013): 213.

2 The origins of the smock are therefore perhaps not as ecologically sound as it first appears.

3 See B. Lemire, 'Reflections on the Character of Consumerism, Popular Fashion and the English Market in the Eighteenth Century', *Material History Bulletin* 31 (Spring 1990): 67.

4 B. Yates, 'Rural Dress in Norfolk', Strata of Society, Proceedings of the Seventh Annual Conference of the Costume Society, 6–8 April 1973 (London: V & A, 1974): 8, © reproduced with permission of The Licensor through PLSclear.

5 J. Lewis-Stempel, *The Running Hare: The Secret Life of Farmland* (London: Doubleday, 2016), 213, also 23.

6 Workwear is clothing worn over other clothing for protection, as an overall. Denim jeans were first worn in this way too and called 'waist overalls' until the 1950s.

7 P. Cunnington and C. Lucas, *Occupational Costume in England, from the 11th Century to 1914* (London: Adam and Charles Black, 1976), 336.

8 Britains, toy manufacturers, produced such lead farm figures from 1921 to 1966.

Bibliography

Individual newspaper, magazine and online articles plus archive sources are referenced in the notes.

Anon., *Working Class Costume: From Sketches of Characters by William Johnstone White*. 1818. Reprinted with notes. Ed. P. Clabburn. London: Costume Society reprint, 1971.

Anon., By a Lady. *The Workwoman's Guide, Containing Instructions to the Inexperienced…* 1838. Reprinted. London: Simpkin, Marshall, and Co., 1840.

Anon., *Smocking, Traditional and Modern*. 1955. Reprinted. Ipswich: National Federation of Women's Institutes, 1959.

Ablett, W. *Reminiscences of an Old Draper*. London: Sampson Low, Marston, Searle and Rivington, 1876.

Addison, R. 'Liberating Fashion: The Aesthetic Portraits of George Frederick Watts'. In *Liberating Fashion: Aesthetic Dress in Victorian Portraits*, ed. R. Addison and H. Underwood, 46–73. Guildford: Watts Gallery, 2015.

Alcock, N. W., and N. Cox. *Living and Working in Seventeenth Century England: An Encyclopedia of Drawings and Descriptions from Randal Holme's Original Manuscripts for the Academy of Armory (1688)*. London: British Library, 2000, CD ROM.

Andersson, P. K. *Streetlife in Late Victorian London: The Constable and the Crowd*. Basingstoke: Palgrave Macmillan, 2013.

Andrews, M. *The Acceptable Face of Feminism: The Women's Institute as a Social Movement*. London: Lawrence & Wishart, 1997.

Anthony, I. E. *The Countrymen's Smocks in the Welsh Folk Museum*. Reprint from AMGUEDDFA, *Bulletin of the National Museum of Wales* 18 (Winter 1974): 1–7.

Arch, J. *The Autobiography of Joseph Arch*. 1898. Reprinted. London: MacGibbon & Kee, 1966.

Armes, A. *English Smocks with Directions for Making Them*. Leicester: Dryad Press, 1928.

Arnold, J. 'Smocks, Shirts, Falling Bands and Mantuas: Evidence of Loosely-Fitting Garments and Neckwear produced for the Ready-to-Wear Market, c. 1560–1700'. In *Per Una Storia della Moda Pronta, Problemi e Ricerche*, 17–27. Milan: Pitt Immagine, 1990.

Arnold, J. *Patterns of Fashion 4: The Cut and Construction of Linen Shirts, Smocks, Neckwear, Headwear and Accessories for Men and Women, c. 1540–1660*. London: Macmillan, 2008.

Ashelford, J. *The Art of Dress*. London: National Trust, 1996.

Bailey, P. '"Will the Real Bill Banks Please Stand Up?" Towards a Role Analysis of Mid-Victorian Working-Class Respectability'. *Journal of Social History* 12, no. 3 (1979): 336–53.

Barrell, J. *The Dark Side of the Landscape: The Rural Poor in English Painting 1730–1840*. Cambridge: Cambridge University Press, 1983.

Barrett, D. W. *Life and Work among the Navvies*. 1880. Reprinted. Kettering: Silver Link Book, not dated.

Barringer, T. *Men at Work: Art and Labour in Victorian Britain*. New Haven: Yale University Press, 2005.

Barwick, C. *A Century of Style*. London: George Allen & Unwin, 1984.

Baumgarten, L. *What Clothes Reveal: The Language of Clothing in Colonial and Federal America*. Williamsburg: Colonial Williamsburg Foundation, 2002.

Baverstock, A. H. *The English Agricultural Labourer*. London: Vineyard Press, 1912.

Begiato, J. 'Moving Objects: Emotional Transformation, Tangibility, and Time-Travel'. In *Feeling Things: Objects and Emotions through History*, ed. S. Downes, S. Holloway and S. Randles, 229–42, Oxford: Oxford University Press, 2018.

Begiato, J. *Manliness in Britain, 1760–1900*. Manchester: Manchester University Press, 2020.

Bermingham, A. *Landscape and Ideology: The English Rustic Tradition, 1740–1860*. Berkeley: University of California Press, 1989.

Blackman, C. 'Colouring the Claddagh: A Distorted View?' *Costume* 48, no. 2 (2014): 213–35.

Breward, C. *The Hidden Consumer: Masculinities, Fashion and City Life, 1860–1914*. Manchester: Manchester University Press, 1999.

Breward, C. 'The Dandy Laid Bare: Embodying Practices and Fashion for Men'. In *Fashion Cultures, Theories, Explorations and Analysis*, ed. S. Bruzzi and P. Church Gibson, 221–38. Abingdon: Routledge, 2000.

Breward, C. 'The Politics of Fashion and the Pleasures of Youth, Young Men and Their Clothes, 1814–1914'. In *Artist, Rebel, Dandy: Men of Fashion,* ed. K. Irvin and L. A. Brewer, 73–87. New Haven: Yale University Press, 2013.

Bright Rix, M. *Boars Hill, Oxford*. Oxford: Hall the Printer, 1943.

Bronstein, J. L. *Caught in the Machinery: Workplace Accidents and Injured Workers in Nineteenth-century Britain*. Stanford: Stanford University Press, 2008.

Brooke, D. *The Railway Navvy: 'That Despicable Race of Men'*. Newton Abbot: David & Charles, 1983.

Brooke, D. 'The Railway Navvy – a Reassessment'. *Construction History* 5 (1989): 35–45.

Brough, W. *A Phenomenon in a Smock Frock*. London: Thomas Hailes Lacy, 1852.

Brown, M. *Somerset Smocks*. Reprint from *Notes & Queries for Somerset & Dorset* 30, part 305 (March 1977): 1–10.

Buck, A. 'The Countryman's Smock'. *Folk Life* 1, no. 1 (1963): 16–34.

Buck, A. 'Clothes in Fact and Fiction, 1825–1865'. *Costume* 17, no. 1 (1983): 89–104.

Buck, A. 'Buying Clothes in Bedfordshire: Customers and Tradesmen, 1700–1800'. *Textile History* 22, no. 2 (1991): 211–37.

Burman, B., and A. Fennetaux. *The Pocket: A Hidden History of Women's Lives*. New Haven: Yale University Press, 2020.

Capper, H. *Capper's South Australia: Containing the History of the Rise, Progress and Present State of the Colony, Hints to Emigrants … Embellished with Three Maps Showing the Maritime Portion of the Located Districts, the … Districts of Adelaide and Encounter Bay, and the City of Adelaide.* London: H. Capper, 1839.

Carden, S. 'Cable Crossings: The Aran Jumper as Myth and Merchandise'. *Costume* 48, no. 2 (2014): 260–75.

Cave, O. *Traditional Smocks and Smocking.* London: Mills and Boon, 1979.

Chapman, S. 'The Innovating Entrepreneurs in the British Ready-made Clothing Industry'. *Textile History* 24, no. 1 (1993): 5–25.

Chapman, S. 'The "Revolution" in the Manufacture of Ready-made Clothing 1840–60'. *London Journal*, 29, no. 1 (2004): 44–61.

Charpy, M. 'Adjustments, Bodies and Clothing in Standard Industrial Sizes during the 19th Century'. *Modes Pratiques, Journal of Clothes and Fashion History*, Special Issue in English (January 2018): 180–209.

Chartres, J. 'Rural Industry and Manufacturing'. In *The Agrarian History of England and Wales, VII, (part II), 1850–1914,* ed. E. J. T. Collins, 1101–49. Cambridge: Cambridge University Press, 2000.

Child, L. *The Little Girl's Own Book.* Edinburgh: Robert Martin, 1847.

Clark, A. *The Struggle for the Breeches: Gender and the Making of the British Working Class.* London: University of California Press, 1997.

Coe, B. *A Victorian Country Album: The Photographs of Joseph Gale.* Sparkford: Oxford Illustrated Press, 1988.

Corn, W. M. *Georgia O'Keeffe: Living Modern.* New York: DelMonico Books, 2017.

Craik, J. *The Face of Fashion: Cultural Studies in Fashion.* London: Routledge, 1994.

Craik, J. *Uniforms Exposed: From Conformity to Transgression.* Oxford: Berg, 2005.

Cramer, L. 'Diggers Dress and Identity on the Victorian Goldfields, Australia, 1851–1870'. *Fashion Theory, The Journal of Dress, Body & Culture*, 22, no. 1 (2018): 85–108.

Crouch, P. 'Entrepreneurs, Manufactories and Small Industrial Communities, 1850–1914'. PhD thesis, University of Leicester, 2010.

Cunningham, H. 'The Metropolitan Fairs: A Case Study in the Social Control of Leisure'. In *Social Control in Nineteenth Century Britain,* ed. A. Donajgrodzki, 163–84. London: Croom Helm, 1977.

Cunnington, P., and C. Lucas. *Occupational Costume in England, from the 11th Century to 1914.* London: Adam and Charles Black, 1976.

Davies, P. 'Clothing and Textiles at the Hyde Park Barracks Destitute Asylum, Sydney, Australia'. *Post-Medieval Archaeology* 41, no. 1 (2013): 1–16.

de Marly, D., *Working Dress: A History of Occupational Clothing.* London: B. T. Batsford, 1986.

Duff-Gordon, Lady. *Discretions and Indiscretions.* London: Jarrolds Publishers, 1932.

Elson, G. *The Last of the Climbing Boys.* London: John Long, 1900.

Elson, V., and R. Shirley. *Creating the Countryside: The Rural Idyll Past and Present.* London: Paul Holberton Publishing, 2017.

Evans, N. *The East Anglian Linen Industry: Rural Industry and Local Economy 1500–1850*. Aldershot: Gower Publishing, 1985.

Ewart Evans, G. 'Dress and the Rural Historian'. *Costume* 8, no. 1 (1974): 38–40.

Ewart Evans, G. *Ask the Fellows Who Cut the Hay*. 1956. Reprinted. London: Faber and Faber Limited, 2018.

Ewing, E. *History of Children's Clothing*. Tiptree: Anchor Press, 1977.

Farwell, A. 'A Gathering of Smocks'. *Countryman* 70, no. 1 (1968): 77–83.

Faure, A. 'The Working Man's Blouse in 19th Century Paris, The Norms of Dignity'. *Modes Pratiques, Journal of Clothes and Fashion History*, Special Issue in English (January 2018): 88–113.

Finn, M. 'Men's Things: Masculine Possession in the Consumer Revolution'. *Social History* 25, no. 2 (2000): 133–55.

Finn, M. *The Character of Credit: Personal Debt in English Culture 1740–1914*. Cambridge: Cambridge University Press, 2003.

Finney, E., N. Hely-Hutchinson and A. Mackenzie. *Smocks from the Hereford Museum Collection*. Hereford: Herefordshire Heritage Services, 2005.

Fitzrandolph, H., and M. Hay. *The Rural Industries of England and Wales: Decorative Crafts and Rural Potteries*. Volume 3. Oxford: Oxford University Press, 1927.

Fowler, C. 'Robert Mansbridge, A Rural Tailor and His Customers 1811–1815'. *Textile History* 28, no. 1 (1997): 29–38.

Gawade, K. 'Fashioning Aestheticism: Ellen Terry, Photography and Fashion'. In *Ellen Terry, the Painter's Actress,* ed. V. F. Gould and K. Gawade, 49–76. Guildford: Watts Gallery, 2014.

Ginsberg, M. 'The Tailoring and Dressmaking Trades, 1700–1850'. *Costume* 6, no. 1 (1972): 64–71.

Godley, A. 'Introduction. The Development of the Clothing Industry: Technology and Fashion'. *Textile History* 28, no. 1 (1997): 3–10.

Godley, A. 'Comparative Labour Productivity in the British and American Clothing Industries 1850–1950'. *Textile History* 28, no. 1 (1997): 67–80.

Gosse, P. H. *The Romance of Natural History*. London: James Nisbet, 1860.

Gosset, A. L. J. *Shepherds of Britain: Scenes from Shepherd Life*. London: Constable, 1911.

Grayzel, S. R. 'Nostalgia, Gender, and the Countryside: Placing the "Land Girl" in First World War Britain'. *Rural History* 10, no. 2 (1999): 155–70.

Grey, E. *Cottage Life in a Hertfordshire Village*. St Albans: Fisher, Knight, n.d [1935].

Hall, M. *Smocks*. Princes Risborough: Shire Publications, 1979.

Hamilton, P. 'The Beautiful and the Damned'. In *The Beautiful and the Damned: The Creation of Identity in Nineteenth Century Photography,* ed. P. Hamilton and R. Hargreaves, 1–15 and 109–15. Aldershot: Lund Humphries, 2001.

Harden, R., and J. Hashagen. *Laura Ashley: The Romantic Heroine*. Bath: Fashion Museum and North East Somerset Council, 2013.

Hardy, T. *Far from the Madding Crowd*. 1874. Reprinted. Ware: Wordsworth Editions, 2000.

Hargreaves, R. 'Putting Faces to the Names: Social and Celebrity Portrait Photography'. In *The Beautiful and the Damned: The Creation of Identity in Nineteenth Century Photography*, ed. P. Hamilton and R. Hargreaves, 17–55. Aldershot: Lund Humphries, 2001.

Harrod, T. *The Crafts in Britain in the Twentieth Century*. London: Yale University Press, 1999.

Harvey, K. 'Craftsmen in Common: Objects, Skills and Masculinity in the Eighteenth and Nineteenth Centuries'. In *Gender and Material Culture in Britain since 1760*, ed. H. Greig, J. Hamlett and L. Hannan, 68–89. London: Palgrave, 2016.

Helland, J. 'Rural Women and Urban Extravagance in Late Nineteenth-Century Britain'. *Rural History* 13, no. 2 (2002): 179–97.

Holman, G. *Made in East Anglia: A History of the Region's Textile and Menswear Industries*. Pasold Resource, no. 1, 2015. http://www.pasold.co.uk/resource-page.

Honeyman, K. 'Gender Divisions and Industrial Divide: The Case of the Leeds Clothing Trade, 1850–1970'. *Textile History* 28, no. 1 (1997): 47–66.

Honeyman, K. *Well-suited: A History of the Leeds Clothing Industry, 1850–1990*. Oxford: Oxford University Press, 2000.

Hood, A. 'Material Culture and Textiles: An Overview'. *Material History Bulletin* 31 (Spring 1990): 5–10.

Howell, M. *The Handbook of Dress-Making: Including Correct Rules for the Pursuit of the above Art, and Concisely Illustrating the Mode of Fitting at Sight*. London: Simpkin, Marshall, and Co., 1845.

Howitt, W. *Rural Life in England*. Volume 1. London: Longman Orme Brown Green & Longmans, 1838.

Howitt, W. *The Hall and the Hamlet: Or Scenes and Characters of Country Life*. Volume 2. London: Henry Colburn, 1848.

Howkins, A. 'The Discovery of Rural England'. In *Englishness: Politics and Culture, 1880–1920*, ed. R. Colls and P. Dodds, 62–88. London: Croom Helm, 1986.

Howkins, A. *Reshaping Rural England, A Social History 1850–1925*. London: HarperCollins Academic, 1991.

Hudson, P. 'Industry, Working Lives, Nation and Empire, Viewed through Some Key Welsh Woollen Objects'. In *History Matters: History after Hobsbawm; Writing the Past in the Twenty-first Century*, ed. J. Arnold and M. Hilton, 160–83. Oxford: Oxford University Press, 2017.

Hussey, D. 'Guns, Horses and Stylish Waistcoats? Male Consumer Activity and Domestic Shopping in Late-Eighteenth and Early-Nineteenth-Century England'. In *Buying for the Home: Shopping for the Domestic from the 17th Century to the Present*, ed. D. Hussey and M. Ponsonby, 47–69. Aldershot: Ashgate Publishing, 2008.

Jefferies, R. *The Toilers of the Field*. London: Longmans Green, 1907.

Jekyll, G. *Old West Surrey*. 1904. Reprinted. East Ardsley: S. R. Publishers, 1971.

Johnson, P. 'Conspicuous Consumption and Working-Class Culture in Late-Victorian and Edwardian Britain'. *Transactions of the Royal Historical Society* 38 (1988): 27–42.

Jones, A. *The Rural Industries of England and Wales: Wales*. Volume 4. Oxford: Oxford University Press, 1927.

Kennedy, J. *Authentocrats: Culture, Politics and the New Seriousness*. London: Repeater Books, 2018.

Kenny, R., J. McMillan and M. Myrone. *British Folk Art*. London: Tate Publishing, 2014.

Kershen, A. *Uniting the Tailors: Trade Unionism amongst the Tailoring Workers of London and Leeds, 1870–1939*. Ilford: Frank Cass, 1995.

King, S. 'The Clothing of the Poor: A Matter of Pride or Shame?' In *Being Poor in Modern Europe: Historical Perspectives 1800–1940,* ed. A. Gestrich, S. King and L. Raphael, 365–87. Oxford: Peter Lang, 2005.

Kuchta, D. *The Three-Piece Suit and Modern Masculinity: England 1550–1850*. London: University of California Press, 2002.

Lambert, M., and E. Marx. *English Popular Art*. London: B. T. Batsford, 1951.

Lebart, L. *Gold and Silver: Daguerreotypes, Ambrotypes and Tintypes from the Gold Rush*. Paris: RVB Books, 2018.

Lee, Y. S. *Masculinity and the English Working Class: Studies in Victorian Autobiography and Fiction*. Abingdon: Routledge, 2007.

Lemire, B. 'Developing Consumerism and the Ready-made Clothing Trade in Britain, 1750–1800'. *Textile History* 15, no. 1 (1984): 21–44.

Lemire, B. 'Reflections on the Character of Consumerism, Popular Fashion and the English Market in the Eighteenth Century'. *Material History Bulletin* 31 (Spring 1990): 65–70.

Lemire, B. *Fashion's Favourite: The Cotton Trade and the Consumer in Britain 1660–1800*. Oxford: Oxford University Press, 1991.

Lemire, B. *Dress, Culture and Commerce: The English Clothing Trade before the Factory, 1660–1800*. Basingstoke: Macmillan Press, 1997.

Lemire, B. '"In the Hands of Work Women". English Markets, Cheap Clothing and Female Labour, 1650–1800'. *Costume* 33 (1999): 23–35.

Lemire, B. *The Business of Everyday Life: Gender, Practice and Social Politics in England, c. 1600–1900*. Manchester: Manchester University Press, 2006.

Lemire, B. 'A Question of Trousers: Seafarers, Masculinity and Empire in the Shaping of British Male Dress, c. 1600–1800'. *Cultural and Social History* 13, no. 1 (2016): 1–22.

Levitt, S. *Victorians Unbuttoned: Registered Designs for Clothing, their Makers and Wearers, 1839–1900*. London: George Allen & Unwin, 1986.

Levitt, S. 'Bristol Clothing Trades and Exports in the Georgian Period'. In *Per Una Storia della Moda Pronta, Problemi e Ricerche,* 29–41. Milan: Pitt Immagine, 1990.

Levitt, S. 'Cheap Mass-Produced Men's Clothing in the Nineteenth and Early Twentieth Centuries'. *Textile History* 22, no. 2 (1991): 179–92.

Lewis-Stempel, J. *The Running Hare: The Secret Life of Farmland*. London: Doubleday, 2016.

Lloyd, C. F. 'Liberty's Embroidery Workrooms'. *Costume* 10, no. 1 (1976): 86–90.

Maidment, B. '101 Things to Do with a Fantail Hat: Dustmen, Dirt and Dandyism, 1820–1860'. *Textile History* 33, no. 1 (2002): 79–97.

Maidment, B. *Dusty Bob: A Cultural History of Dustmen, 1780–1870.* Manchester: Manchester University Press, 2007.

Marshall, B. *Smocks and Smocking.* Sherborne: Alphabooks, 1980.

Matless, D. *Landscape and Englishness.* London: Reaktion Books, 2016.

Mayhew, H., and J. Binny. *The Criminal Prisons of London and Scenes of Prison Life.* 1862. Reprinted. London: Frank Cass, 1968.

Maynard, M. *Fashioned from Penury: Dress as Cultural Practice in Colonial Australia.* Cambridge: Cambridge University Press, 1994.

McConkey, K. *George Clausen and the Picture of English Rural Life.* Edinburgh: Atelier Books, 2012.

Medick, H. 'Plebeian Culture in the Transition to Capitalism'. In *Culture, Ideology and Politics: Essays for Eric Hobsbawm,* ed. R. Samuel and G. Stedman Jones, 84–113. London: Routledge and Kegan Paul, 1982.

Metcalfe, H. 'Recalling the Comforts of Home: Bachelor Soldiers' Narratives of Nostalgia and the Re-creation of the Domestic Interior'. In *Martial Masculinities: Experiencing and Imagining the Military in the Long Nineteenth Century,* ed. M. Brown, A. M. Barry and J. Begiato, 58–81. Manchester: Manchester University Press, 2019.

Mida, I., and A. Kim. *The Dress Detective: A Practical Guide to Object-Based Research in Fashion.* London: Bloomsbury, 2015.

Milhous, J. 'Gravelot and Laguerre: Playing Hob on the Eighteenth-Century English Stage'. *Theatre Survey* 43, no. 2 (2002): 149–75.

Miller, A. *Dressed to Kill: British Naval Uniform, Masculinity and Contemporary Fashions 1748–1857.* London: National Maritime Museum, 2007.

Mitchell, I. *Tradition and Innovation in English Retailing, 1700 to 1850: Narratives of Consumption.* Farnham: Ashgate Publishing, 2014.

Mitchell, I. 'The Victorian Provincial Department Store: A Category too Many?' *History of Retailing and Consumption* 1, no. 2 (2015): 149–63.

Morgan, M. 'Jam Making, Cuthbert Rabbit and Cakes: Redefining Domestic Labour in the Women's Institute 1915–60'. *Rural History* 7, no. 2 (1996): 207–19.

Newton, S. M. *Health, Art and Reason: Dress Reformers of the Nineteenth Century.* London: John Murray, 1974.

Nichols, M. *Smocks in Luton Museum.* Luton: Borough of Luton Museum and Art Gallery, 1980.

North, S. *Sweet and Clean? Bodies and Clothes in Early Modern England.* Oxford: Oxford University Press, 2020.

Parker, R. *The Subversive Stitch: Embroidery and the Making of the Feminine.* London: Women's Press, 1996.

Pass, O. *Dorset Feather Stitchery.* London: Mills & Boon, 1957.

Payne, C. *Toil and Plenty: Images of the Agricultural Landscape in England 1780–1890*. London: Yale University Press, 1993.

Payne, C. *Rustic Simplicity: Scenes of Cottage Life in Nineteenth-Century British Art*. London: Lund Humphries Publishers, 1998.

Payne, C. '"Murillo-like Rags or Clean Pinafores": Artistic and Social Preferences in the Representation of the Dress of the Rural Poor'. *Textile History* 33, no. 1 (2002): 48–62.

Payne, S. *The Gurteens of Haverhill: Two Hundred Years of Suffolk Textiles*. Cambridge: Woodhead-Faulkner, 1984.

Payne, S., and R. Pailthorpe, eds. *Barclay Wills' The Downland Shepherds*. Gloucester: Alan Sutton Publishing, 1989.

Rachlin, A. *Edy was a Lady*. Kibworth Beauchamp: Matador, 2011.

Reay, B. *Microhistories, Demography, Society and Culture in Rural England, 1800–1930*. Cambridge: Cambridge University Press, 2002.

Reay, B. *Rural Englands*. Basingstoke: Palgrave Macmillan, 2004.

Rees, M. G., and C. Stevens. 'Smocks in the Welsh Folk Museum Collection'. *Medel* 3, Cardiff, National Museum of Wales (1986): 32–8.

Richmond, C. *Oxford Gaol, Prisoner Portraits 1870–1881, Volume One: Crimes in West Oxfordshire*. Witney: Oxfordshire Black Sheep Publications, 2005.

Richmond, V. *Clothing the Poor in Nineteenth-Century England*. Cambridge: Cambridge University Press, 2013.

Richmond, V. 'Stitching Women: Unpicking Histories of Victorian Clothes'. In *Gender and Material Culture in Britain since 1760*, ed. H. Greig, J. Hamlett and L. Hannan, 90–103. London: Palgrave, 2016.

Roche, D. *The Culture of Clothing: Dress and Fashion in the Ancien Regime*. Cambridge: Cambridge University Press, 1996.

Rose, C. 'Bought, Stolen, Bequeathed, Preserved: Sources for the Study of 18th-century Petticoats'. In *Textiles and Text, Re-establishing the Links between Archival and Object-based Research,* ed. M. Hayward and E. Kramer, 114–21. London: Archetype Publications, 2007.

Rose, C. *Making, Selling and Wearing Boys' Clothes in Late-Victorian England*. Abingdon: Routledge, 2016.

Ross, E. *Love and Toil: Motherhood in Outcast London, 1870–1918*. Oxford: Oxford University Press, 1993.

Rowntree, B. S., and M. Kendall. *How the Labourer Lives: A Study of the Rural Labour Problem*. London: Thomas Nelson and Sons, 1913.

Rudd Putman, T. 'Joseph Long's Slops: Ready-Made Clothing in Early America'. *Winterthur Portfolio* 49, no. 2/3 (2015): 63–91.

Ryott, D. *John Barran of Leeds 1851–1951*. Leeds: John Barran, 1951.

Sayer, K. *Women of the Fields: Representations of Rural Women in the Nineteenth Century*. Manchester: Manchester University Press, 1995.

Schorman, R. *Selling Style: Clothing and Social Change at the Turn of the Century*. Philadelphia: University of Pennsylvania Press, 2003.

Severa, J. *Dressed for the Photographer: Ordinary Americans and Fashion, 1840–1900*. Kent: Kent State University Press, 1995.

Shannon, B. *The Cut of His Coat: Men, Dress, and Consumer Culture in Britain, 1860–1914*. Athens: Ohio University Press, 2006.

Sharpe, J. 'History from Below'. In *New Perspectives on Historical Writing*, ed. P. Burke, 24–41. Cambridge: Polity Press, 1992.

Sharpe, P. 'De-industrialization and Re-industrialization: Women's Employment and the Changing Character of Colchester, 1700–1850'. *Urban History* 21, no. 1 (1994): 77–96.

Sharpe, P. '"Cheapness and Economy": Manufacturing and Retailing Ready-made Clothing in London and Essex 1830–50'. *Textile History* 26, no. 2 (1995): 203–13.

Sharpe, P. *Adapting to Capitalism: Working Women in the English Economy, 1700–1850*. Basingstoke: Macmillan Press, 2000.

Shine, C. 'Scalping Knives and Silk Stockings: Clothing the Frontier, 1780–1795'. *Dress* 14 (1988): 39–47.

Shrimpton, J. *British Working Dress: Occupational Clothing 1750–1950*. Oxford: Shire Publications, 2012.

Smiles, S. 'Defying Comprehension: Resistance to Uniform Appearance in Depicting the Poor, 1770s to 1830s'. *Textile History* 33, no. 1 (2002): 22–36.

Snell, K. *Annals of the Labouring Poor: Social Change and Agrarian England, 1660–1900*. Cambridge: Cambridge University Press, 1987.

Spielman, M. H., and G. S. Layard. *The Life and Work of Kate Greenaway*. London: Bracken Books, 1986.

Spufford, M. *The Great Re-clothing of Rural England: Petty Chapmen and Their Wares in the Seventeenth Century*. London: Hambledon, 1984.

Spufford, M. 'The Cost of Apparel in Seventeenth-Century England, and the Accuracy of Gregory King'. *Economic History Review* 53, no. 4 (2000): 677–705.

Spufford, M., and S. Mee. *The Clothing of the Common Sort, 1570–1700*. Oxford: Oxford University Press, 2017.

Squire, G. 'E. W. Godwin and the House of Liberty'. *Costume* 34, no. 1 (2000): 81–99.

Steedman, C. 'Englishness, Clothes and Little Things'. In *The Englishness of English Dress*, ed. C. Breward, B. Conekin and C. Cox, 29–44. Oxford: Berg, 2002.

Steedman, C. *An Everyday Life of the English Working Class: Work, Self and Sociability in the Early Nineteenth Century*. Cambridge: Cambridge University Press, 2013.

Stevens, C. 'Welsh Costume: The Survival of Tradition or National Icon?' *Folk Life* 43 (2004–5): 56–70.

Styles, J. 'Design for Large-Scale Production in Eighteenth-Century Britain'. *Oxford Art Journal* 11, no. 2 (1988): 10–16.

Styles, J. 'Product Innovation in Early Modern London'. *Past and Present* 168, no. 1 (2000): 124–69.

Styles, J. 'Custom or Consumption? Plebeian Fashion in Eighteenth-Century England'. In *Luxury in the Eighteenth Century,* ed. M. Berg and E. Eger, 103–15. Basingstoke: Palgrave Macmillan, 2003.

Styles, J. *The Dress of the People: Everyday Fashion in Eighteenth-Century England*. London: Yale University Press, 2007.

Sykas, P. 'Fustians in Englishmen's Dress: From Cloth to Emblem'. *Costume* 43 (2009): 1–18.

Tagg, J. *The Burden of Representation: Essays on Photographies and Histories*. Minneapolis: University of Minnesota Press, 1988.

Tankard, D. 'Giles Moore's Clothes: The Clothing of a Sussex Rector, 1656–1679'. *Costume* 49, no. 1 (2015): 32–54.

Tankard, D. '"They Tell Me They Were in Fashion Last Year": Samuel and Elizabeth Jeake and Clothing Fashions in Late Seventeenth-Century London and Rye'. *Costume* 50, no. 1 (2016): 20–41.

Tankard, D. *Clothing in 17th-century Provincial England*. London: Bloomsbury Visual Arts, 2019.

Tanner, H. 'Smocks and Smocking'. *Countryman* 48, no. 1 (1953): 82–9.

Tarrant, N. *Smocks in the Buckinghamshire County Museum*. Aylesbury: Buckinghamshire County Council, 1976.

Tayler, W. *Diary of William Tayler, Footman 1837*. Ed. D. Wise, London: St Marylebone Society, 1987.

Thirsk, J. 'Popular Consumption and the Mass Market in the Sixteenth to Eighteenth Centuries'. *Material History Bulletin* 31 (1990): 51–8.

Thom, M. *Smocking in Embroidery*. London: B. T. Batsford, 1972.

Thompson, F. *Lark Rise to Candleford*. 1945. Reprinted with notes and introduction. London: Penguin Books, 2000.

Thornton, N. 'Enigmatic Variations: The Features of British Smocks'. *Textile History* 28, no. 2 (1997), 176–184.

Toplis, A. 'The Manufacture and Provision of Rural Garments, 1800–1850: A Case Study of Herefordshire and Worcestershire'. *Textile History* 40, no. 1 (2009): 152–69.

Toplis, A. *The Clothing Trade in Provincial England, 1800–1850*. London: Pickering and Chatto, 2011.

Toplis, A. 'The Smock Frock: The Journey from Fieldwork to the Pages of Vogue'. *Textile History* 49, no. 1 (2018): 71–91.

Tosh, J. 'Masculinities in an Industrializing Society: Britain, 1800–1914'. *Journal of British Studies* 44, no. 2 (2005): 330–42.

Twigger Holroyd, A. *Folk Fashion*. London: I. B. Tauris, 2017.

Twinch, C. *Women on the Land: Their Story During Two World Wars*. Cambridge: Lutterworth Press, 1990.

Ugolini, L. *Men and Menswear: Sartorial Consumption in Britain 1880–1939*. Aldershot: Ashgate Publishing, 2007.

Vaisey, D. G. 'A Charlbury Mercer's Shop, 1623'. *Oxoniensia* 31 (1966): 107–16.

Verdon, N., *Working the Land: A History of the Farmworker in England from 1850 to the Present Day*. London: Palgrave Macmillan, 2017.
Wahl, K. *Dressed as in a Painting: Women and British Aestheticism in an Age of Reform*. Durham: University of New Hampshire Press, 2013.
Walsh, C. 'Shop Design and the Display of Goods in Eighteenth-Century London'. In *The Retailing Industry Volume I, Perspectives and the Early Modern Period*, ed. J. Benson and G. Shaw, 361–88. London: I. B. Tauris, 1999.
Whitlock, T. C. *Crime, Gender and Consumer Culture in Nineteenth-Century England*. Aldershot: Ashgate Publishing, 2005.
Wilson, A. E. *The Lyceum*. London: Dennis Yates, 1952.
Wilson, R. 'Trade, Industry and Domestic Activity at the Old Clothing Factory Site, Abingdon'. *Oxoniensia* 54 (1989): 279–86.
Wilson, S. 'Away with the Corsets, on with the Shifts'. In *Simply Stunning: The Pre-Raphaelite Art of Dressing*, 25–36, exhibition catalogue. Cheltenham: Cheltenham Art Gallery and Museums, 1996.
Wise, S. *The Italian Boy: Murder and Grave-Robbery in 1830s London*. London: Jonathan Cape, 2004.
Woods, K. S. *The Rural Industries Round Oxford: A Survey*. Oxford: Oxford University Press, 1921.
Woolman Chase, E., and I. Chase. *Always in Vogue*. London: Victor Gollancz, 1954.
Worth, R. 'Rural Labouring Dress, 1850–1900: Some Problems of Representation'. *Fashion Theory, The Journal of Dress, Body & Culture* 3, no. 3 (1999): 323–42.
Worth, R. 'Rural Working-Class Dress, 1850–1900: A Peculiarly English Tradition?' In *The Englishness of English Dress*, ed. C. Breward, B. Conekin and C. Cox, 97–112. Oxford: Berg, 2002.
Worth, R. *Dress and Textiles (Discover Dorset)*. Wimborne: Dovecote Press, 2002.
Worth, R. 'Clothing the Landscape: Change and the Rural Vision in the Work of Thomas Hardy (1840–1928)'. *Rural History* 24, no. 2 (2013): 199–215.
Worth, R. *Clothing and Landscape in Victorian England: Working-Class Dress and Rural Life*. London: I. B. Tauris, 2018.
Wright, M. *Everyday Dress of Rural America, 1783–1800: With Instructions and Patterns*. Mineola: Dover Publications, 1992.
Wuchatsch, R. *John Muston: Draper, Squatter, Speculator in Colonial Australia*. Pirron Yallock: Stony Rises Run, 2017.
Yates, B. 'Rural Dress in Norfolk'. *Strata of Society, Proceedings of the Seventh Annual Conference of the Costume Society, April 6–8, 1973*. London: V & A (1974): 6–9.
Young, L. 'The Experience of Convictism: Five Pieces of Convict Clothing from Western Australia'. *Costume* 22 (1988): 70–84.
Zakim, M. 'Sartorial Ideologies: From Homespun to Ready-made'. *American Historical Review* 106, no. 5 (2001): 1553–86.
Zakim, M. *Ready-Made Democracy: A History of Men's Dress in the American Republic, 1760–1860*. London: University of Chicago Press, 2003.

Index

Abingdon 25, 41–6, 59, 61, 112, 161 n.139. *See also* Hyde; Oxfordshire
advertising 91. *See also* branding; clothing on trial; shops
   Australian 104–6
   for children's wear 115
   by shops 31, 39, 41, 43, 46–52, 56–70
   twentieth century 124, 126–9
   for waterproofing 87
   window display 57, 66, 68, 110
aesthetic dress 113–14, 116–17, 134
agricultural labourer 3, 12–18, 38, 59, 91, 119. *See also* farm servant
   as wearers of smocks 29, 40, 70–1, 96, 111, 136
Anglo-Saxon origins 21–2, 139 n.2
Armes, Alice 14, 129–30
army clothing 100–1, 180 n.180. *See also* naval clothing
army clothing contracts 24, 38, 54, 59, 84, 99
artist's smock. *See* smock, artist's
artistic dress. *See* aesthetic dress
Arts and Craft associations 122–3, 129. *See also* craft
Ashley, Laura (1925–85) 131
Atkinson & Company 51
auctions of clothing 24, 48, 64, 105, 152 n.11
Australia 47–8, 51, 84, 104–7, 182 n.19. *See also* Axe Brand; bush clothing
Avery, Claire (1879–1927) 123–4
Axe Brand 50–2, 107. *See also* Bousfield; Favell and Bousfield

Barnsley 57. *See also* Yorkshire
Barran, John (1821–1905) 67
beadwork 89
Bedfordshire 6, 37, 81, 87
   clothing sellers 62, 64, 68

beer consumption 3, 35, 71–3, 76, 102–3. *See also* public house
Berkshire 47, 61, 63, 73, 89, 116. *See* also Reading
best clothing 68, 89, 94, 98, 115, 150 n.85. *See also* mourning attire; respectability; Sunday smocks; wedding wear
   buying of 64, 70
Birmingham 4, 62, 67, 103. *See also* Warwickshire
bleaching. *See* laundry
boots 73, 96, 105, 111, 175 n.87
Bousfield 47–52, 65, 93, 106–7. *See also* Axe Brand; Favell and Bousfield
branding 50–2, 56, 107. *See also* advertising; Axe Brand
breeches 25–6, 31, 111, 119, 126, 128
Bristol 5, 39, 62
Buck, Anne (1910–2005) 6, 21, 32–3, 53, 56, 80
Buckinghamshire 17, 61, 63, 65–6, 81, 119
bush clothing 47, 105–7. *See also* Australia
butcher 25, 54, 67, 104, 128
buttons 25, 29–30, 89–91, 92, 94–5, 103

canal 52, 80, 91
canvas 22–3, 25–6, 52, 86–7, 98, 176 n.87
   smocks for export 39, 100, 105, 179 n.164
carter 22–3, 98, 114–15, 136, 171 n.13, 180 n.170. *See also* waggoner
   smocks sold in shops 31, 39
   as wearers of smocks 26, 71, 73, 172 n.35, 178 n.146
chapman 22, 23. *See also* pedlar
charity provision 69, 77, 99, 112–13
Chelmsford 72, 93–4. *See also* Colchester; Essex

Chesterfield 39, 56–7, 62. *See also* Derbyshire
childhood 13–16, 19, 69, 89, 131–4, 136. *See also* nostalgia
children's wear 19, 122–3, 129, 133, 136, 187 nn.116, 117
  late nineteenth century 114–15
chimney sweep 98
cleanliness. *See* laundry
clothes dealer 41, 53, 56, 67, 73, 157 n.79. *See also* clothier; outfitter; ready-made clothes; salesman
clothes labelling. *See* labelling
clothier 48, 54, 58, 62, 64, 67. *See also* clothes dealer; outfitter; ready-made clothes; salesman
  in Essex 52, 72, 93
clothing, female. *See* petticoat; shift; smock, female
clothing, male. *See* boots; breeches; coat; frock; gaiters; Guernsey; handkerchief; hat; jacket; jumper; shirt; shoes; smock; suits; trousers; waistcoat
clothing repair 18, 35, 40, 77, 89–91, 137. *See also* mending
clothing on trial 65–6
clothing warehouse. *See* warehouse
coat 22–5, 62, 68–9, 87–8, 91, 136
  as fashion, also 27, 29–31, 84, 119, 126
  manufacturers of, 44, 50–1
Cobbett, William (1763–1835) 13, 102
Colchester 41, 44, 49, 52, 156 n.55, 157 n.68. *See also* Chelmsford; Essex; Hyam shop 61
colonial clothing 24, 47–8, 103, 104–7
corduroy 45, 98, 104, 111, 160 n.131
cost of fabric 25, 40, 44
cost of smocks 2, 52, 58, 62–7, 69–72, 75–8
  in Australia 104
  revival 122
Country Life magazine 12, 15, 120, 123, 128, 130
craft 14–17, 19, 55, 58, 112–13
  revival 122–3, 129–34, 136–7

Craig, Edith (1869–1947) 117, 123–4, 134. *See also* Terry, Ellen
Crimean War (1853–6) 44, 87, 100, 180 n.180
cutter of smocks 43–4, 163 n.178

dandy dressing 29–31, 98. *See also* fashion for men
Derbyshire 31, 57, 72, 93–5, 99. *See also* Chesterfield
Devon 5, 43, 68
dictionaries 2–3, 24
disguise 25, 73, 79–80, 99, 101–3, 107
Dorset 13, 17–18, 82, 87, 113. *See also* Hardy, Thomas
  revival 122, 130
dowlas 67, 86
drabbet 52–5, 57, 64–5, 86
draper 4–5, 39–43, 56–8, 61–8, 70, 89–91. *See also* linen draper; shops
  in Australia 47, 106
dress reform. *See* aesthetic dress; rational dress movement
dressmakers 114, 128, 148 n.46. *See also* home sewing; seamstress
drover 79–80, 101, 103, 180 n.170
Dryden John (1631–1700) 23
dustmen 98–9, 107, 142 n.18, 144 n.38
dyeing of smocks 24, 52, 55–6, 124, 163 n.179. *See also* laundry; smocks, coloured

East India Company 24
ecclesiastical garments 5, 21, 121, 182 n.32
education. *See* school needlework
embodiment of clothing 18, 108
embroidery 31–6, 49, 89, 94, 119. *See also* needlework; smock design process
  embroidered designs 13–15, 55–6, 69, 80, 82, 122
  on female smocks 22, 24
  lack of 27–9, 40, 52, 84, 106
  revival 115, 117, 122–4, 128–30
  selling embroidered smocks 64–5, 67, 73

employment, female, in smock trade 44–5, 49, 53, 55, 59, 153 n.25. *See also* dressmaker; outworker; seamstress; smock maker; wages, female
late nineteenth century 113
employment, male 38, 59, 70, 92, 119–20. *See also* cutter of smocks; occupational clothing; wages, male
engineer 47, 55, 93, 100, 157 n.77
Englishness 1, 11–17, 19, 129
　association with nationalism 22, 28, 119, 128, 135
Essex 37, 52, 54, 82, 84, 122. *See also* Chelmsford; Colchester; Hyam
exhibitions, international and local 15, 45, 55, 85, 112–13, 122–3

fabric. *See* canvas; corduroy; dowlas; drabbet; flax; fustian; hemp; moleskin
factory 25, 40, 43–7, 48–50, 53–8, 67. *See also* cutter of smocks; outworker
　prison manufactory 48
fairs 30, 68–9, 79–80, 87, 102, 151 n.102. *See also* markets
fancy dress 115
farm servants 2, 38, 70, 90, 101. *See also* agricultural labourer; servants
　runaways 88
　selling to 65, 69, 104
farmers clubs 57, 96
farming 13, 25, 103–4, 109, 119, 127–8
　lead toys 136
fashion magazines 28, 123–6, 128–9, 134
fashion for men 29–31, 91, 105–6, 109–10, 119–20, 135–7. *See also* dandy dressing
fashion for women 28, 35, 112–14, 118, 123–9, 131–4
Favell and Bousfield 47–8, 50–1, 106. *See also* Axe Brand; Bousfield
feather stitch 34, 130. *See also* embroidery; needlework
flax 25, 153 n.20, 155 n.40, 163 n.183. *See also* hemp
folk art 9, 14–15, 18

folk culture 11–12, 19
folk dress 8, 14–15, 107, 119, 135
France 2, 15, 59
frock 5, 22–6, 29, 36, 39, 61
　American usage 103–4
　nineteenth-century usage 65
funeral wear. *See* mourning attire
fustian 23–5, 27, 31, 84, 104
　textiles 52, 63
　trousers 30, 79, 93, 95–6

gaiters 13, 15, 63, 64, 111, 126
Galliano, John 131–2
gardening 33, 123–6, 128–9, 131, 134
Gloucester 31, 61, 68–9, 164 n.3
Gloucestershire 74, 92, 101, 113
Goddard, Molly 131–2, 134
goldfield miner 59, 104–6
Grantham, William (1866–1942) 5, 121–2
Greenaway, Kate (1846–1901) 114
Grey, Edwin (c. 1860–1955) 89, 91
grocers 62–3, 89, 94
Gucci 134
Guernsey 105, 177 n.132
Gurteens 52–5, 57

Hamilton's 113–14
Hampshire 5, 26, 33, 72, 76, 121
handkerchief 29–31, 63, 73, 79, 92–4, 99
　necktie 69
Hardy, Thomas (1840–1928) 13–14, 80, 87, 131. *See also* Dorset
hat 5, 21, 68, 94, 99, 103, 109
　buying 71
　children's hats 115
　doffing of 12
　hatter/hat seller 39, 62–4
Haverhill 44, 52–5
hawker 63. *See also* chapman; pedlar
hemp 52, 86. *See also* flax
　manufacturing 25, 26, 43, 153 n.20, 155 n.40
Herefordshire 49–51, 62–3, 65, 102, 110, 153 n.25
　wearers of smocks in 31, 40, 70, 72, 75–6

Hertfordshire 3–4, 32, 89, 102, 117, 122
   selling of smocks in 47, 66
Holme, Randle (1627–99) 23
home sewing 19, 37–8, 59, 104, 117.
   See also dressmaker
   twentieth century 124–5, 128–30, 136
honeycomb smocking 27–8, 31, 35, 131, 183 n.39. *See also* smocking, revival
Houndsditch, London 47–8, 77. *See also* London; second-hand clothes
Howitt, William (1792–1879) 13, 30, 55, 68, 80, 87
Hyam 41, 49, 52, 156 n.54, 157 n.68. *See also* Colchester
Hyde 41–7, 49, 54, 65, 165 n.28. *See also* Abingdon

India 24, 100–1
Ipswich 27, 61, 110. *See also* Suffolk
Italian Boy murder 73
itinerant selling. *See* chapman; pedlar

jacket 29–30, 50–1, 63, 69, 92, 98–9
   duck 3, 67, 84–5
   as fashion 74, 111, 119, 126
   fustian 25, 31, 104
Jekyll, Gertrude (1843–1932) 88
jumper 5, 105, 128

Kent 24, 61, 49, 87, 100
   Small Hythe 117, 124
King, Gregory (1648–1712) 23

labelling of clothing 50–2, 65, 68
land girl. *See* Women's Land Army
laundry 22, 28, 82, 88–9, 91, 110.
   See also dyeing
   bleaching 86
Leeds 39, 43, 50, 57, 58, 67. *See also* Yorkshire
Leicestershire 2–3, 61, 64, 73, 79, 92
Liberty 114–16, 126, 129, 184 n.53
Lincolnshire 2–3, 25–6, 54, 56, 72, 120
   shops 39, 49, 65, 76
   wearers of smocks in 30, 35, 89–90, 94

linen draper 23–4, 62, 66, 164 n.3. *See also* draper; shops
Liverpool 39, 100, 177 n.114
London 41, 47–51, 67, 73, 111–14, 123.
   See also Houndsditch
   fashion 117, 119, 128–9, 131
   manufacturers 50, 84, 86–7, 106–7
   wearers of smocks in 94, 98–9

mackintosh. *See* waterproofing
Manchester 87
manufacturers. *See* factory
markets 61–2, 67–8, 76, 102–3, 111.
   See also fairs
masculinity 9, 30–1, 64, 74, 97–9, 134–7
   and modernity 70–1, 91, 105–6, 109
measurements, nails 44. *See also* sizing
mechanisation 39–40, 43–4, 46, 49, 53–4, 109–10
mending 33–4, 90–1, 137. *See also* clothing repair
military clothing. *See* army clothing; naval clothing
milkman 111, 114, 117
miners. *See* gold rush miners
moleskin 51, 94, 105, 160 n.123
Moses 49, 60, 139 n.10
mourning attire 94, 121
museum collections, establishment of 17–18, 58, 80, 111, 121–2, 137
music hall 111–12, 133. *See also* theatre costume

naval clothing 25, 38, 84, 99. *See also* army clothing; sailor's clothing
navvy 3–4, 59, 67, 80–1, 89–97, 104–6
   manufacturers of clothing for 45, 47
neckerchief. *See* handkerchief
needlework 2, 18, 27, 32–7, 45, 58. *See also* embroidery
   revival 113–14, 123, 129, 131
Newark-on-Trent 55–6, 68, 76, 87, 156 n.57, 165 n.28. *See also* Nottinghamshire
Nicoll 50, 156 n.54
Norfolk 54, 61, 127

Northamptonshire 44, 61, 175 n.82
nostalgia 13–19, 36, 107, 118–20, 132–4, 136–7. *See also* childhood
Nottinghamshire 31, 39, 75, 173 n.38, 178 n.151, 182 n.19. *See also* Newark-on-Trent
Rolleston 183 n.41

occupational clothing 7, 29–30, 79–80, 86, 135. *See also* agricultural labourer; butcher; carter; chimney sweep; drover; dustman; engineer; farm servant; goldfield miner; milkman; navvy; ploughman; road worker; shepherd; waggoner; woodman
 manufacture of 47, 54, 59
O'Keeffe, Georgia (1887–1986) 125
outfitter 48, 57, 62, 67, 105, 107. *See also* clothes dealer; clothier; salesman
outworker 38, 41, 43–6, 48, 55, 58–9, 74. *See also* employment, female; smock maker
 named outworkers 53, 68
 twentieth century 129
Oxford 39, 41, 45, 46–7
Oxfordshire 25, 61, 63–4, 81, 130. *See also* Abingdon
 wearers of smocks in 71–3, 75, 84

paintings of smocks 17, 28, 81, 95–7, 112
patents 87
pattern blocks 53, 56, 174 n.70
pawnbroker 162 n.158
pawning 39, 66, 68, 76–7, 88, 159 n.102
peasant life 12, 14–15, 80, 104, 120, 129–30
pedlar 63, 146 n.8. *See also* chapman
petticoat 58, 144 n.47, 148 n.46, 153 n.21
A Phenomenon in a Smock Frock, play (1852) 111–12. *See also* theatre costume
philanthropy 45, 54–5, 58, 114, 123
photography of smocks 17, 81–5, 95, 110, 119, 126–7
pickpockets 102–3. *See also* theft of clothing

plain dressing 11, 29–30, 70, 103–4
plain sewing 33, 34, 40. *See also* embroidery; school needlework
ploughman 30, 57, 80
poaching 80, 91, 101
pockets 8, 30, 91, 103
policing 3, 44, 73, 101–3
Poor Law provision 26, 37, 63, 65, 69–70, 78, 110. *See also* workhouse clothing
 as employers 40, 91
posture 30
price of smocks. *See* cost of smocks
price tickets. *See* labelling of clothing
prize giving 57, 112–13, 122
public house 3, 71–4, 76–7, 79–80, 98, 101–3. *See also* beer consumption

rail workers. *See* navvy
rational dress movement 114, 122, 184 nn.47, 59. *See also* aesthetic dress
Reading 4, 39, 43, 47–9, 93. *See also* Berkshire
ready-made clothing. *See also* clothier; factory; outfitter; salesman; slops
 sixteenth-century 22, 38
 seventeenth-century 2, 22–4, 38
 eighteenth-century 2, 24–5, 37, 61, 99
 nineteenth-century 17, 32, 37–78, 80, 104–7, 135
 twentieth-century 123–8
 shops 4–5, 31, 84, 93, 114–15
repair. *See* clothing repair
respectability 8, 22, 30–2, 54, 70–1, 112. *See also* best clothing; Sunday smocks
Ritchie, James Ewing (1820–98) 54
road worker 75, 80, 96
runaways clothing 3, 22–3, 26, 31, 88, 164 n.8
rural idyll 6, 12–15, 54, 107, 118–19

sailor's clothing 24, 64, 91, 99, 101, 115. *See also* naval clothing
 trousers 2
salesman 24, 41, 44, 61, 69, 73. *See also* clothes dealer; clothier; outfitter; shops; tailor

savings club 72
school needlework 33–4, 53–4, 116. *See also* plain sewing
Scotland 57–8, 62
seamstress 23, 48, 54, 82. *See also* dressmaker; employment, female; outworker
second-hand clothes 2, 40–1, 47, 61, 75–7, 89. *See also* Houndsditch
servants 34, 72–3, 80, 117, 163 n.185, 185 n.80. *See also* farm servants
sewing. *See* home sewing
sewing machines 44, 46, 49–50, 53–4, 67
sewing by men 90–1, 108
Sheffield 3, 39, 57. *See also* Yorkshire
shepherd 15, 21, 23, 38–9, 85, 136
   as wearers of smocks 32, 35, 68, 79–80, 82, 88
shift 22, 24, 27
shirt construction 1–2, 33, 82
shirt manufacture 24, 37–40, 51, 59, 114
shoes 45, 48, 68, 176 n.90
shopping, male 69–77
shops 61–75, 77–9. *See also* advertising; clothier; draper; linen draper; outfitter; salesman; shopping; tailor; warehouse
   city, also 3, 46, 50, 105–6, 124, 128
   department store, also 51, 115–16, 127, 129
   provincial, also 4–5, 24, 39, 42–3, 93–4, 120
   rural, also 23, 89
Shropshire 3, 50, 68, 72, 88
sizing 44, 58–9, 70, 75. *See also* measurements
   in shops 24, 39, 51, 64–5, 67
slops 2–5, 84–5, 91, 96, 123. *See also* clothier; factory; outfitter; ready-made clothing; salesman
   eighteenth century 25, 39, 99
   manufacture of 41–3, 45, 47–8, 52–3, 55–6, 105–7
   selling of 61–2, 64, 67–8, 93

smock, artist's 11, 117–18, 124–5
smock, coloured 64–5, 87–9, 94, 102, 122, 124–7
   blue 2, 55–7, 77, 87–8, 99, 136
   green 54, 87, 104, 122, 125, 131
   sellers of blue smocks, also 31, 39, 64, 67, 128
smock construction 1–2, 38, 40, 58, 130
smock design process 53, 58, 161 n.139. *See also* embroidery, embroidered designs
smock, female 3, 22, 24, 26
smock maker (individual) 39–40, 49, 53, 112–14, 121–2. *See also* employment, female; outworker
smocking, revival 5, 14, 112–15, 122–3, 126, 129–30. *See also* honeycomb smocking
sociability 69, 72, 74–5
Somerset 3, 5, 47, 111, 176 n.103
Staffordshire 39, 73, 103
stage costume. *See* theatre costume
stitches. *See* embroidery; feather stitch
stolen clothing. *See* theft of clothing
Suffolk 21, 39, 52–5, 71. *See also* Ipswich
suits 17, 57–9, 109–11, 134, 135
   wearers of 85, 98, 120
Sunday smocks 2, 32, 36, 62, 89, 96. *See also* best clothing; respectability; wedding wear
   wearers of 30, 35, 74
Surrey 33, 61, 88, 94
Sussex 5, 14, 89, 101, 133
   sellers in, 22, 68, 129
   smock 27, 33, 120–2

tactility of cloth 86, 88
tailor 4, 40–1, 45, 71, 80, 98. *See also* draper; linen draper; salesman; shops
   eighteenth century 41, 61
   shop 39, 56, 58, 62, 64, 67–8, 91
Tasmania (Van Diemen's Land) 47–8, 104–5. *See also* Australia
Terry, Ellen (1847–1928) 115–18, 122–4, 132, 134. *See also* Craig, Edith

textile production 40–1, 53, 57. *See also* factory
textiles. *See* canvas; corduroy; dowlas; drabbet; flax; fustian; hemp; moleskin
theatre costume 25–6, 36, 111–12. *See also* music hall
theft of clothing (smocks) 3–5, 25, 39–40, 53, 66, 99. *See also* pickpockets
   of a jacket 49–50
   from other men, also 73, 75–7, 87–8, 90, 100
   from retailers, also 61, 68, 102
Thornycroft, Hamo (1850–1925) 117–18
tickets for clothing. *See* labelling of clothing
trousers 30, 69, 79, 93–6, 100–1, 104–5
   female wearers 124
   manufacture of 44–5, 54, 57, 59
   seventeenth and eighteenth centuries 2, 29

uniform, prison 81. *See also* army clothing; naval clothing; workhouse clothing
United States 44, 59, 84, 103–5, 116, 148 n.56
   twentieth century 123–6, 129, 134, 169 n.110

village shows 112–13. *See also* exhibitions

wages 37, 55, 68–9. *See also* employment
   female 40, 45–6, 48–9, 53, 122–3, 129
   male 62, 71–2, 75, 92, 94, 149 n.64
waggoner 28, 52, 67, 79–80, 151 n.98. *See also* carter
waistcoat 3, 26, 30–1, 69

manufacturing of 44–5, 51, 54
selling of 62–3, 65, 152 n.11
wearing of 76, 79, 92, 102
Wales 2–3, 33, 62, 89–90, 143 n.29, 163 n.183
warehouse 22, 24, 47–8, 50, 57. *See also* shop
   as a retailer 31, 39, 41–3, 63–4, 87, 93
   as a retailer in Australia 107
Warwickshire 55, 61, 68–9, 88, 119, 154 n.34. *See also* Birmingham
washing of clothing. *See* laundry
waterproofing 57, 86–8, 107, 177 n.130
Watts, George Frederick (1817–1904) 113, 117
weaving 40–1, 57, 129, 153 n.18, 161 n.137, 179 n.157
wedding wear 32, 40, 69. *See also* best clothing; Sunday smocks
Wiltshire 39, 66, 68, 79, 87
   wearers of smocks in 26, 71, 88
window display *see* advertising
Women's Institute (WI) 18, 129–30
Women's Land Army (WLA) 126–8
woodman 80, 89, 122
Worcestershire 31, 39–40, 48, 67, 76–7, 102–3
   shops in, also 61–4, 69–70, 115
workhouse clothing 41, 51, 69–70, 78, 110, 121. *See also* Poor Law provision
workhouse manufactories 48

yokel 1, 11, 19, 107, 109, 133
York 57, 67–8
Yorkshire 3–4, 61, 66–7, 88, 119, 172 n.25. *See also* Barnsley; Leeds; Sheffield